INSTRUCTIONAL GUIDE

to accompany

BECOMING A MASTER MANAGER
A Competency Framework

Quinn / Faerman / Thompson / McGrath

Laurie Newman DiPadova

Graduate School of Public Affairs
Nelson A. Rockefeller College of Public Affairs and Policy
State University of New York at Albany

JOHN WILEY & SONS
New York   Chichester   Brisbane   Toronto   Singapore

ISBN 0-471-51911-1
Printed in the United States of America

10 9 8 7 6 5 4 3 2

Printed and bound by Malloy Lithographing, Inc.

PREFACE

Writing the Instructional Guide for *Becoming A Master Manager* has been a most exciting and energizing project. The book conveys a meaningful expression of the Competing Values approach, a theory which appeals to both the academic and the practitioner. Further, the text's ALAPA learning model format enhances management/business education. We are living in times of immense social and political changes, and of growing urgent concerns for the physical environment. These changes and concerns pose momentous challenges for U.S. firms that will only accelerate during the coming decades. However, I am convinced that the resources--many of these being creative resources in the individuals who work in organizations--are available to meet those difficulties successfully. This text represents a superb effort to educate our future managers to face these challenges.

Finally, this text represents efforts to enhance learning and to affirm the student-teacher relationship. Because of the ALAPA learning model, the text is interaction-intensive. The traditional learning model, with the teacher-as-lecturer and student-as-note-taker format has its merits, but that format may reinforce distance between teachers and students. In contrast, the ALAPA model functions to reduce that distance, advancing more interaction in the classroom, and a more honest degree of sharing among students and teachers. As such, ALAPA affirms a student-teacher relationship which is at once candid and sharing, viewing all concerned as pilgrims on a journey of discovery. It implicitly rejects one-way communication, which magnifies the already existing status barriers between students and teachers. The text, then, gives the student-teacher relationship the increased emphasis it deserves. Our teachers are mentors who have opened up doors of understanding, and played pivotal roles in affirming our creative and intellectual abilities. ALAPA also allows students to know, understand, and subsequently appreciate each other better.

I would like to express my gratitude to Bob Quinn, Sue Faerman, Michael Thompson and Michael McGrath for giving me this opportunity to write this Instructional Guide, and for helping and encouraging me in this endeavor. Literally hours of telephone conversations and tape recorded responses to questions--not to mention mail from 7,000 miles away--have gone into this effort. A special thanks goes to Sue Faerman, who I've worked most closely with. Sue originally suggested that I take on this assignment. I have relished learning from her; her classroom and group skills have been a source of knowledge and inspiration.

While working on this manual, I recalled some of my own professors--past and present--and what they mean to me. I realized that those using this Instructional Guide are to their students what my professors are to me. Two of these professors--who I had in graduate school two decades ago--still play active roles in my life. Their ideas still influence my thinking. Dr. Lowell Bennion advocated the ALAPA learning model-- although he did not call it that. A noted teacher and Weberian scholar, this sociology professor had two guiding principles of good teaching: 1) instead of going into the classroom and thinking "What will I teach?", go in there thinking, "What will students learn?" Remember that we teach students, not subject matter; and 2) good teaching is one idea, well organized, illustrated, developed, practiced and applied in students' lives. Dr. Sterling McMurrin encouraged excitement over ideas and the cultivation of rationality and knowledge. He maintains that there is no standardized way of teaching: the essence of good teaching is to use whatever way you best communicate; employ methods which are natural to you and be yourself with the students. As you can see from this brief description, *Becoming A Master Manager* nurtures teaching with these principles.

In addition to my indebtedness to the authors, and to the teachings and examples of professors past and present, I am grateful to those who contributed to this Instructional Guide: Dan Denison, University of Michigan; Bill Metheny, North Texas State University; Larry Michaelsen, University of Oklahoma and Deborah Wells, Creighton University; additionally, Dan Denison and Luke Holmann, University of Michigan, for their work with the software.

I am grateful to the Division of Developmental Services at the New York State Governor's Office of Employee Relations for permission to use materials from the Advanced Human Resources Development Program, now called the **Advanced Program**.

A special thanks goes to the editors at John Wiley and Sons: Cheryl Mehalik and Barbara Heaney. They offered ideas and support. Also, to Robert Epps at John Wiley for his work on the software instructions, and for words of encouragement.

Also, friends and colleagues have willingly assisted on a number of things, from word-processing to idea clarification. I am indebted to Tom Darling, Ted Peters, Patricia Reagan, Dr. John Rohrbaugh, and Sandor Schuman of the Department of Public Administration and Policy, State University of New York at Albany, as well as to Michael Cooper of the Nelson A. Rockefeller Institute of Government. These individuals freely interrupted their busy schedules to give important and needed assistance when asked.

Finally, a special note of appreciation to my husband Ted, whose love and support--both emotional and culinary--sustained me along the way. While I willingly take responsibility for the contents of the Instructional Guide, I am deeply grateful for the support and assistance that I've been granted to bring this effort to completion.

Laurie Newman DiPadova

CONTENTS

Competency 1: Taking Initiative

Competency 2: Goal Setting

Competency 3: Delegating Effectively

Competency 1: Personal Productivity and Motivation

Competency 2: Motivating Others

Competency 3: Time and Stress Management

Competency 1: Reducing Information Overload

Competency 2: Analyzing Information With Critical Thinking

Competency 3: Presenting Information: Writing Effectively

Competency 1: Understanding Yourself and Others

Competency 2: Interpersonal Communication

Competency 3: Developing Subordinates

Competency 1: Team Building

Competency 2: Participative Decision Making

Competency 3: Conflict Management

Competency 1: Living With Change

Competency 2: Creative Thinking

Competency 3: Managing Change

Competency 1: Building and Maintaining a Power Base

Competency 2: Negotiating Agreement and Commitment

Competency 3: Presenting Ideas: Effective Oral Presentations

PART 1

INSTRUCTIONAL GUIDE

This **Instructional Guide** accompanies *Becoming A Master Manager: A Competency Framework* by Robert Quinn, Sue Faerman, Michael Thompson, and Michael McGrath. The purpose of this guide is to empower instructors in using the text, rather than to prescribe ways of teaching from it.

The Instructional Guide as a Decision Making Tool: The text contains more material than can reasonably be taught in one semester. As such the text provides flexibility, enabling you to tailor your course in a way you find comfortable. This **Instructional Guide** is designed to help you make necessary decisions in using the text. As such, effort has been made to exclude information which is probably on your bookshelves (such as more discussion on MBO), while including considerable detail on what may not be as assessible to you, such as specifics suggestions on processing each individual case.

Further, we recognize that you are the sole best assessor of your students, your classes, and your teaching style; obviously we cannot presume to provide you with answers, but we are anxious to provide you with the best of our thinking. In developing this guide, I have engaged in extensive dialogue with the authors, seeking their perceptions on a number of issues related to teaching with this text. Their experience and considered responses are reflected throughout these pages, as they are throughout the textbook.

The Instructional Guide is divided into three parts:

Part 1: Discusses the key features of the text and its relevance for business and management education, how to use the ALAPA learning model, classroom management, guidelines for group facilitation, and advice from the authors. It should be pointed out that the basic explanation of the Competing Values framework and the ALAPA learning model is provided in chapter 1 of the text; explanations in Part 1 of this guide build on the discussion in the text. A list of references is also included.

Part 2: Presents contributions from reviewers of the text specifying how they would use it in their classes. They share numerous excellent teaching suggestions including recommendations for setting up groups and for evaluating students.

Part 3: Features specific assistance on the text chapters and on the processing of each activity. A 1-page Activity Flow Sheet and a complete Process Guide is provided for each of the 101 skill activities in the text.

Your input is welcomed: This guide is viewed as part of an interactive effort between the authors and instructors using the text. We share with you a keen interest in advancing business/management education. As such we welcome your experiences and thoughts as you teach from the text. You can be assured that your perceptions and feelings will be very much appreciated as well as receive thoughtful study. I will be coordinating this effort and compiling your responses for future use. What is meant by "future use" is somewhat vague at the moment, but possibilities range from inclusion in future revisions of the **Instructional Guide** to the publication of a newsletter-type of addendum to this guide which would be distributed to those who have adopted the text.

If you decide to participate, and I hope you do if you are so inclined, please include the following information in addition to your name and address:

For what course did you use the text?

How many students were in your class?

What was the schedule format of your class? i.e. quarter or semester system? How many weeks? How many days per week, and minutes per class?

Were your students traditional college students, or were they adult learners with jobs and professions?

Did you use supplemental texts? If so, what did you use?

Did you assign any other supplemental articles or readings?

My address is:

Laurie N. DiPadova
Department of Public Administration and Policy
Rockefeller College of Public Affairs and Policy
University at Albany, State University of New York
135 Western Avenue
Albany, New York 12222

Or, if you prefer, feel free to contact either of the following authors and they will convey salient information to me:

Dr. Sue R. Faerman
Department of Public Administration and Policy
Rockefeller College of Public Affairs and Policy
University at Albany, State University of New York
135 Western Avenue
Albany, New York 12222

Dr. Michael Thompson
569 Tanner Building
Marriott School of Management
Brigham Young University
Provo, Utah 84602

We sincerely hope to hear from you.

KEY FEATURES OF THE TEXT

Becoming A Master Manager: A Competency Framework
has a number of distinguishing features:

1. The grounding of competency-based learning in a solid organizational theory. One of the most compelling strengths of this text is that it incorporates competency-based learning in a theoretical context. The Competing Values Framework offers an approach which facilitates student comprehension of the major issues in organizational theory and their current relevance. Focusing on the paradoxes and tensions inherent in organizational life, this framework assists students in conceptualizing key managerial skills and competencies.

Although the need to include skills in management education has been widely acknowledged, it has been difficult to find a competency-based text which incorporates a recognized model of organizational theory. This text, based on the Competing Values Framework of Managerial Effectiveness, does precisely that. The organizational effectiveness model, roles and competencies have basis in research as well as in theory. References not included in the text can be found in Part 3 of this guide.

2. Use of a well-defined and proven learning model. Through the application of the ALAPA learning model, students are permitted to interact fully with the material for optimal learning, interest, and long-term retention. The ALAPA learning model, which is explained on pages 20-22 of the text, was developed (as PLAPA)* by Whetten and Cameron (1984, 3-5). In addition to its widespread classroom use, ALAPA has also been used extensively in management development education nationally and internationally.

This model enhances learning by providing students with opportunities to interact with and apply the concepts to their experiences. It approaches what is available to students in the physical sciences. Chemistry students, for instance, are expected to learn chemistry with the aid of experiences in the laboratory. In the lab they manipulate and test the chemical compounds and become comfortable with the world of chemistry. In much the same way, the ALAPA model permits students to find their laboratory in classroom activities as well as in their own life experiences.

While I am not implying that management is as discrete and precise as the physical sciences may appear, the point is that there are identified competencies than can be developed by students. The ALAPA model provides the structure through which the competency-based learning takes place.

*Parenthetically, it should be noted that the only difference between the Whetten and Cameron model and ALAPA is that PLAPA terms Preassessment as its first step, while ALAPA refers to it as Assessment. Conceptually the two are identical.

3. Heightened perceived relevance of the text by students. Sometimes textbooks, as disseminators of data and information, can easily become regarded as valuable only for the duration of the course. In contrast, this text has explicit value to the student beyond the course requirements. This value is apparent for two reasons:

a) Relevance of the concepts is immediately discernable. Students will not have to wait until their first job to experience the pertinence of the ideas covered by the course content. For instance, most students will find immediate applicability of reflective listening skills; most will be able promptly to put stress and time management strategies into their lives; many will find current benefit from conflict management skills.

b) Experiencing course concepts as currently relevant adds to the heightened perception that the concepts are meaningful for their intended future use, as well. Any portions of the text not covered in class are more likely to be studied independently by students.

This textbook, by its interactive design, readily lends itself to being regarded by students as relevant after the course is completed. As such the text enhances the students' perception of the course as being relevant to their future as well as to their lives.

4. Flexibility of the text. This text is appropriate for use in a number of courses, including: Organizational Behavior, Principles of Management, Executive Skills, and various hybrid courses. Furthermore, it can be used as the main text alone, or in conjunction with another text. It can also be used in its entirety, or you may select chapters or competencies according to the needs of your students. As such, it permits greater reliance on your judgment, enhancing your freedom to tailor your courses without jeopardizing continuity.

Additionally, the text is so flexible that the ALAPA model does not have to be followed completely; the Competing Values framework is independent of the learning model. While ALAPA is the ideal, the text is organized in such a way that it easily accommodates to any level of approach to experiential education.

5. Skills-based learning and its value in American business education. Management skills is an issue facing business schools today. With the approach of the 21st century, American business faces new challenges, and so does American business education. The Porter and McKibbin study (1988), commissioned by the American Assembly of Collegiate Schools of Business, expressed concern that business education is deficient in several dimensions which may prove critical to American business into the next century. This textbook is a step towards meeting those needs. Students learn competencies that reflect the paradoxes and dilemmas of organizational life. As such they will begin to develop judgment and discretion, using critical analysis, creative thinking, and their experiences.

The text as it relates to the Porter and McKibbin Study:

It is appropriate to consider briefly the major curriculum concerns highlighted in the Porter and McKibbin study, and how the text relates to them. According to the study, of the areas which were identified as undernourished in the American business school curriculum, six were specified by Porter and McKibbin to be the most important:

1. Breadth: There is a need to emphasize a broad education rather than too much business specialization. The concern is that business schools seem to be turning out focused analysts who are interested only with the "bottom line". Other consequences of outcomes are not seriously considered.

While the text does not address this point directly, it does so implicitly. Unlike the traditional management education approach, the content does not focus most heavily on the internal functions of planning, organizing, and controlling. Instead the text expands the managerial role to a balance of many competencies which are important for effectiveness. By doing so the text advances the need for a broad-based understanding of managerial effectiveness and expands what is considered necessary for sound management behavior.

2. The External Environment of Organizations: Related to the call for breadth is the call for a better balance in the curriculum between the "internal environment" and the external environment. Porter and McKibbin note that business education tends to focus on the internal functions of operational effectiveness. However, the reality of the situation is that the boundary between firms and their external environment is becoming more and more blurred. The competitive business environment, as well as government regulations, societal trends, and international developments, require that firms increasingly interact with their environment.

The text promotes this balance. In the Competing Values Framework, the importance of the external focus is recognized, balancing the internal focus. The boundary spanning roles of broker and innovator are given equal attention to the internal process roles of monitor and coordinator.

The importance of the balance in the text between internal and external process cannot be overstated. Students gain their understanding of what constitutes legitimate concerns for managers from the content of basic business/management courses. These courses provide for students the fundamental expectations of the managerial role. Of course students' programs of study may include additional courses in areas related to the external environment. However, the ability of such courses to address this concern of Porter and McKibbin is limited as long as the overriding definition of managerial effectiveness is confined to the traditional concepts. Only by broadening the definition of managerial expectations, as implicitly suggested by Porter and McKibbin, into basic management courses, can the concern of attention to the external environment be met.

3. The International Dimension: This point is a call for increased emphasis in the business school curriculum on a global perspective. It is a logical extension of the first two concerns, considered above. Recognized in this concern is the increasing competitiveness of other countries with U.S. businesses. As the decade of the 1990's begins, there seems to be heightened expectations that some of our future prime competitors are just now being born. Progress is being made on 1992 European Economic Community. New markets are rapidly developing in the Eastern Bloc. The probable economic unification of East and West Germany will present a formidable competitive force not only to Europe, but to the United States as well. Turning our attention to expanding markets and competition with Japan, China, and the other Asian countries, the need for internationalizing the business school curriculum becomes even more salient.

The U.S. business community tends to divide business into American business and international business. The Japanese have no such divisions: business **is** international business. Porter and McKibbin advance this more global perspective.

While the text appropriately does not directly address international and global issues, it does succeed in advancing concern for them in three ways:

1. The text advances this concern by redefining the managerial role in business education as having an external focus equal in importance to the internal focus. The recognition of the external focus as appropriate for the managerial role lends legitimacy to increasing the interest of the individual manager in global matters and international issues.

2. Many cases and examples in the text are based on multinational corporations, encouraging students to consider global matters.

3. The competencies in the text include many skills that managers need in order to function effectively in a world of intensifying change and innovation.

4. The Information/Service Society: This point recognizes the increasing information-intensive nature of society, as well as the related advancement of service industries. With regard to MIS, Porter and McKibbin advocate a halt to separate courses in information management, and an increased integration of these skills into the curriculum as a whole. No part of the organization - no manager - will be exempt from the need for skills in information management.

The text responds to this concern by incorporating information management into the managerial roles. This emphasis is found primarily in the monitor role and in the coordinator roles. Unlike Porter and McKibbin's first three concerns, which seem to advocate a decreasing emphasis on the internal organizational environment and processes, this point strengthens attention to internal process by advancing the need fully to integrate information management in the curriculum.

5. Cross-functional Integration: Porter and McKibbin emphasize here a need for an integrated approach. This point is beyond the generalist vs. specialist dichotomy. Instead, this concern addresses the issue of integrating specific functions into a coherent framework. As they point out, with increasing entrepreneurial trends, a specialized approach will not be adequate. Students must be aware of integration and how functional areas relate.

The Competing Values Framework, as discussed in the text, provides a basis for integration. The approach furnishes a graphic portrayal of how opposite roles are necessary, and how a number of specialized competencies are required to form an effective whole. For example, in becoming aware of the intricacies of the Broker Role, students are able to discern some of the qualities of the Monitor Role; in understanding the basis for the Mentor Role, they are assisted in understanding the dynamics of the Director Role. The framework makes clear that in managerial decision-making, the most troubling choices may be from among good alternatives. As they cognitively understand that the reality is one of paradox and dilemma, of tensions between important values, they can increase their discernment, their effectiveness, and their abilities to cope and adapt.

6. "Soft" People Skills: This last major concern is that people skills need to be advanced. The very nature of organizations as well as the composition of the workforce, is experiencing rapid change. Organizations are becoming less hierarchical and by extension are relying less on autocratic authority. At the same time, the workforce is becoming more diversified. It is estimated that by the year 2000, white males will comprise the definite minority. Managing a culturally diverse workforce poses tremendous challenges, and "people skills" are a must.

Porter and McKibbin point out that business schools have the challenge of incorporating more people skills without diminishing the necessary quantitative and analytical skills so valued by the corporate community. Several approaches are suggested, including greater utilization of interpersonal activities in class.

The text, with its basis in experiential learning, provides increased opportunities for students to advance their people skills. Not only is the development of such skills explicitly involved in 30-50 percent of the competencies, but often such interactive activities are used in learning the other competencies.

Summary: These six concerns seem to be grounded in a fundamental discrepancy between the expectancies of the managerial role taught in business education, and the expectancies of the role which are needed in the corporate and business world. The view traditionally espoused in business education is that the expectations of good managers are confined to the areas of internal organizational processes (planning, organizing, and controlling), as well as leadership. What Porter and McKibbin seem to be saying is that a broadening of those expectations is necessary. The needs of firms have changed, as the world has changed. The Quinn, et al. text penetrates the very definition of the managerial role, broadening it to an array of competencies, thereby materially addressing the concerns raised by Porter and McKibbin.

In sum, the text promotes a broadening of the definition of the effective manager from concern with internal process to concern with a number of different demands, roles, and perspectives. It places the management of information squarely within the managerial role, but integrated into a fuller dynamic system. And by virtue of its content and method, people skills receive considerable emphasis and modeling.

A final note is that the text has long-term value to students, preparing them for their changing roles in their careers. It is highly unlikely that graduates will stay in the positions in which they are initially hired. Further, the demands of the workforce are changing so rapidly that the content of specializations are sometimes quickly outdated; the content they learn in college may be quite different from the content they work with in ten years. Furthermore, job changes are likely, as buy-outs, take-overs and organizational restructuring become increasingly a fact of life for U.S. firms. Projections indicate that more business graduates may become entrepreneurs, requiring many diversified organizational and managerial skills. Indeed, we can expect that change will be the constant in the careers of graduates. Students need to be prepared for their changing work demands and their changing roles in their careers. The multifaceted and dynamic approach of the text can assist students as they face their future.

USING THE INSTRUCTIONAL GUIDE

Part 3 of the **Instructional Guide** is organized parallel to the text. The central 8 chapters (2-9) each address a key managerial role. As you have noticed from examining the text, 3 competencies are discussed in each role. Following the ALAPA model, for each competency there are 5 activities, 4 of which are skills-based and the other is the learning activity. The learning activity is the cognitive content for the competency.

Using ALAPA: ALAPA refers to five different activities: Assessment, Learning, Analysis, Practice, and Application.

Assessment: The assessment activities allow students to respond to scales and questionnaires and other activities, gaining a sense of their level of comfort with the competency. Please note that these activities are not included for the purpose of scientific measurement, but function instead to enhance student interest and awareness. As such the assessment activities provide natural transitions into the learning activity.

Learning: Learning activities involve conceptual content. After responding to the assessment activity, students read the learning activity to discover concepts relevant to concerns which may have been raised in the assessment. The content of the learning activities is supplemented by the instructor in class.

Analysis: After exposure to the concepts, the analysis activity allows students to work with the learning material, engaging in further learning and discovery.

Practice: The practice activity permits reinforcement of the learning through practicing the skill.

Application: Finally, the application affords students the opportunity of applying the competency to an appropriate personal or work situation.

It is important to note that assessment and application activities may be assigned as homework, or they may be completed in class if you prefer. If students complete the assessment activity and read the learning activity as homework, the basis is formed for class discussion the next session. After discussing the assessment and the learning portions, the analysis and practice activities can take place in class. Then students may be assigned to do the application as homework, along with the assessment and learning activities of the following competency.

A Possible Class Activity Schedule

If you follow the entire ALAPA model, you could anticipate taking a minimum of two 50-minute class periods to complete one competency, or two weeks to complete one chapter. Under such circumstances, a possible schedule would look like this:

Day 1: Students attend class having completed the assessment and read the learning activity. The assessment activity can be discussed as a warm-up. You could initiate discussion by asking the class questions such as:
What did you learn from the assessment?
What surprised you?
Then learning material could be presented, followed by the analysis activity and discussion.

Day 2: Summarize the analysis activity by asking questions such as:
What are we seeing with the results of the analysis?

This discussion may be used as a warm up before proceeding to the practice activity. Complete it and assign the application for homework, along with the next assessment and learning reading.

As you will recognize, this learning method constitutes an exploration/induction type of approach, which is variable depending on your emphasis. The activities vary widely according to the time it takes to do them and the time you choose to allot to their meaningful processing. Therefore I want to emphasize strongly that the above 2-day schedule is not concrete by any means.

Integrating Supplemental Texts

As can readily be seen from the possible schedule of 2-days per competency, students have ample homework between Day 2 and Day 1. During this time they may be assigned to complete the application activity of the former competency, as well as complete the assessment activity and the reading for the upcoming competency. However, in between Day 1 and Day 2, there is no assigned reading. This is a good place to assign supplemental reading material related to the competencies.

For the sake of illustration, a tentative assignment schedule is detailed below for using the Quinn, et al. text with another text in organizational behavior: James L. Bowditch and Anthony F. Buono, *A Primer on Organizational Behavior*, 2nd edition, New York: John Wiley & Sons, 1990.

Quinn, et al. text	Bowditch & Buono text
Chapter 1: Models	Chapter 1: pp. 1–29 Chapter 9: pp. 250–259
Chapter 2: Producer	Chapter 11: pp. 300–334
Chapter 3: Director	Chapter 3: pp. 52–81
Chapter 4: Coordinator	Chapter 9: pp. 218–237
Chapter 5: Monitor	Chapter 2: pp. 30–51 Appendix B: pp. 350–376
Chapter 6: Mentor	Chapter 4: pp. 82–105 Chapter 5: pp. 106–126
Chapter 7: Facilitator	Chapter 6: pp. 127–155 Chapter 7: pp. 175–187 Chapter 11: pp. 284–299
Chapter 8: Innovator	Chapter 9: pp. 237–249
Chapter 9: Broker	Chapter 7: pp. 156–175 Chapter 8: pp. 188–217
Chapter 10: Mastery	Chapter 10: pp. 260–283

Two portions of the Bowditch and Buono text are concerned specifically with assessing data and information: Chapter 2, The Research Process in Organizational Behavior, and Appendix B: How to Read a Research Oriented Journal Article. While not directly related to the Monitor Role, these two sections were placed there because of the common focus on assessing data and information.

Notice that the role with the least related readings is the Innovator Role. You could choose to supplement reading for this role further with articles or materials directly related to such topics as organizational change. There are a number of suggestions in the textbook at the end of each chapter, as well as in the chapter 10 summary of each role.

Chapter Organization

A. The role and competency learning activities: Several pages of information on the role and its relation to the effectiveness model, and the three learning contents of the three competencies begin each chapter discussion of the guide. Other competencies which are a part of this role but not included in the textbook are identified, along with the rationale of why the authors chose these three specifically. Furthermore, since it is unlikely that you will be able to cover in your class each competency (they total 24), you can expect to be faced with the potentially troublesome decision of which ones to cover and which ones to omit. That question was posed to the authors, and their judgments of which one, or two competencies they would choose, are included. Additionally the relationship of this role to various issues in business and in organizations are noted here.

B. For each skills activity: After the above pages of discussion, you will find, for each activity (assessment, analysis, practice, and application), the following:

1. A 1-page Activity Flow Sheet. This is designed to give you salient information at a glance regarding the activity. For easy reference and identification, the Activity Flow Sheet is headlined with the chapter, role, and competency. This is followed by the type of activity (assessment, analysis, practice, and application). The format of the sheet, including an explanation of its information, is:

Type of Activity: Name of Activity
Activity Flow Sheet

PURPOSE: Abbreviated purpose of the activity as it relates to the learning section. This is designed to assist you in making the transition from the activity to your class lectures and discussions. An elaborate version of the purpose is included in the Process Guide.

KEY TOPICS: Specifies key topics from the learning section illustrated by the activity.

TIME ESTIMATE: Obviously time estimates are very imprecise. Much depends on how many students are in the class, and how you might choose to frame the activity. But experience provides some basis for estimating, so here is our best estimate. Please keep in mind that it is only a ball-park figure and you have considerable control as to how much time you wish to spend here. Also, whenever you assign part of an activity as homework, the class time is diminished.

FORMAT: This is the group format of the activity, and includes whether it is an individual or group activity, size of groups, dyads, role-play, etc. **PLEASE NOTE:** observation sheets and other material related to an activity will be attached following the Process Guide.

SPECIAL NEEDS: Things you may need to have on hand to complete the activity, such as observation sheets, diagrams, other instructional sheets, etc.

SEQUENCE: A summary of the steps in process. These steps are further elaborated in the Process Guide.

VARIATIONS: Variations in the activity format, including which parts can be assigned as homework, group sizes, etc.

KEY POINTS: A summary of key discussion points.

WATCH FOR: Discusses possible cautions such as the basis for anticipated student resistance, and suggestions of how to handle such resistance. Included only when needed.

It is hoped that this flow sheet will provide you at a glance with the most salient information you need in using the activities. Furthermore, we understand that you may have to decide which of the activities to omit from your course. Hopefully this flow sheet will assist you in making this decision efficiently by summarizing key information on one page regarding the activity.

2. Process Guide: Following the activity flow sheet is a 1 to 3 page process guide which provides the steps in the sequence in greater detail along with discussion questions. Effort was made to furnish many discussion questions, providing considerable choice. There is no intention implied that you use every question. Again, you can frame the process to your liking; this process guide is intended only to present ideas of how the activity has been done - not to prescribe how you should do it.

Additionally, this process guide may provide further information in deciding whether to use the activity. For quick reference and identification, it is headed in the same fashion as the activity flow sheet.

The following is the sequence of pages in Part 3, for each of the chapters.

1. Discussion of role, competencies and the learning sections
2. Competency 1:
    Assessment Activity
        One-page Activity Flow Sheet
        Process Guide
    Analysis Activity
        One-page Activity Flow Sheet
        Process Guide
    Practice Activity
        One-page Activity Flow Sheet
        Process Guide
    Application Activity
        One-page Activity Flow Sheet
        Process Guide
3. Competency 2: (same as above)
4. Competency 3: (same as above)

Any observation forms, diagrams, etc. which may be necessary for the activity are included between the Activity Flow Sheet and the Process Guide.

GROUP FACILITATION

As you know, the Quinn, et al. text is designed for the extensive use of group facilitation as a teaching method. Like many other current texts, it provides exercises to be used in class. In addition, using the ALAPA learning model, skills activities are integrated into the very learning fabric of the book.

It is recognized that many instructors already use group facilitation in classes; many believe that learning is enhanced with the use of such methods. However, some instructors may be hesitant to use experiential learning for a variety of reasons.

There are many excellent discussions of the value of process courses, or experiential learning, as compared with the traditional lecture approach. Especially in business education, the need for learning which more closely approximates situations in the real world is recognized. My intent in this section is not to reiterate these discussions in fine detail, but to acknowledge briefly some of the more salient points.

My purpose in this section of the **Instructional Guide** is to advance the use of group facilitation as a teaching method. To do this, some general guidelines will be summarized.

Guidelines for Successful Group Facilitation in the Classroom

1. Chapter 6: The Mentor Role and Chapter 7: The Facilitator Role. Fortunately an excellent source of information on the skills involved in group facilitation is chapters 6 and 7 of the text. Competencies included in chapter 6 are Interpersonal Communication and Developing Subordinates. Chapter 7 includes the competencies of team building, participative decision making, and conflict management. Reviewing the points of these two chapters is recommended for those who wish to decrease their discomfort with the use of facilitation as a teaching method.

2. Provide clear instructions. Ambiguous instructions make it difficult for students understand what is expected of them. This is one of the more common hindrances to the successful completion of activities.. In order to be certain that students understand the instructions, you may not want to rely on their reading the directions in the text. Instead, read the directions to them. Procedural questions are more likely to be surfaced when the directions are read aloud.

3. Provide a safe environment for their responses. Structured classroom group experiences are in many ways *real* experiences emotionally. Students need to feel safe in this environment, not subject to condescension or ridicule by others. Only then can they risk their free expression of ideas. You, as the instructor, set the tone by how you respond to their questions, ideas, and concerns. Genuinely reflecting the attitude that "There is no such thing as a stupid question" is critical.

In addition, however, you may decide to set some ground rules, which could include how to respectfully disagree with someone else. One way is to suggest that students acknowledge the validity of the viewpoint or idea, or to express appreciation for that perspective, and then proceed to express specific disagreement and why. Too much attention to this detail may just stifle discussion, but a gentle reminder may be in order.

4. How to arrange small groups. Small group work within the classroom setting provides a real laboratory for learning. After all, much of what is work in organizations is accomplished in group settings. Further, in a real sense, the class is an organization.

One issue facing instructors using group facilitation as a teaching method is whether to set up permanent groups of students, or different groups for each activity. It is exciting to see classes formed into teams of 4-5 students who work on projects and engage in peer evaluation. The Managerial Practices Survey (see the discussion of chapter 1 in the **Instructional Guide**) has been used at the University of Michigan for this. While this text does not include long-term projects, instructors can include them, dividing the class members into long-term group teams. The contributors in Part 2 of the **Instructional Guide** address this issue and share their experiences.

If short-term groups are used, the optimum group size is 4-6 students, depending upon the task. Until the students seem to know one another well and are comfortable getting into groups, you may want to put them into groups, rather than have them do it. For instance, if you give the class members instructions to get into groups of 5, students typically will gravitate towards people they know. Some students may drift around, trying to find a group to join. These moments may be tense and awkward. When they do find a group, they may already feel that they are not equal participants, that somehow the others belong together.

One way to avoid these difficult moments, and to ensure that students who tend to sit together join different groups, is to divide the class by having everyone count off in turn. For instance, if there are 50 students, there can be 10 groups of 5. Have each student count themselves in turn, from 1 to 10. This will happen 5 times before everyone has a number. Then put all the one's together, all the two's, etc. In this way, every person comes to the group with an equal sense of legitimacy to being a part of the group.

More importantly, however, forming heterogeneous groups (age, work experience, major, etc.) is highly recommended. This requires that you take information from each student and assign them to groups. Sometimes professors have students fill out an index card, or a short form, gathering relevant responses from the students in order to form heterogeneous groups. Several of the contributors (Part 2 of this **Instructional Guide**) discuss in detail the mechanics of forming groups.

5. What to do during the group activities. Instructors sometimes feel hesitant to use group facilitation because they may feel awkward in the classroom which is filled with groups at work. They feel that they are not doing anything while the groups are involved. Several points should be made here.

a) Students need to know that you care very much about what happens in their groups. For at least the first part of the activity, it may be important to rotate among the groups, listening to be sure that they are on the right track, and being available to clarify any points.

b) Often facilitators report that their most successful groups are sometimes the ones where they "did the least". The key is the nature of the task, careful structuring of the activity, as well as clear directions. The point here is: don't be deceived into thinking that not much is happening just because you are not doing it. One of the most exhilarating moments in group work is to witness the excitement generated by groups actively engaged in dialogue and discovery.

6. Guidelines for role playing. Role playing is an activity format used frequently in the text. The technique is recognized as effective in helping students place themselves in a "real world" situation. Role plays permit students to apply and consider concepts beyond the cognitive environment of the traditional classroom. They also tend to be fun.

Effective use of role plays requires that you make several decisions in advance:

1. What format do you wish to use? Basically there are three possibilities. You may want everyone to play a role, in which case you put the class into dyads. Or you may wish to incorporate the role of observer, and place the class into small groups of role players and observers. Or you may wish to have a "fishbowl" activity, where one role play takes place in front of the class, while the other students observe.

These three formats are related to five variables to consider, as indicated by the chart below:

	DYADS	SMALL GROUPS w/observers	FISHBOWL
PLAYER RISK	low	medium	high low: see pt #2
INSTRUCTOR CONTROL OF CONTENT	low	medium	high
CLASS INVOLVEMENT IN ACTIVITY	high	high medium/observers	low
OBSERVER ROLE	low	high	high
APPROPRIATE FOR VERY LARGE CLASSES	high	high	low

1. **Player risk** in completing the activity refers to the extent to which players are placed in a situation where they are likely to feel that their performance is evaluated by others. Possibly the higher the risk, the greater the chances for student resistance to the activity. In the dyads, there is no one but their partner, who is also involved in a role. Student risk is slim, especially compared with the fishbowl where they are being observed by the entire class. In the small group the players to have a few observers, so the risk is medium.

2. **Instructor control of the content** of the activity is a direct function of the instructor's ability to hear and respond to the content of the interaction. In dyads this control is the lowest. In contrast, with the fishbowl, the players have the undivided attention of the instructor who could intervene if necessary. If the content of the activity is sensitive, or is judged to benefit from instructor monitoring, then use of the fishbowl would be most appropriate. Conceivably, player risk might be lessened in a fishbowl with instructor monitoring than in a small group.

3. **Class involvement** is the potential of the activity to directly involve every class member. If this is desired, than dyads are recommended. However, if the point is to demonstrate a concept or illustrate dynamics, then the fishbowl might be more useful.

4. **The role of the observer(s)** is important because in the organizational setting, we are often observers, and we typically derive information about our situation by noting how someone else's situation is handled. While often in role play activities, observers may feel that they do not have a "real role to play", it is important for them to note their feelings as well as observations.

Have the observers complete a form, or respond to questions regarding their observations. In processing the activity, you might ask them for their feelings as well as their observations. An observation form is provided in Part 2 of this guide with every activity that calls for this type of role play.

One more note on observers: have them sit close enough to the role players to hear and observe, but positioned in such a way that they do not distract role players and are not naturally brought into the interaction among the role players.

5. Appropriateness for very large classes is related to student risk as well as the ability of class members to hear and observe what happens in the activity. Obviously in a very large class, a fishbowl activity might be less effective due to inability of students to hear the dialogue or to observe the non-verbal cues, facial expressions, and the like.

Hints for conducting role plays

1) Consider how you wish to select the players. You may just call on individuals or ask for volunteers. Selecting individuals gives you some control, permitting a degree of "type-casting". If you ask for volunteers, there is always the chance that you may not get any. Some very effective role players may be too shy to volunteer. Sometimes the same people will always volunteer.

In small groups, how are role players and observers designated? At the beginning of the course, you may need to designate who does what. As students gain more experience with one another throughout the course, however, they will probably handle this themselves. When this happens is a judgment call on your part.

2) Give students prior notice. When possible, especially at the beginning of the course, let students know in advance that they will be role players in the following class.

3) Clarify your intentions. If you use the small group with observers, will everyone take turns playing the roles? If you use dyads, will students be able to switch roles? If so, be sure you have enough time. Its more important to have one role play, with observers, properly processed, than to have rotations so that everyone can play a role but the processing is compromised.

4) Set a time limit. Sometimes roles plays could continue for longer than you would like. Time limits frequently are helpful in role plays and in other group exercises for a variety of reasons, not the least of which is class management.

5) Give players a few moments to get into their roles before beginning. After assigning the roles and before starting the activity, allow the players a few moments to think about their role and some of the implications of it. In some cases there will be instructions for them to read, clarify their role.

6) Possibilities with the fishbowl. The fishbowl format provides numerous instructional possibilities. For instance, you can interrupt at any time and:

    a) allow the players to discuss their feelings.
    b) allow the class members to make observations.
    c) let other students step into the roles.
    d) make instructional points about what is happening.

ADDITIONAL SUGGESTIONS FOR CLASSROOM MANAGEMENT: The previous pages have covered a number of classroom management issues. Below is a summation and a few additional items you may wish to consider.

1. Explicit Course Expectations. The course design should be explained clearly to students on the first day of class, supplemented in writing on the syllabus. Expectations are different for a skills course, and they need to be explicit.

2. Class Attendance. Using group facilitation as a teaching method requires that students attend class on time. It is not unreasonable to make class attendance a requirement. This should be clearly stated on the syllabus.

3. Keeping a Journal. On Table 10.1 of page 322 of the text, the authors present an agenda for self-improvement. You may wish to review this agenda on the first day of class and have students immediately begin to keep the journal. The journal could include their skill application exercises as well as their feelings about the other activities. They will find this an invaluable source of data for learning about themselves at the end of the course.

4. Homework Activities. This is a reminder that the assessment and application activities can be used as homework. But of course you may use them in class if you prefer.

5. Guest Speakers. Guest speakers from the local business community may be a welcomed addition to the course. You may know some business people who have become known in the community for their performance in a particular role. This not only heightens relevance, but also serves to strengthen ties with the business community.

6. Evaluation of Students. There are a variety of ways to evaluate students in a competency-based course. Traditional testing is still an option; after all, there is ample content material in the text to allow for plenty of questions. Besides, in traditional lecture courses, instructors routinely grade for class participation. This course would be no exception.

Additionally, there are a number of discussion questions on the process guides for the skills activities. Obviously you will not want to use all of them; they are presented merely as a smorgasbord. However, some may be appropriate as test questions.

You may, of course, choose to evaluate student's on the completion of their activities; the most likely activities to be graded are the applications. It is recommended that, in so doing, instructors not grade students for successful application of the competency as much as for successful discussion of what they did, how it went, and the relation of the activity to the concepts. In this way there is a focus on the process of application and not on the content.

Part 2 of this guide includes essays from professors who are using the text, along with their evaluation methods.

Advice from the Authors

The question was posed to the authors: Pretend that a friend and valued colleague comes to you for advice on teaching from this text. This friend has never used experiential methods in teaching. **What advice would you offer to help your friend teach from this book?**

Responses from them include the following suggestions:

1. Review the first chapter of the text. Understand the Competing Values Framework.

2. Read what you plan to do a week or so in advance.

3. Make sure you think through what you need for the classes 2 days ahead.

4. Most important: Don't be afraid to trust the process. Its hard to let go of the straight lecture method. Trust that students learn from doing the exercises as much as they learn from listening to you.

5. Be flexible. If you find something is not working, don't keep going in that direction.

6. Remember that, as instructor, you are a facilitator. Be a good role model. Students will be frustrated if they do not see the principles they are learning being followed. This may sound negative, but I've seen this happen, where an instructor teaching the facilitator role never once asked students to respond to questions of other students and always gave the "expert advice."

7. Balance small group discussions, large group discussions, and group exercises. It is important for students to get feedback, whenever possible, from their peers as well as from the instructor. Try to structure exercises to allow for feedback.

8. Value and affirm students' experiences in organizations, whether they are work experiences, or experiences in student organizations, community or religious groups, sports teams, etc. Whenever possible, students should draw from their experiences.

9. Recognize the importance of the application exercise as more than an opportunity to assign a grade. I think that this is one of the most important parts of the students' learning experience. Encourage students to use this opportunity to grow and develop as managers (or managers-to-be).

10. As we have gone into organizations, the common complaint is that communication is too often one-way, from the top down. All too often this experience mirrors the classroom. When we use facilitated learning in the classroom, we model what organizations need, and thereby train future managers in these important skills.

REFERENCES

Balk, Walter L. "Organization Theories As Instigators of Public Productivity Improvement Action," in Marc Holzer, ed., *The Public Productivity Handbook*. N.Y.: Marcel Decker, Inc., 1990.

Bowditch, James L. and Anthony F. Buono. *A Primer on Organizational Behavior*. 2nd edition. New York: John Wiley & Sons, 1990.

Cameron, Kim S. "Effectiveness as Paradox: Consensus and Conflict in Conceptions of Organizational Effectiveness." *Management Science*, Vol. 32, No. 5, May 1986, pp. 539-553.

Cheit, Earl F. "Business Schools and Their Critics." *California Management Review*, Vol. 27, No.3, Spring 1985.

Dumaine, Brian. "What the Leaders of Tomorrow See." *Fortune*, July 3, 1989.

Faerman, Sue R., R. E. Quinn, and M. P. Thompson. "Bridging Management Practice and Theory." *Public Administration Review*, 1987, 47 (3), 311-319.

Getting Work Done Through Others: The Supervisor's Main Job. Advanced Human Resources Development Program, New York State Governor's Office of Employee Relations and CSEA, 1987.

Guzzardi, Walter. "Wisdom from the Giants of Business." *Fortune*, July 3, 1989.

Main, Jeremy. "B-Schools Get a Global Vision." *Fortune*, July 17, 1989.

Miles, Raymond F. "The Future of Business Education." *California Management Review*, Vol. 27, No. 3, Spring 1985.

Nelton, Sharon. "Molding Managers for the Tests of Tomorrow." *Nation's Business*, April 1984.

Porter, Lyman W. and Lawrence E. McKibbin. *Management Education and Development: Drift or Thrust into the 21st Century?* New York: McGraw-Hill Book Co., 1988.

Quinn, Robert E. *Beyond Rational Management*. San Francisco: Jossey-Bass Publishers, 1989.

Weisbord, Marvin R. *Productive Workplaces: Organizing and Managing for Dignity, Meaning and Community*. San Francisco, CA: Jossey-Bass, 1989.

Whetten, David A. and Kim S. Cameron. *Developing Management Skills*. Glenview, Illinois: Scott, Foresman and Company, 1984.

Woditsch, Gary A., Mark A. Schlesinger, and Richard C. Giardina, "The Skillful Baccalaureate" *Change*, November-December 1987.

PART 2

FOUR CONTRIBUTORS SHARE IDEAS AND INSIGHTS

FOR TEACHING WITH <u>BECOMING A MASTER MANAGER</u>

**Page 23: "Notes on Teaching with <u>Becoming A Master Manager:</u>
<u>A Competency Framework</u>"
Dr. Daniel R. Denison, University of Michigan.**

In this contribution, Dan Denison describes his use of the Quinn text in a hybrid course of OB content and OB skills. He discusses specific readings, films, and class activities for each model in the competing values framework. Dan demonstrates how materials which are familiar to instructors may be incorporated into the competing values framework.

**Page 27: "Using Quinn, et al. in Large Management Classes"
Dr. William M. Metheny, North Texas State University**

Bill Metheny shares a strategy for using the Quinn text in large principles of management classes. He addresses the issue of evaluating students in an experiential course and describes using Quinn to enhance experiential learning through assessments, cases, and applications.

**Page 31: "Team Learning and Development of Leadership Competencies"
Dr. Larry K. Michaelsen, The University of Oklahoma.**

This contribution describes the use of Quinn, et al. with the Team Learning method. Larry describes how to build a class into an organization, the Team Learning Instructional Activity Sequence, and evaluation procedures for a competency-based course. He also includes several integrative application oriented exams.

**Page 43: "Experiential Learning in the Classroom"
Dr. Deborah Wells, Creighton University.**

This contribution explores a number of ideas for using the Quinn text in various courses. Noting that the text includes more activities than could be completed in one semester, Deborah shares what roles and competencies she would choose and why. She provides a discussion of handling experiential learning in the classroom. Her essay closes with a chart which details how she would use Quinn, et al. with other texts.

Notes on Teaching with
BECOMING A MASTER MANAGER: A COMPETENCY FRAMEWORK

Dr. Daniel R. Denison
University of Michigan

For several years I have taught organizational behavior as a "hybrid" - a mix of OB **content** and OB **skills**. For this reason, I was particularly pleased to see this new text. It is, from my perspective, the best attempt thus far to bringing these two approaches together in the classroom.

By OB content, I mean traditional topics in OB such as leadership, motivation, group process, culture, work and organization design, organizational development, and so on. The classic difficulty with teaching this material, particularly with students who have not had much work experience, is the lack of common experience that can be used to illustrate the theories. To overcome this, I typically grouped students into project teams and had them do diagnostic projects with organizations. This gave us two common points of reference: the groups that they had worked in and the organizations they had studied.

This worked well, but did not include what I consider to be the other important component of a successful OB class: an experiential approach to interpersonal, group, and leadership skills. To incorporate this, I typically tried to introduce a series of exercises that focused on forming groups, establishing group norms, analysing group process, and so on.

The problem with this approach is that many students have trouble integrating it all: The skills exercises are great, but how do they fit together? The experiential learning is exciting, but how does it relate to "content" of the course? Analysing a case or an organization is terrific, but what should I study? Leadership? Culture? Work design? Motivation?

The beauty of this text and the competing values framework is that it integrates these approaches and resolves many of the problems of teaching such a "hybrid" class. By doing so, the "content" sections become a way of understanding a particular management role, the exercises build skills in an area where the student may be weak or strong, and the diagnosis of a case or company can rely on the model. Slowly it begins to come together.

The following sections describe in some detail the approach I've taken recently with a large (N=60), required MBA class at the University of Michigan, titled **Human Behavior and Organizations**. The class used the text as a base, but often included other materials as supplements. In general, for each quadrant of the model, I went through some variation of the following sequence:

1. Present some of the background research supporting the perspective;

2. Discuss the managerial skills emphasized in that quadrant;

3. Do an exercise or two to build those managerial skills;

4. Present a case that shows a manager or situation emphasizing those skills;

5. Analyse a video clip of a manager with respect to those roles and skills.

Introduction and Overview of the Model

The fundamental point to make in an overview of the model and the book is the centrality of paradox and balance to the leadership role. Bob Quinn, in his classes, shows video clips from the films Patton and Ghandi and then discusses leadership. We've also used a video tape of Allan Gilmour, Executive Vice President of Ford Motor Company in which he says, "You ask which is more important, cost or quality?" "The answer is yes." "Timeliness or customer service?" "The answer is yes." A presentation of the model, a discussion of the roles, and a discussion of paradox and balance makes the framework for the course very clear to most students. If additional material is needed to elaborate any of the theoretical perspectives in Chapter One, I suggest drawing from a reader like Shafritz and Whitbeck's *Classics of Organizational Theory*. Introducing students to the Competing Values Skills Assessment software package at this stage also helps them to personalize the roles and model. Once they get data about themselves, they are highly motivated to understand and apply the model and the skills presented in the book.

The Open Systems Model

As background for the open systems model, I discussed Kanter's *The Change Masters* (particularly her ten rules for stifling innovation) and Katz and Kahn's *The Social Psychology of Organizations*. Material on intrapreneurship (Pinchot or Burgelman, for example) or the 3M "post-it" clip from the first **"In Search of Excellence"** video could also be used to make the point. These materials or others can be used to describe both the innovator and broker roles and the open systems model.

A creativity exercise is a must. One of my favorites is to ask students to answer the questions, "When was the last time you did something creative?" "What was it?" One time a manager answered this question by saying that the last time he was creative was six months ago when they found a new way to **drive home from work.** The message of this exercise is that the simple finding that people who **think** that they are creative, are creative. I sometimes follow this with a lateral thinking exercise described by Van Oech in his delightful little book, *A Whack on the Side of the Head*. My colleague Poppy McLeod often asks her students to work in groups to design products that would be in high demand if people doubled their height and weight. The textbook also contains several excellent exercises on creativity.

A case on entrepreneurship, such as People Express Airlines or an excerpt from *Odessey* by John Sculley, will continue to drive the message home. The People Express video clip is available from the Harvard Business School. At Michigan, we used a case study on People Express that is in my book *Corporate Culture and Organizational Effectiveness*, and a paper by Cameron and Quinn on organizational life cycles ["Organizational Life Cycles and Shifting Criteria of Effectiveness: Some Preliminary Evidence" *Management Science*, 1983] that uses the competing values approach. This usually allows for an excellent discussion of the changing balance that occurs as firms develop and the need for a different mix of skills at different points in their evolution.

Another Harvard case, the **Center for Machine Intelligence**, focuses on a joint venture between General Motors and EDS to develop computer-aided conference room technology. This case allowed for simultaneous discussion of organizational innovation and group process in meetings. By presenting background, skills, exercises, and video, students get a thorough exposure to this first quadrant.

The Human Relations Model

The Human Relations Model is often what students expect to hear about in an OB class. Our course began with several classes on culture, human resource management, managing diversity, and the contribution of these factors to creating competitive advantage for a firm. We read my paper, **"Bringing Corporate Culture to the Bottom Line,"** Dave Ulrich's work on **"Human Resources as a Source of Competitive Advantage"**, and the **Workforce 2000** report. Coupled with the description of the human relations model in Chapter One of the text, these readings help give the student the necessary perspective.

After an introduction to the mentor and facilitator roles and their associated skills, we did two exercises in class: a Human Synergistics exercise called **The Project Management Situation**, which serves as a great example of the facilitator role, and the exercise on facilitating conflict management in the text. We closed this segment by discussing the **Suzanne de Passe at Motown Productions** case, along with the Harvard video.

The Internal Process Model

This segment began by looking back to the introductory chapter and reviewing the origins and nature of bureaucracy, and then going on to discuss the design of control systems and organizations in general. David Halberstam's discussion of Ed Lundy and the McNamara "Whiz Kids" at Ford Motor Company in *The Reckoning* makes a great supplement to this material. A reading from *Classics on Organizational Theory* might also be useful here.

After discussing the monitor and coordinator roles, I focused primarily on organizational design as a key skill. It is a subject that I like to teach, so I integrated some material on design and structure at this point in the course. As an exercise, we used a very short case, **The Dashman Company**, that required groups of students to design a control system and then present their plans to the class.

We then discussed the Citibank A&B cases, which focus on John Reed's role in restructuring the Citibank back office during the mid-1970's. The case addresses control systems and organizational design issues, leadership styles, strategies for managing change, and even leadership succession. We also made a video of a recent presentation Reed made at Michigan to contrast his style in this case with his development as a manager.

The Rational Goal Model

For the final section, we focused first on the concept of economic rationality, and contrasted the assumptions of neo-classical economics with Simon's concept of bounded rationality. I found Etzioni's new book, *The Moral Dimension*, to be useful both in presenting a clear statement of what economic rationality **is**, and to provide examples that contradict economic rationality.

The discussion in the text of the producer and director roles and related skills focused primarily on goal setting, delegating, and the expectancy theory of motivation. I did two exercises to try to build an understanding of these skills: One concentrated on motivation and asked students to compare the job design, goal setting, and expectancy theories of motivation, and then write down their own theory of motivation. It was surprising how few students had a confident answer to such a central question. The second question asked students to think of a time when they had tried to delegate work and then comment on what worked well and what did not. It focused their attention on an area that they all felt quite uncertain about.

The case that we discussed in this section was the HBS Hercules case. Included along with this case was a video of the CEO. The CEO tends to emphasize a task and control approach to managing the organization and has fundamentally restructured the company over the past decade. He has a clear vision for the organization, but, unfortunately, it is less clear if it is the right vision, or if the rest of the organization is behind him.

A few final comments:

As the reader can see from my description, I used the textbook for three purposes:

1. A framework for discussing organizations and managerial leadership.

2. A set of roles and skills that operationalize leadership in a highly specific way.

3. A source of cases and exercises that parallel the model.

Many other resources were incorporated into the class and allowed me to teach the OB "content" in a way that was familiar and worked best for me. Fitting this content into the framework generally strengthened it; contrasting one perspective with another or personalizing the content by relating it to a managerial role all helped to pull things together.

My initial apprehension about this book was that much of the OB content that I valued so highly (and knew so well!) would be lost in taking a skills approach. After trying it once, I see it quite differently: there are many ways in which familiar materials can be incorporated into the competing values framework, and doing so tends to give greater integration to that material and link it directly to managerial skills.

USING QUINN, ET AL. IN LARGE MANAGEMENT CLASSES

Dr. William M. Metheny
North Texas State University

Introductory management classes provide an excellent opportunity to share the excitement of management with a diverse group of students. The Principles of Management course is required of all business students in most schools. Students from disciplines other than business are also required to study management or are allowed to take the course as an elective in many institutions. In my classes, for instance, I teach students from all of the business disciplines, political science, psychology, art, music, and other departments. With limited resources, serving all these constituencies often requires the use of large classes (mine have ranged in size from 120 to 220 students, though some are much larger). The anomie of such large classes, added to the diversity of backgrounds, can be a challenge to an instructor.

To take advantage of the differing strengths and interests of such a varied group of students, I ask them to actually use the principles they are studying throughout the semester. The procedure is to break them into heterogeneous groups, then assign tasks which require them to both study and practice management as a team. Managing this small organization is their real introduction to the topics of management. Texts help them understand the processes they are experiencing and explain reasons for their successes or disappointments. This reinforces their learning.

The Quinn text assists this process in two ways. First, the **competing values framework** helps students appreciate others in the group who enter the management class with a different perspective than theirs. Over the semester, different tasks will also allow group members to experiment with an assortment of management models and roles. Varying levels of success give them an incentive to compare their experiences with the theories presented.

Second, the Quinn, et al text provides a rich source of material to enhance experiential learning. **Assessments** allow the students to measure their attitudes and discuss them with other group members. **Cases** offer concrete examples of the managerial actions being discussed. The chapters provide **specific suggestions** on developing particular competencies. **Applications** help shorten or eliminate the lengthy process of designing exercises which offer students new ways to learn.

SOME SPECIFICS

Textbook

Most recently, I have been using Stephen Robbins' text, *Management*, 2nd ed., from Prentice-Hall. This offers a functional approach to the study of management. The Quinn approach blends well with the Robbins approach and an emphasis on experiential learning.

Conduct of the Class and Evaluation

In the first two sessions of the semester, the instructor assigns students to groups. Students fill out a questionnaire listing their major field, personal background, weaknesses, and strengths. The instructor and teaching assistant assign students to groups by selecting a mix of their backgrounds, interests, and abilities. Groups have from 5-7 students each. After the groups take a few minutes to get acquainted, then send representatives to determine the grading system for the semester. Within limitations set in advance, the class may elect any mix of the following grade components:

Individual Performance_____	%
.Examinations	
Group Performance_____	%
Examinations	
Group Projects	
Peer Evaluation_____	%
(Ratings by team members)	

TOTAL   100%

Individually, and in groups, students study assigned reading material. There is no formal lecture. After studying a block of material, students take a brief test. When all individuals have completed the test, the group takes the same text. Exams are mechanically graded, and returned as soon as the last group has finished. While the groups write appeals on those answers which they disagree, the instructor analyzes the overall results. If there are areas of misunderstanding, then an immediate mini-lecture is presented on that material. The individuals receive the grade they made on the test. Also, each group member receives the group grade on that exam as a component of the group grade for the semester.

During subsequent class periods, groups work together on assignments which give them an opportunity to apply the material they have studied. These assignments could be an analysis of a case, an interview of a practicing manager, or a description of their experience with one facet of managing a small group. All group members receive the group grade on the project. Members whose performance is exceptional in either direction are rewarded through their peer evaluation grades.

Using Quinn, et al. As A Supplement

The first reading assignment in the Robbins text is normally chapters one through four. To many students, "The Evolution of Management Thought" is an exercise in memorization. Yet the topic is crucial to the understanding of management. Adding Chapter 1 of Quinn will help the students integrate the large amount of information without reducing their study to rote memorization.

As an introductory exercise, the group could be asked to turn in their written responses to the following exercise:

ASSIGNMENT: Throughout this semester, your group will be required to hand in answers to exercises concerning your readings. This is the first exercise. Your group should turn in **one paper** for each exercise. All of you will receive the same grade for that paper.

You are now beginning the management of a small organization. At this point, there is probably no single manager in your organization; you are sharing the managerial tasks. Like other organizations, yours has ultimate goals. In the case of your group, ultimate goals might be to learn the basics of management and to receive good grades for your efforts. There are always intermediate goals that must be accomplished in order to attain the ultimate goals. This assignment is one of those.

Quinn lists a number of the roles performed by managers in Table 1.2.

   a. What part will these roles play in the management of your group this semester?

   b. Which roles do you feel will be the most important?

   c. Which roles will be the least important?

   d. Did you have difficulty getting some members to agree on the most or least important roles? Could it be that they subscribed to competing models of management? If so, try to explain the competing models.

   e. Now look at Mintzberg's managerial roles in Table 1-1 of your Robbins text. Some of these have different names than the roles described by Quinn. Compare Mintzberg's roles with those in Quinn.

A Second Use

The first example used the first chapter of Quinn to supplement the first chapter of Robbins. Of course that simple pattern doesn't follow. The Quinn section, **Seeing Things As We Really Are** (chapter 5), ties in with Robbins' chapters on decision making (4) or communication (14), depending on instructor preferences. I would assign this section during the communication chapter. At this point in the semester, many of my students are beginning to wonder about the value of all the "behavioral stuff." Quinn does an excellent job of focusing on the importance of communication in the decision making process. Rather than writing an assignment this time, the instructor could assign the practice section, **Argument Mapping**. That would reinforce the study of communication from a managerial perspective.

Assessments

The group development process, of course, includes one or more stages of "Storming." To many of our students, this confrontation portends the imminent demise of their team. In the past, I've worked in some form of personal style assessment in weeks five and fifteen to help them understand the sources of conflict. Copying costs for the instruments and explanations, alone, were very high. The Quinn text is a rich source of instruments which point to the uniqueness of individuals. This reduces costs to the school, offers a wider variety of instruments, and frees up class time that was spent in distributing and administering the assessments.

SUMMARY

This section has briefly discussed how one professor might use the Quinn text in conjunction with the Robbins text on management. It discussed, briefly, one approach to teaching management experientially. Within that framework, one specific example was presented showing the integration of the Quinn text. A broader example showed the flexibility of the text. Finally, this section explained how the assessments in the Quinn text could save money and classroom time.

TEAM LEARNING AND DEVELOPMENT OF LEADERSHIP COMPETENCIES

Dr. Larry K. Michaelsen
The University of Oklahoma

In recent years, there has been an increasing interest in group-oriented instruction. This probably stems from a number of factors. These include: an increased use of teams and task forces in the work place, the growing recognition of the deficiencies of business school graduates' interpersonal and group skills (eg. see Porter and McKibbin, 1988), an increased awareness of the usefulness of group interaction in the development of higher level learning and problem solving skills (eg. Kurfiss, 1989), a growing number of students who are critical of professors who waste their time by going over material that they can read in a text. When the primary instructional objective is to increase students' mastery of leadership competencies, however, the simple fact is that the opportunity to work in small groups is an absolutely essential part of the process. They can't become better leaders if they don't have the opportunity to practice leading.

Unfortunately, simply having students work in groups is no guarantee that either they will learn more or that they will be more satisfied with the instructor. In fact, just the opposite can occur. Unless the groups are structured properly and group activities are designed and managed effectively, they ban both be an obstacle to learning and a source of considerable student frustration.

One of the ironies of group oriented instructional formats is that, as group interaction becomes more intensive, the potential for both positive and negative outcomes also increases. As the groups become more "real" they provide an increasingly valuable source of data from which students can learn about themselves and about the way they interact with others. The danger is that the learning comes from making mistakes and the pain can be so great that the learning never occurs. The key is providing students with the opportunity to experience working in an "organization like" situation that promotes successes but also provides support when the inevitable failures occur.

Two Approaches for Bringing the Organization into the Classroom

There are tow basic approaches for providing students with the opportunity to practice using the leadership competencies in a classroom setting. These are:

1. Engaging in activities that, in effect, bring a "slice" of the organization into the classroom. Some of the most common of these types of activities are cases, role plays and simulations.

2. Organizing the class in a way that causes it to take on the properties of a real organization. This approach requires the use of:

   - "Permanent" groups
   - A grading structure in which group work really "counts".
   - Activities that ensure individual accountability to the groups.

There are significant advantages and disadvantages to both approaches. For example, bringing the organization into the classroom through the use of cases, role plays and simulations can be very effective in helping students to develop a cognitive understanding of specific leadership competencies and learn from observing and experiencing the impact of specific leadership competencies in a low-risk situation. On the other hand, they may experience the activities as a series of "games" to be played. When this occurs, the intensity of students' involvement is usually so low that students may not become introspective enough that they seriously examine their own strengths and weaknesses. In addition, focusing on competencies can inhibit students' ability to see the "big picture" issues such as how the organizational context affects the appropriateness of the various competencies.

What is and isn't in the Quinn book

In my judgment, the Quinn book contains:

1. Excellent cognitive material on the various models of competent leadership.

2. Well presented material about some of the key theoretical approaches that relate to the leadership competencies.

3. An effective model for aiding students in the development of leadership competencies.

4. A wide variety of examples, short cases, and role plays to help students:

    - develop a cognitive understanding of specific leadership competencies.
    - learn from observing and experiencing the impact of specific leadership competencies in a low-risk situation.

In my judgment, the Quinn book does **not** (and should not) contain two items that are critical from a teaching perspective. These are:

1. An approach to managing the instructional process so that the class itself provides a real-life opportunity for students to experience the concepts they are learning about.

2. Material and/or activities that will allow students to actively struggle with the "big picture" issues of:

    - how competencies relate to each other.
    - how the organizational context affects the need for different leadership competencies.

USING TEAM BUILDING TO BUILD THE CLASS INTO AN ORGANIZATION

The Team Learning format (see Michaelsen, Cragin, Watson & Fink, 1985) seems to me to be a near ideal way to meet the instructional needs of a course whose primary objective is to increase students' mastery of leadership competencies and also utilize the strengths of the Quinn book. Team learning, by its very nature, ensures that:

1. Students will develop a working familiarity with key course concepts and terminology using an absolute minimum (approximately 20%) of class time.

2. The class will quickly become very much like an ongoing organization due to the fact that the vast majority of groups will take on the characteristics of highly effective task teams (i.e. they become a very powerful source of motivation for students to complete reading assignments, attend class and participate in group activities.

3. Virtually all of the class time will be spent in group activities in which students will have the opportunity to observe and practice using specific competencies and to experience the relationship between the competencies in a wholistic way.

Essential Elements of the Team Learning Model

The team learning model has been used with many subjects in a wide variety of settings. The degree of success you can achieve by using the model, however, depends on:

1. Availability of appropriate reading material. (The Quinn book is key here. It provides most of the material I would use the first time through, although I would probably use some additional readings in specific topics later on.)

2. Immediate feedback on both individual and group performance. (*See* instructional activity sequence below.)

3. A grading system that provides incentives for group work. (I would use the "Setting Grade Weights" -- see Michaelsen, Cragin & Watson, 1981 -- to establish a grading system for the class. This exercise is a highly effective way to build group cohesiveness, clearly demonstrates that both the teacher and student roles in the class will be different from most other courses, and ensure that both group performance and a peer evaluation are an important part of the grading process.)

4. Individual accountability for pre-class preparation. (This is largely accomplished through a combination of an appropriate grading system and the individual mini-tests -- see instructional activity sequence below.)

Key questions in developing a course using Team Learning:

1. What do I want students to be able to do when they have completed this unit of instruction (or course, program of study, etc.)? This identifies the desired outcome(s) of the instructional process. In the case of a Leadership Competencies course they would include making sure that students were able to do such things as:

- Describe each of the key leadership competencies and the kinds of situations in which they would be critical to organizational success.

- Observe others' behavior and correctly identify their strengths and weaknesses with respect to the leadership competencies.

- Gain a sufficient level of self understanding that they can correctly identify their own strengths and weaknesses with respect to the leadership competencies.

- Use the learning model as a means of improving degree of mastery of one or more of the leadership competencies.

- etc.

2. What will students have to know to be able to do #1? This questions the content that will have to be covered in the readings or in some other way. (Fortunately, the Quinn book does a terrific job on this one.)

3. How can I tell what students have already learned on their own so I can build from there (rather than assuming that they don't know anything and starting from scratch)? This question guides the development of:

- Mini tests (see instructional activity sequence below).

- Application exams and projects (see instructional activity below).

Forming groups

I always form groups and, in doing so, attempt to ensure that: 1) they are as heterogeneous as possible and 2) both the key members assets (eg. full time work experience) and member liabilities (eg. limited fluency in English) are evenly spread across the groups (see Michaelsen et al., 1985 for additional information). In my judgment, allowing class members to form their own groups is asking for trouble for a variety of reasons (see Fiechtner & Davis, 1985).

Team Learning activity sequence

Team Learning employs a six-step instructional activity sequence that is repeated for each major unit of instruction (see Michaelsen et al., 1985). These steps are shown in Figure 1. With the Quinn book, I will probably divide my course into five instructional units (a unit on the introductory chapters plus a unit on each of the four models in the framework). Thus I will go through the sequence five times.

Probably the most unique overall feature of this sequence is that there is no input from the instructor until very late in the instructional process. This is possible because of the mini tests, steps 2-5 (see the discussion on Informative Tests in Michaelsen et al., 1985). This sequence, which takes approximately an hour to an hour and a half to complete (thus consuming approximately 20% of the total available class time) virtually eliminates time that is often wasted in "covering" material. The instructor can be certain whether or not students have mastered the key concepts by designing appropriate test questions. Furthermore, by providing immediate feedback, he or she can correct any misconceptions before students move on to other activities or material for which they are inadequately prepared (see Michaelsen et al., 1985).

Figure 1
Team Learning Instructional Activity Sequence

Individual Study
(over assigned reading material)

⬇

Individual Mini Test
(15-20 multiple choice questions; scored during group test)

⬇

Group Mini Test
(same questions as individual mini test; scored immediately)

⬇

Preparation of Written Appeals
(open book; from groups only)

⬇

Instructor Input
(in response to students' remaining questions or the instructor's perceptions of the issues about which additional input is needed)

⬇

Application Oriented Activities, Projects and Exams
(would include many of the cases and activities from the Quinn book plus at least two or three major integrative group exams -- see below)

In addition to ensuring that students develop a sound understanding of course concepts, the mini tests also accomplish two other important objectives with respect to the management of the class. One is that they are extremely effective at building cohesiveness. As a result, you can count on group norms to provide a motivation for individual study and class attendance. The other is that, due to the fact that the individual and group scores have an impact on both course grades and group status, the mini tests provide multiple opportunities for students to engage in group decision making and conflict resolution in a situation that **is** real life. Every question provides an opportunity to practice a wide variety of interpersonal and group skills while, at the same time, developing an understanding of the course content.

Due to the efficiency of the mini test process, approximately 80% of the class time can be spent on application oriented class activities (eg. role plays, case discussions, etc.) which should be designed and executed so that they:

1. Provide a structured situation that is focused on the application of specific competencies.

2. Ensure that students have the opportunity to gain both a cognitive and an affective understanding of the leadership competencies.

3. Provide vehicles that allow students to examine the relationship between the cognitive and affective aspects of the leadership competencies.

Effective application oriented activities, projects and exams:

A factor that has a tremendous impact on the success or failure of group work is the nature of what they are being asked to do. (Fortunately, the Quinn book has many excellent application oriented activities.) In case you decide to create some of your own, the following general guidelines should be helpful. Group activities are likely to be very effective if they:

1. Require participants to produce a visible product (preferably one that could be graded even though you may not actually grade it).

2. Can **not** be successfully completed unless participants understand the concept(s).

3. Are difficult enough that they can not be successfully completed by any of the group members working alone.

4. Require the groups to do things they do well (collect and process information) and minimize the effort they have to put into things they do very poorly (eg. create a polished written document while sitting together as a group).

5. Simulate as closely as possible the kind of activities participants will experience in their work situation.

INTEGRATIVE APPLICATION ORIENTED EXAMS

In addition to the integration oriented activities that focus on specific competencies, in my judgment, it would be extremely important to use two or three major application oriented exams that give students the opportunity to focus on the relationship between the competencies. In general these would be based on "cases" that portray a complex organizational situation over time and in which organization members exhibit a wide range of leadership competencies. The purpose of these integrative exams would be to:

1. Help students to develop a sound understanding of the leadership competencies by observing and classifying a variety of contrasting approaches to leadership behavior.

2. Ensure that students have the opportunity to observe the impact of the organizational context on the need for different leadership competencies.

In most cases, I use case examples from either novels or full-length feature films (in which case I show the entire film so that students are exposed to the entire context and have to learn to separate the important from the unimportant). These are open-book exams and I typically allow the groups at least two hours of class time to work on the exams. I also hand out the exams a week or so in advance so that they can work on them longer if they want. Most groups get so involved that they work on the exam 6-8 hours outside of class in addition to the designated class time. Three examples of integrative application exams are shown below.

The Bridge Over the River Kwai

I would give a group exam over this movie following the introductory unit of the course. My primary objective would be to ensure that students had a basic understanding of the four models of the competing values framework. In addition, this movie provides two special bonuses. One is that it does an excellent job or portraying the organizational costs of having an unbalanced set of competencies (most of the principal characters are nearly one-dimensional). In addition, it clearly shows the personal cost of having a rigid view of what is appropriate.

The "Bridge Over the River Kwai" is an Oscar-winning movie that portrays the lives of a group of British POWs in a Japanese prison camp in Burma during WWII. The principal characters of the movie are:

- Colonel Saito: the Japanese camp commander

- Colonel Nicholson: the British POW commander

- Captain Reeves: Nicholson's immediate subordinate; a trained engineer

- Major Hughes: Nicholson's immediate subordinate; an excellent administrator

- Major Clipton: Nicholson's immediate subordinate; an M.D.

- Commander Warden: the leader of a British Commando team that was sent to destroy the Kwai bridge

In general terms, the movie is a story about Nicholson's initial refusal and subsequent adoption (for the POWs) of the project of building a Japanese railroad bridge over the Kwai River. Each of the British officers plays a consistent role throughout the film. In contrast, Saito, who fails to make progress on the bridge using the director role (because of Nicholson's stubbornness), later shifts to the role of supporting Nicholson in his role of directing the building of the bridge.

In the exam, I would ask the following:

1. Identify the principal competency quadrant(s) for each of the principal characters in the film. (Please provide specific examples to justify your conclusions.)

2. In what way, if any, is the effectiveness of the organizations portrayed in the film affected by an imbalance in the competencies of their leaders? (Please provide specific examples top justify your conclusions.)

3. In what way, if any, are the individuals portrayed in the film personally affected by an imbalance in their own leadership competencies? (Please provide specific examples to justify your conclusions.)

The Golden Gate (a novel by Alistair MacLean, Fawcett)

The Golden Gate is an adventure novel about an incident in which a bus, containing the President, several Cabinet members and a couple of oil sheiks is kidnapped and held for ransom in the middle of the Golden Gate Bridge. The principal characters in the novel are:

- Branson: the leader of the hijackers

- Hagenbach: the head of the FBI

- Revson: a top FBI agent who is on the bridge posing as a reporter

- The President

- General Cartland: the President's chief of staff

I would give this as an open book exam near the end of the term. As with the earlier integrative exam, I would give the exam out in advance and also give the groups at least two hours to work on the exam in class. In the exam itself, I would ask the following:

1. Identify the principal competency quadrant(s) for each of the principal characters in the book. (Please provide specific examples to justify your conclusions.)

2. In what way, if any, is the effectiveness of the organizations portrayed in the book affected by an imbalance in the competencies of their leaders? (Please provide specific examples top justify your conclusions.)

3. In what way, if any, are the individuals portrayed in the book personally affected by an imbalance in their own leadership competencies? (Please provide specific examples to justify your conclusions.)

4. In what way did changing circumstances affect the appropriateness of relying on different leadership competencies? (Please provide specific examples to justify your conclusions.)

There are two principal differences between this and the Kwai Bridge assignment. One is that several of the characters are much more well rounded. The other is that the organizational conditions change dramatically over the course of the book. Also, by the time the exam is given, I would expect the groups to be able to do a much better job of dealing with the first three questions. In addition, I think it would be important to ask a question that causes the groups to think through the relationship between the organizational situation and the appropriateness of various competencies.

The Flight of the Phoenix

This feature film is about the survivors of a plan that crashed in the Arabian Desert, who rebuilt the plane and flew it to safety. The principal characters in the film are:

- Captain Towns: the pilot, played by Jimmy Stewart

- Lou Moran: the co-pilot

- Heinrich Dorfman: an aeronautical engineer who is among the stranded passengers

I would probably use this film as an individual final exam. This would give me the opportunity to evaluate how well the individuals in class had been able to develop competencies in working with the course concepts. In this case the three principal characters are adept at different competencies and very poor in most of the others. In the exam, I would ask:

1. Identify the principal competency quadrant(s) for each of the principal characters in the film. (Please provide specific examples to justify your conclusions.)

2. In what way, if any, is the effectiveness of the organizations portrayed in the film affected by an imbalance in the competencies of their leaders? (Please provide specific examples top justify your conclusions.)

3. In what way, if any, are the individuals portrayed in the film personally affected by an imbalance in their own leadership competencies? (Please provide specific examples to justify your conclusions.)

4. In what way did changing circumstances affect the appropriateness of relying on different leadership competencies? (Please provide specific examples to justify your conclusions.)

5. Given the fact that no one in the group was very balanced with respect to leadership competencies, how do you explain the fact that the group was able to make it back to safety? (Please provide specific examples to justify your conclusions.)

A unique contribution of this film is that it dramatically portrays the fact that group effort can overcome obstacles that are created by individual members' weaknesses but not without considerable cost. In addition, it clearly portrays the importance of having someone who is skilled at handling the interpersonal conflicts that keep threatening to blow the group apart.

TEAM LEARNING RESOURCE READINGS

1. Fiechtner, S. B. and Davis, E. A. Why some groups fail. The Organizational Behavior Teaching Review. 1985. 9 (4), 58-73.
   Helpful in thinking through the implications of utilizing different types of group activities and grading strategies.

2. Mallinger, M. A. and Elden, M. Improving the quality of working life in the classroom: QWL as self-managed learning. The Organizational Behavior Teaching Review. 1987, 11(2), 43-45.
   A description of the Team Learning process using QWL terminology and examples.

3. Michaelsen, L. K., Watson, W. E., and Cragin, J. P. Grading and anxiety: A strategy for coping. Exchange: The Organizational Behavior Teaching Journal. 1981, 6(1), 8-14.
   Describes the "Grade Weight Setting" activity that we use to get the groups started off on the right foot.

4. Michaelsen, L. K., Watson, W. E., and Schraeder, C. B. Informative testing: A practical approach for tutoring with groups. The Organizational Behavior Teaching Review. 1985, 9(4), 19-33.
   The key article on Team Learning. It outlines the theoretical rationale for the process, what to do to get started, and what to watch for along the way.

5. Hackman, R. E. The design of work teams. In Handbook of Organizational Behavior, J. W. Lorsch, ed. Prentice-Hall, Englewood Cliffs, N. J., 1987, pp. 315-342.
   Provides a conceptual rationale for and research evidence which supports the value of many aspects of the Team Learning process.

OTHER REFERENCES

Kurfiss, J. G. (1988). Critical Thinking: Theory, Research, Practice, and Possibilities. Washington, D.C., ASHE-ERIC Higher Education, Report No. 2.

Porter, L. W. & McKibbin, L. E. (1988). *Management Education and Development: Drift or Thrust into the 21st Century*. New York: McGraw Hill.

"Experiential Learning in the Classroom"

Dr. Deborah Wells
Creighton University

Some General Comments and Ideas:

First, let me say that I really like this book. Its greatest strength is its organization around four management models, the roles associated with those models, and then the competencies that might logically accompany each role. That is an excellent structure, and so rational! In fact, I could imagine a whole course for non-traditional students (typical adult night class students, for example) that progresses through this entire book. My fear is that if you use bits and pieces of it as supplements to a regular text in a lecture format course, you'll destroy the effect that this excellent organizational heuristic creates.

The second really nifty thing about this book is its inclusion of critical thinking, analyzing information, writing, and oral communication skills as important competencies. Thanks to the authors for doing that! It's about time those skills were directly addressed as an integral part of a management text (and thus a management course) instead of saying, "Hey, that's a problem for the English department."

The third strength of this book is its presentation of background material on each of the competencies in the "learning" section (the L in ALAPA). This will make the professor's job easier because it has already pulled together for him or her theoretical and conceptual material most relevant to each competency. It also reinforces for students why and how this competency would be important for them as practicing (or potential future practicing) managers. Because of this, Quinn would not only make an excellent supplement, but a "stand alone" text as well.

I can actually see Quinn used three different ways: as a supplement to *Management for Productivity* by Schermerhorn, as a supplement to *A Primer on Organizational Behavior* by Bowditch and Buono, or alone. Because it provides background on each topic, it could be used in a second management course for undergraduate students (assume they've already had a principles course) as either a supplement to Bowditch and Buono or even to a Schermerhorn, Hunt, and Osborn. Or, it could stand alone as a text. Here at Creighton all juniors take MGT 301 (Management and Organization Behavior) and then all management majors must take MGT 341 (Advanced Organizational Behavior). Nonmanagement majors may also choose this as a management elective course. I could use Quinn alone as the text for 341 (Advanced OB) because it does provide background on each topic. In fact, it would be super to be able to do that because there is so much redundancy in management principles and OB texts. Quinn stands in contrast to the experiential paper I currently use (*Experiences in Management and Organizational Behavior* by Lewicki, Bowen, Hall, & Hall; John Wiley) in the advanced OB class because it does have some readings included (the learning sections that accompany each competency).

How I teach my courses:

The principles of management course is basically a lecture course. I talk about all of the substantive topics; students listen and take notes. But I have to break the monotony of constant lecturing with activities that involve the students in some way other than note taking, so I try to use appropriate and relevant self-tests, exercises, and cases. I haven't asked students to buy two books for that class - just the Schermerhorn text, and then I hand out or verbally direct exercises. Because this is a first course and there is so much material to cover, I'm not sure that I would attempt to use the Quinn book in my class the way I teach it, but if an instructor wanted to, there are lots of things in Quinn that would be good complements for lectures. For example, lectures on control can be really dull. The assessment exercise for role 3 (Coordinator) competency 3 (Controlling) would be very good for personalizing the notion of control, since it asks students to list areas in their lives they think there have relatively complete control over.

The organizational behavior course (MGT 341) really deemphasizes lecturing (although I've had to do more of it than I wanted to set up the experiential exercises in Lewicki, et al.). I do use Schermerhorn, Hunt, and Osborn's *Managing Organizational Behavior* in that class, but I wouldn't have to if I used Quinn. To have students really benefit from experiential exercises they need some background information to anchor the exercise to whatever topic it was relevant. Otherwise, experiential stuff is like eating cotton candy: "Gee, that was fun, but I didn't really get anything out of it." The questions you ask afterward and the discussion do this, too.

Another strength of Quinn is the number of self-assessment instruments it provides. Students really like self-assessment, because it answers "Who am I -- what am I like compared to other people?" (Some norm). Because a lot of my students are very competitive, self-assessment goes over well. Students would really like, for example, the role 4 (Monitor) competency 1 (Reducing Information Overload) application that requires them to analyze themselves as monitors. Or the Monitor competency 2 that asks them to analyze how good their own critical thinking processes are.

What roles and competencies I'd use and why:

Korn/Ferry International, an international headhunting firm, conducted a survey of international executives in 1988 to explore the traits that CEO's of the future will need. Among those skills that will be needed and demands that will be placed on future execs are visionary leadership, rather than traditional managerial skills, the need to communicate frequently with employees, promotion of management training and development, concern over planned management succession, and a global outlook ("How the next CEOS will be Different," Lester B. Korn, *Fortune*, May 22, 1989).

There is no doubt that all eight roles presented in the Quinn text are important. The first four are historically important and present some very basic skills all managers must have. With an eye toward the future, however, the last four roles presented by Quinn become very important. If you look back to the paragraph above, the results of Korn/Ferry's survey indicate that vision, good relationships with subordinates, communication, negotiation, and so on will be increasingly important. So will the Mentor, Facilitator, Innovator, and Broker Roles, and all 12 competencies associated with them.

Being creative: Innovator Role, Creative Thinking Competency
Ability to Think Critically and Analyze Information: Monitor Role, Analyzing Information with Critical Thinking Competency
Writing Skills: Monitor Role, Presenting Information Competency
Oral Communication Skills: Mentor Role, Interpersonal Communication Competency; Broker Role, Presenting Ideas Orally Competency
How to Motivate, Train, and Develop Others: Producer Role, Motivating Others Competency; Mentor Role, Developing Subordinates Competency
How to Manage Conflict and Negotiate: Facilitator Role, Conflict Management Competency; Broker Role, Negotiating Agreement and Commitment Competency
Skills in Managing Time and Planning: Producer Role, Time and Stress Management Competency; Coordinator Role, Planning Competency

Topics from the other books that I would combine with the competencies from Quinn:

Please see attached chart at the end of this essay.

How to mesh a traditional text with experiential learning and tips on how to handle what's likely to happen:

The chart referred to above addresses the how-to question from the standpoint of what to use with what topics. In general, try to make sure the experiential exercise you choose is closely related to the subject it is supposed to illustrate so that students see the relevance. You'll have to set up almost every exercise by providing some lecture-type instruction, although this can often be fairly brief especially in an advanced course where what you're doing is essentially reviewing material presented once before (in an OB class, for example, for topics covered in a previous principles of management course). Also, be sure to follow up exercises with a discussion or questionnaire or some other form of evaluation to make sure that the point came across. In some ways, the follow-up is the most important part, and the hardest part, because it is tempting to say to yourself, "Well, we've done that - now it's over" or to cut the follow-up short for exercises that the class really gets into or that are time consuming.

If you use any experiential or self-assessment type activities in a class, students tend to become impatient on the days that are mostly lecture. Warn them at the beginning of the semester that the course format will require a good deal of input, cooperation, and participation from them but that they will also have to take notes some days as they would have to do in a more traditional class. You have to be able to count on your students to behave maturely and truly participate or the whole class can become just a "blow off" for them. Crack down on goof-offs very early in the semester to set an example, if you have to.

How to adapt exercises:

Much of Quinn won't require adaptation, with the exception of the assessments and exercises geared toward practicing managers and students with lots of work experience. For these assessments and exercises, you'll have to tell students to think of the roles they've played that involved management or management-related skills in some form or another; groups in school, clubs and organizations, part-time jobs, sports teams, hobby groups, scouting, church activities - whatever.

How I would evaluate my students on their grasp of the material:

I have been giving exams composed of multiple choice and short essay questions. I would like to get away from that. In fact, I can envision teaching a very experiential course that doesn't have traditional exams at all. The problem with that is getting students to read if you don't test them over the material. One approach might be to have them be the teachers - after all, training or teaching is a part of managing people - and make them present the brief "learning" section to their classmates. This would reinforce the "Presenting Ideas Orally" competency that appears in Quinn in the Broker Role and would give them more practice at that. The more involved projects suggested in Quinn would be good substitutes for exams. They are very experiential in nature and will cause students to do some first hand exploration of management in action. Possible candidates would be, for example, conducting an interview with a person, and writing it up in 3-5 pages (Director Role, competency 1: Taking Initiative). Or, conducting a 45-minute interview with a delegator (Director Role, competency 3: Delegating Effectively). This approach would reinforce the "Writing Effectively competency presented as part of the Monitor Role. This would also allow the professor to give good feedback on written communication skills at the same time.

I've wrestled with the problem of how to acknowledge participation in experiential activities from semester to semester when I have taught the OB course. I have tried awarding points for each exercise assigned. That gets to be a clerical nightmare is you have a lot of students and you do a lot of exercises, particularly when you try to deal with students who miss class and then need to do some kind of make up. This semester, I decided to award a "bunch" of points (50 points total) for attendance and participation in the assigned experiential exercises. Some students didn't buy the experiential book as a consequence, because they didn't need to study it directly to do well on exams (the primary determinant of final course grade). After trying it both ways, I really believe you do have to award points for every exercise or you just don't get much effort out of students. Get clerical help in keeping track of points and who was absent, etc.

How could students evaluate themselves?

The last chapter of Quinn (Total Integration and Mastery) provides a ready answer to this question. The assessment exercise asks students to return to previous chapters and reevaluate their profiles, putting the result into a convenient matrix that will reveal their strengths and weaknesses. What could possibly be a more fitting cap for the course than such a comprehensive self-evaluation? The application appearing at the end of this chapter is also excellent and takes students to the final step. After all, it isn't enough just to know their own weaknesses, they need to plan to do something about the,. The final overall project for the course should be writing an improvement plan and long-term improvement strategy, based in the self-evaluation matrix, as the authors suggest. This is another illustration of the way in which Quinn, et al. succeed in personalizing the management experience (and why I maintain the whole book is really a simulation as I suggest in a later paragraph) for students.

Long-term or short-term groups:

I tend to favor short-term groups for two reasons: first, they give students a chance to get to know and work with many more classmates than do permanent groups assigned for the entire semester. Secondly, you may by chance or by design (if you don't use a seating chart and students sit by friends) end up with a group that is particularly hard to manage and non-functional. This has happened even when there is just one students in the group with a bad attitude. Bad attitudes seem to be infectious, and pretty soon the whole group has a "This experiential stuff is stupid and isn't teaching me anything" attitude. The opposite can happen, too. A group of really high-powered "get in there and give it all its worth" students will form. It is better to spread these energetic, insightful, and bright students out through the rest of the class so they can enthuse their classmates.

Another reason for not using permanent groups for the exercises in the Quinn text is that the activities require different sized groups. For example, the Broker Role practice section task force role play requires groups of 6; the Facilitator conflict management role play requires groups of 5, and so on. Assigning students randomly to groups by asking them to "number off" about 50% of the time, and then allowing them to self-select into groups about 50% of the time seems to strike a good balance between forcing them to meet and work with new people and letting them work with people they know and like.

Business Games or Projects:

Becoming a Master Manager is so loaded with experiential "stuff" that a professor really need not include a business game as well. That would be overkill, in my opinion. In fact, I would characterize the entire Quinn book as a simulation of the role of a manager because of the systematic way it takes students through all these needed competencies. After all, a game is just one format for presentation of experiential learning.

There are great project ideas sprinkled throughout Quinn in the application (the last A in ALAPA) section associated with each competency. If instructors are using Quinn as a second book with a primary text as well, they should pick their favorite of these projects and assign one or two. In a way, there are more projects in Quinn than you could possibly assign in a semester unless you make it the focus of the course and use it as the stand alone. Many of these projects require a 3-5 page written report following an interview or some other form of in-organization data gathering. Instructors will have to be judicious in balancing the demands placed upon students as the select potential projects to assign, as well as the grading and evaluation demands they place upon themselves.

Texts

Topical "Clusters"	Schermerhorn Mgmt for Productivity	Schermerhorn, et al Mng O.B.	Bowditch Buono	Lewicki, et al.	Quinn, et al.
General Background - History, Models Evolution, etc.	Chap. 2	Module A	Chap. 1		Chap. 1
Nature of Mgmt.	Chap. 1	Chap. 1			
Planning, Strategic	Chap. 4				Chap. 4, Comp. 1
Planning	Chap. 5				
Planning Change		Chap. 17		Exer. 43, 44	Chap. 8, Comp. 1
Managing Change					Chap. 8, Comp. 3
Creativity	Chap. 17				Chap. 8, Comp. 2
Critical Thinking					Chap. 5, Comp. 2
Innovation		Chap. 9			Chap. 2, Comp. 2
Decision Making				Exer. 18	Chap. 7, Comp. 2
Problem Solving	Chap. 3	Chap. 13		Exer. 2	
International	Chap. 19				
Human Resources - General, Staffing	Chap. 9				
Ethics/Social Responsibility	Chap. 20		Chap. 1	Exer 30	
Organizing	Chap. 6				
Org. - Environment		Chap. 11	Chap. 8		
Org. Structure				Exer. 38, 39	
Org. Design	Chap. 7	Chap. 12		Exer. 9, 41	
Job Design		Chap. 6	Chap. 9	Exer. 7	Chap. 4, Comp. 2
Work Scheduling					
Org. Culture & Climate	Chap. 8	Chap. 10	Chap. 11	Exer. 31, 42	
Research how-to's		Module B	Chap. 2		
Leadership	Chap. 10	Chap. 16	Chap. 7		
Motivation - Self		Chap. 4		Exer. 3, 23	Chap. 3, Comp. 1
Motivation - Others	Chap. 12		Chap. 3	Exer. 22, 25	Chap. 3, Comp. 2
Delegation				Exer. 26, 27	
Goal Setting					Chap. 2, Comp. 2
Rewards	Chap. 14	Chap. 6	Chap. 11	Exer. 10	
Performance Appraisal		Module C		Exer. 4, 8	Chap. 6, Comp. 3
Power, Politics		Chap. 15		Exer. 32, 33, 34	Chap. 9, Comp. 1

Topical "Clusters"	Schermerhorn Mgmt for Productivity	Schermerhorn, et al Mng O.B.	Bowditch Buono	Lewicki, et al.	Quinn, et al.
Controlling	Chap. 14				Chap. 4, Comp. 3
Information Systems	Chap. 15				
Production/Operations Management	Chap. 16			Exer. 40	
Communication –					
Improving Own	Chap. 11	Chap. 14	Chap. 5	Exer. 36, 35	Chap. 6, Comp. 2
Conflict				Exer. 11, 19	Chap. 5, Comp. 3
Negotiation	Chap. 18			Exer. 12, 21	Chap. 9, Comp. 3
				Exer. 13	Chap. 7, Comp. 3
				Exer. 14, 20	Chap. 9, Comp. 2
Training					
Development – Careers	Chap. 21				
Development – Organization	Chap. 17	Chap. 18	Chap. 10	Exer. 29, 46	Chap. 7, Comp. 1
Learning Reinforcement		Chap. 5			
Individual differences					
Personality		Chap. 3			Chap. 6, Comp. 1
Values			Chap. 4		
Attitudes				Exer. 5	
Job Satisfaction				Exer. 6	
Perceptual Processes		Chap. 2			
Groups –					
Group Design		Chap. 7			
Group Attitudes				Exer. 30	
Group Attitudes			Chap. 6	Exer. 15	
Group Dynamics	Chap. 13			Exer. 16	
Intergroup Relations		Chap. 8			
Stress					
Time Management	Chap. 21	Chap. 17			Chap. 3, Comp. 3
Role Conflict				Exer. 45, 47, 48	
Information Overload					Chap. 5, Comp. 1

Chapter 1 begins the text with two very important tasks. First, it traces the historical development of management theory and details the emergence of the Competing Values Framework. As such the Competing Values Framework, and its eight key managerial roles, are integrated into an historical-theoretical context. The second task is that the chapter explains the ALAPA learning model. This learning model is further discussed in the **Instructional Guide**.

The Competing Values Framework acknowledges the value of the previous management models which have emerged in this century. While affirming that rich heritage, the framework also introduces the concept of paradox as a fundamental context in which organizations and individuals operate and thrive.

While the idea of paradox may be new to some, it is familiar to those acquainted with Eastern thought. The co-existing of opposites is considered basic to reality, and in fact they serve to define one another and to facilitate each other's existence and distinctness. It has been argued that the advancement of the metaphysical notion of paradox has been difficult in Western culture due to the dichotomous structure of the language structure. Western languages tend to be built around a framework of subjects and predicates, nouns and verbs, actors, actions, and the acted upon. Such language structure implicitly espouses a separated view of reality characterized by an "either-or" orientation. In contrast, many Eastern languages are noted for their more integrated view of reality.

Paradox, however, is more than a passing philosophical interest. Reflection affirms that it makes a good deal of common sense. We recognize that the universe is at once characterized by order and chaos, strength and weakness, energy and entropy.

We encounter paradox in our everyday existence. People ordinarily experience opposite feelings and reactions to the same event. For example, we can approach the prospect of marriage with anticipation and trepidation; parenthood with elation and dread; death of a suffering loved one with grief and gratitude. Rather than ask ourselves why we are experiencing such different intense feelings, we are well advised to acknowledge paradox as fundamental to the very nature of existence, including human existence. Such recognition assists us in accommodating the competing demands of the managerial role in organizations.

Each of the competing values not only has legitimacy but is critical to the functioning of organizations. As we learn to live in a world of paradox, of competing values, we find ourselves taking the first steps toward mastery. The textbook provides students with essential and timely assistance to that end.

Topics included in this chapter are:

1900-1925: The Rational Goal Model and the Internal Process Model
        Social Darwinism
        Scientific Management
        Taylor's four principles of management

Assignment: Course Preassessment
Activity Flow Sheet

PURPOSE:
This activity allows students to develop a pre-course profile of their managerial strengths. **SPECIAL NOTE:** At the end of the course, students will have the opportunity to take this assessment again and develop a post-course profile to compare with this profile.

KEY TOPICS:
The eight managerial roles and their key competencies.

TIME ESTIMATE:
In class set up: 15 minutes; outside of class: 45 minutes; in class follow up discussion: 20 minutes.

FORMAT:
Individual activity followed by large group discussion.

SPECIAL NEEDS:
Students will need either the software package that accompanies this **Instructional Guide**, or a hard copy of the instruments and blank copies of the profile graphs. Complete software instructions as well as the hard copies of necessary sheets follow the process guide.

SEQUENCE:
1. Introduce the activity.

2. Remind them that there are no right or wrong answers to this instrument.

3. Explain that the resultant profile is for their use, and will be used again at the end of the course.

4. Conduct a large group discussion after they have finished with the instrument and have their profiles.

5. Summarize.

VARIATION:
If the class is organized with long-term groups, this activity can be used *later in the course* to allow group members to rate one another and receive feedback. See page 59 for a discussion of how this has worked in Dan Denison's classes.

KEY POINTS:
1. People are not born managers; the competencies are learned skills.

2. Identifying competency weaknesses is important to the process of self-improvement.

3. One can self-improve even in areas of strength.

Assignment: Course Preassessment
Process Guide

PURPOSE: This activity allows students to develop a pre-course profile of their managerial strengths.

SPECIAL NOTE: At the end of the course, students will have the opportunity to take this assessment again and develop a post-course profile to compare with this profile. This activity has the effect of generating excitement for the course, as students readily see the application of the course content to their behavior.

STEP #1: Introduce the activity by directing students to the assignment on page 23 of the text. Note that there are two instruments to complete: the 36-item Managerial Practices Survey (which measures responses to the 8 managerial roles) and the 113-item Managerial Skills assessment (which measures responses to the 24 competencies within all eight managerial roles). Give them either the software, or the hard copy of the instrument. Complete instructions for use of the software follow this process guide.

For using the hard copy of the questions, instruct students in the use of the computation sheet for the 36-item Management Practices Survey. Direct them to compute the mean for each role, and locate themselves on graphic Competing Values Skills Assessment Leadership Role Profile. Note that each role has a line which goes to the center of the circle. The slash in the line nearest the center has a value of 1; the outer edge has a value of 7. After students have placed their score on each role line, they can connect the marks to gain a graphic profile. Also note that their individual scores from the Managerial Practices Survey can be used to fill in the role bar graphs.

No computation sheet is necessary for the 113-item Self-Assessment: Managerial Skills instrument. The questions are repeated on the bar graphs; after completing the instrument, students can turn directly to the bar graphs and fill in their scores. Their average score for each competency can be reflected in the first bar of each competency.

After completing the bar graphs for each competency, students can complete the graphic Competing Values Skills Assessment Skills Profile. This Profile, which is filled in like the Leadership Profile, provides them with a graphic representation of their scores.

NOTE: You may want to alert students to the fact that a few items are reverse-scored. That is to say, a response of 6 needs to be calculated as a response of 2. Such items are note by (R) on the instruments.

STEP #2: Remind them that there are no right or wrong answers to this instrument. Although they may have little or no experience in managerial positions, instruct them to think about group experiences where they might have used these skills, or to anticipate as clearly as possible how they would respond.

STEP #3: Explain that the resultant profile is for their use, and will be used again at the end of the course.

STEP #4: Conduct a large group discussion after they have finished with the instrument and have their profile. Ask for volunteers to share what surprised them about the instrument and about their profile. What did they learn form this experience?

A key component of personal growth and development is the ability to share the results of an assessment with others, to discuss the results and to try to understand the results within a context. Students should be encouraged to think about what the results mean for them within an organizational context.

STEP #5: Summarize their major points, and the key points on the activity flow sheet.

SPECIAL NOTE: Later in the course, if you use the variation of having students rate each other, please read carefully Dan Denison's discussion on page 59. Further, the following points are noted:

1. This variation is used only in classes with a long-term or permanent groups format, and is not considered appropriate for temporary groups.

2. Only the role profile, or the Managerial Practices Survey is used. The more lengthy skills self-assessment instrument is not considered appropriate for students to use in rating each other.

3. Allow group members time to meet and discuss their profiles with each other immediately after filling them out.

4. It is important to provide a safe environment so that the feedback is not viewed as critical. Explain to students that the individuals they will be rating will also be rating them. This realization may mitigate any uncharitable tendencies that some students possibly may have in responding to their colleagues. Chances of someone's feeling unjustly treated are thus minimized. On the other hand, you may need to remind students that their candor is important in order for the activity to be of any value.

5. You may wish to remind them of some basic rules of giving feedback. I am indebted to Dan Denison for the following list:

   A. Be sure you talk about behavior and not about individuals' "personality."

   B. In receiving feedback, don't react and defend, but listen before reacting.

   C. This is non-competitive. Since you are working in a group, it is in everyone's interest to improve.

   D. Feedback is good for you, providing a basis for self-improvement. As Al Switzler says, "Feedback is the breakfast of champions."

COMPETING VALUES SKILLS ASSESSMENT:
A SUGGESTED EXERCISE TO ACCOMPANY THE TEXT

Robert E. Quinn and Daniel R. Denison

NOTE: A hard copy of the instruments and blank profile sheets begin on page 68.

COMPETING VALUES SKILLS ASSESSMENT:
A Suggested Exercise to Accompany the Text

Robert E. Quinn and Daniel R. Denison

One of the unique features of this textbook is the **Competing Values Skills Assessment**, a software system designed to assess students' managerial skills with respect to the competing values model. At the end of chapter 1, the book mentions that the instructor may have students complete this assessment. Again, in the last chapter of the text, the book mentions that the instructor may want students to complete the assessment again.

The software has two distinct parts; Part One consists of 37 items that assess student's ability to perform each of the eight managerial roles outlined by the model; and Part Two consists of 113 items that assess student's abilities with respect to three skills associated with each of the eight roles, for a total of 24 skills in all. Indexes are created for each of the roles and skills and the results are then plotted as a profile on the competing values model.

The software is designed to run on nearly any IBM-PC compatible computer with a graphics card. It requires only 256K memory to operate and can print the results on a dot matrix (Epson FX or compatible) or laser (HP Laserjet or Postscript) printer. The program can also be set up on a computer network or student computer lab to allow for easier access. It provides students with a quick diagnosis of their managerial abilities as they begin your class.

One copy of the software accompanies the **Instructional Guide**, as does a hard copy of the instruments. It is designed for the use of students who have purchased the textbook and are using it in your class. Permission is granted to instructors to make copies or other arrangements so that CVSA is available to each student. Any other use of the CVSA software is a violation of copyright. If the instructor chooses to use the CVSA it is the responsibility of the instructor to determine how the software will be made available.

FOR THE INSTRUCTOR: How To Use the Software for Teaching

We've found that the most effective way to use the software is to diagnose students' abilities **as they begin the class**. In the first few classes, when the competing values model is initially presented, students can be instructed to answer the questions in the package and to obtain a skill and role profile about themselves. This accomplishes three key objectives in the course:

It Personalizes the Model. When a student receives personalized data, the model hits home. An abstract presentation of a framework suddenly becomes a statement about their abilities. The data also serve as a very personal statement of **what the book is about,** and force each student to begin building a leadership agenda that they want to pursue in the course. This objective can be effectively underscored by requiring a brief paper in which students comment on their data and whether or not it is consistent with their past experience.

It Provides Diagnostic Data. Once a student has the data, certain parts of the textbook and the course become highly salient. Suppose I discover that I'm a terrible broker because I can't build an influence network, or make good presentations. The broker chapter and the skills described within it suddenly become very important to my future as a manager. In contrast, supposed that I find out that I'm a great monitor: I'm an immediate "expert" in this area and view it as a strength that I can rely upon. In our experience, recognizing either strengths or weaknesses increases motivation to understand and build upon the content of the course.

The Data Can Be Used as a Baseline. There are several ways in which the data can be used as a diagnostic baseline and compared to data collected later in the course. One simple way is to have students answer the role and skill items a second time at the end of the course to measure their progress. A more compelling way to use the data as a baseline, however, is to have group or class members **rate each other**. This works very effectively in classes that have assigned groups working on projects throughout the term. The group members have an extensive knowledge of each other as "managers," and a vested interest in giving each other some feedback. A still more ambitious way to use the data is to have group members rate each other **mid-way through the class**. By doing this, the group can use the feedback in order to improve their performance. This strategy works particularly well if combined with a brief discussion of survey feedback and process consultation. A final assessment at the end of the term may also prove useful.

It should be noted that this current release of the software does **not** support aggregation of the data from multiple respondents. Thus, at this point it is impossible, for example, to have five members of a student group respond about each other and have the program aggregate the data and produce an average score for each member of the group. It is possible, of course, to have one student answer the questions and produce an individual profile for each of the other members of their group. The simplest alternative, in practice, seems to be to pass out blank role profiles and have students **trace role profiles only** for each of the members of their group. Returning to a student the profiles that each of their group members have drawn about them provides a very rich data base from which to begin a group feedback session.

HOW TO USE THE CVSA PROGRAM

This section shows how to install the program and get it running, and then gives an overview of the menus and how they can be used. Appendices to this section give instructions for installing CVSA on a network (Appendix A), and discuss the keyboard (Appendix B) and supported devices (Appendix C).

Hard Disk Installation

This section shows you how to install CVSA on your hard disk. If you plan on running CVSA from the program disk, you may skip to the next section.

CVSA may be installed on your hard disk by:

1. Placing the CVSA program disk into a floppy disk drive. (A: is used in this example)

2. Then enter:

   A:INSTALL

This command will create a directory called CVSA on your C: drive and install the program on that directory.

Appendix A contains more complete information for those who want to install CVSA on a computer network or student computer lab.

Running the Program

To run CVSA from the program disk, simply insert the program disk in drive A: and enter **A:CVSA**. This will start the program. If you have already installed the program on your computer's hard disk (as discussed in the previous section), simply enter **C:\CVSA**. When the program begins you will see a full screen graphic of the competing values model.

Using the Program

Pressing any key will clear the screen of the competing values graphic, and a copyright screen will appear briefly. The next two screens will then present a brief overview of the program. After this overview, pressing the <Enter> key will bring up the student identification screen. Pressing <Enter> moves the user through these demographic questions. Some of this information (name, ID, etc.) will be used to track student responses if they are stored, while other information (working experience, etc.) will be used in future data analysis. None of the information will affect a student's role or skill profile. If information is entered incorrectly, don't worry; it can be changed by selecting **Update Student Information** from the main program menu.

THE MAIN PROGRAM MENU

Once a student has entered demographics, the main program menu appears. This menu is displayed below, followed by a brief description of each selection. The <up arrow> and <down arrow> keys are used to select menu items. For additional information on keyboard functions, see Appendix B.

Management Practices Survey
Self Assessment: Managerial Skills
Write Results to Data File
Read Results from Data File
Display Results in Graphic Format
Print Data
HELP
Update Student Information
Exit the Skill Assessment System

Management Practices Survey. The management practices survey is a set of 37 questions which describe behaviors that managers often use. Whether or not students have had managerial experience, they should use the scale presented with each behavior to describe, as realistically as possible, how frequently you might engage in each behavior. Once students begin to answer a set of questions, they cannot interrupt the session. They should reserve enough time to complete the entire question set. The answers to these questions will be used to compute the 8 indexes presented in the role profile. Indexes will only be computed when 50% or more of the items have been answered. Thus, if some items are not answered, some of the graphs may not present an index value. The <up arrow> and <down arrow> keys are used to select a response and the <left arrow> and <right arrow> keys are used to move back and forth between questions. The <Enter> key records the response and moves to the next question.

Self Assessment: Managerial Skills. The self assessment of managerial skills consists of 113 questions that are designed to assess each student's managerial skills. Each question should be answered in as objective a manner as possible. The questions are divided into three sets of 40 items, 40 items, and 33 items so that the student does not have to complete all 113 questions at one sitting. Remember that once a session is begun, it cannot be interrupted. These items will be used to compute the 24 indexes presented in the skills profile. All three sets of questions should be completed before printing the skills profile.

Write Results to Data File. This function allows you to write your responses to a data file. When this option is selected, CVSA will create a file named from the first 6 characters of the student's last name, the underscore character '_', and the first character of the student's first name. An extension of ".DTA" is appended to the filename. So, for example, George Washington would have a file named: **WASHIN-G.DTA** The program will present a menu listing all the drives that are available in the current system, and the student can select the drive where they would like to store the data. The default drive is the currently active drive, and is displayed as the currently selected menu item. If no demographic information has been entered, the program will store the data file under the name QSTRES.DTA in the currently active drive.

The current date is used to identify each data record and CVSA allows one complete data record to be stored for up to 15 different days. In the event that someone attempts to store more than 15 days, CVSA will store the most recent 15 days.

Read Results from Data File. This function allows a student to read a previously created data record. After selecting this option from the main program menu, a list of the 15 most recent dates that the student has written CVSA data records will be presented. The student should select the desired date to read and press <Enter>. The answers for that date will be read into the program. The student may then view, display, or print the answers, or may re-answer any of the questions in the survey. If questions are re-answered, a new date will be given to the data record. Information written to a file on previous days will not be over-written.

Display Results in Graphic Format. The CVSA system produces several different types of graphs:

1. **The ROLE profile**. This profile presents the results for the 8 role indexes plotted on the competing values model.

2. **The SKILLS profile**. This profile presents the results for the 24 skills indexes plotted on the competing values model.

3. **The BAR GRAPHS for specific questions**. Bar graphs for all of the role and skills questions and indexes can also be presented.

When this function is selected from the main menu, the role profile appears first. The <Space Bar> changes the display from the role profile to the skills profile. The <Pg Up> and <Pg Dn> keys display the bar graphs for the specific role and skills questions. For example, from the role profile display, striking the <Pg Dn> key displays the item and index values for the **innovator** role and for the first skill, **living with change**. Since there is not room on most monitors to display the role and skills questions on one screen, the <up arrow> and <down arrow> keys are needed to display the bar graphs for all items under this role. Pressing the <Pg Dn> key again moves to the broker role, while <Pg Up> once returns to the role profile, and pressing it twice moves to the mentor role. The <Home> key will always return the program to the role profile, and the <Esc> key returns the program to the main menu. <Alt-r> will present bar graphs of all of the role indexes, while <Alt-s> will present bar graphs of all of the skills indexes.

Print Data. This function will print the profiles and bar graphs on any of the following printers:

     1) PostScript
     2) HP LaserJet
     3) HP LaserJet+ or HP LaserJet 500+
     4) Epson FX (or compatible) dot matrix printer
     5) IBM Proprinter

The results will be printed in a graphical format, much like the screen format. Under most conditions, the PostScript printer will produce the highest quality output in the shortest amount of time. Other printers will produce good quality output, but because of the method in which these other printers generate graphical output, they may take more time.

After selecting the print option from the main program menu, choose the type of printer that is connected to your system. If you are running in a networked environment, a system administrator can provide additional instructions for printing.

Help. Selecting help from the main menu will display the following menu:

General Information
Displaying Graphical Data
Student Information
The Keyboard
Reading Data Files
Writing Data Files
Printing Information
Return to Main Menu

Selecting any of the above displayed topics will present a summary of the information contained in this manual on the screen.

Update Student Information. Selecting this option will allow the student to make corrections to the demographic information stored by the program.

Exit the Skill Assessment System. Selecting this option from the main program menu will stop the program and return the user to the DOS prompt.

Additional Information

CVSA was written at the University of Michigan by Luke Hohmann, working under the direction of Daniel Denison and Robert Quinn. If you encounter technical problems that you cannot resolve, please call the John Wiley & Sons College Software Helpline at 212-850-6753.

Appendix A: Advanced Installation Notes

Users who wish to install CVSA on a hard disk other than drive C:, or wish to install CVSA in a networked environment may require the following technical information regarding the program.

CVSA requires three files for correct operation:

CVSA.EXE   The executable file. It is required for running the basic program.

CVSA.MSG   The message file, which contains important descriptive information about the program. Without this file, the program will run, but will not have the **HELP** function or descriptive screens.

MODERN.FON   The Microsoft supplied information about screen fonts. This file is required for correct operation of CVSA.

For maximum effectiveness, these files should be placed within the same subdirectory. This directory can then be incorporated into your current path environment or network menuing system.

If CVSA is installed on a network, it can record the responses of all of the students in the class through the use of a log file. It operates so that a copy of each student's responses is copied to the log file whenever they student saves a copy of their work to a local data file. This log file capability is enabled through the use of a special command line option described below.

To enable the log file option, invoke CVSA with the command line:

CVSA LGF=D:/DIRNAME/DIRNAME/FILENAME.EXT

where:

LGF stands for "Log File"

D: is the drive that will contain the log file

DIRNAME is the name of any appropriate subdirectory name

FILENAME.EXT is a normal file name and extension

It is recommended that you grant write access permissions to the user group who will be updating this file, but that you restrict read and delete privileges.

CVSA maintains the log file by appending student information to the end of the file in one stream of information. Each record is date stamped for further processing.

Appendix B: The Keyboard

The following is a brief summary of the keyboard functions for CVSA:

1. **Moving through Menus.** To move to a different item within a menu, press the (up arrow> or <down arrow> keys.

2. **Selecting a Menu Item.** When you press the <Enter> key on menu item, that menu item will be selected.

3. **Answering a Survey Item.** When a survey item is first presented, the default response will be displayed in a blue background. When you press the <Enter> key to respond to a survey items, the highlighted response will change in color from the default blue background to a red background. This is how you can determine which questions you have actually answered - the questions that you have answered will be displayed in with a red background, while those that have not yet been answered will be displayed in a blue background.

4. **Moving through the Survey Questions.** The <right arrow> and <left arrow> keys move forward and backward between different questions in the survey. You may change your answer at any time; the most recent answer will always be displayed with a red background.

5. **Moving Through the Graphical Displays.**

KEY STROKE	GRAPH DISPLAYED
<ESC>	Return to the Main Menu
<Home>	Role Profile
<Space Bar>	Skills Profile
<Alt-r>	Bar Graph of Role Indexes
<Alt-s>	Bar Graph of Skill Indexes
<PgDn>	Next Role/Skill Bar Graph
<PgUp>	Previous Role/Skill Bar Graph
<down arrow>	Next Screen of Role/Skills Graph
<up arrow>	Previous Screen of Role/Skills Graph

Appendix C: Supported Devices

CVSA runs on any IBM PC-compatible computer running MS-DOS Version 2.1 or higher with the following graphical display standards:

Color Graphics Adapter   (CGA)
Enhanced Graphics Adapter   (EGA)
Video Graphics Adapter   (VGA)

CVSA does not require the use of a printer, although access to one of the following printers is recommended:

PostScript
HP LaserJet
HP Laserjet+/500+
Epson FX (or compatible) dot matrix printer
IBM Proprinter

COMPETING VALUES MANAGEMENT PRACTICES SURVEY

Listed below are some statements that describe managerial practices. Indicate how often you engage in the behaviors, using the scale below to respond to each statement. Please place a number from 1 to 7 in the space beside each question.

Almost never	1	2	3	4	5	6	7	Almost always

As a manager, how often would you

_____ 1. Come up with inventive ideas.
_____ 2. Exert upward influence in the organization.
_____ 3. Ignore the need to achieve unit goals.
_____ 4. Continually clarify the unit's purpose.
_____ 5. Search for innovations and potential improvements.
_____ 6. Make the unit's role very clear.

_____ 7. Maintain tight logistical control.
_____ 8. Keep track of what goes on inside the unit.
_____ 9. Develop consensual resolution of openly expressed differences.
_____ 10. Listen to the personal problems of subordinates.
_____ 11. Maintain a highly coordinated, well organized unit.
_____ 12. Hold open discussion of conflicting opinions in groups.

_____ 13. Push the unit to meet objectives.
_____ 14. Surface key differences among group members, then work participatively to resolve them.
_____ 15. Monitor compliance with the rules.
_____ 16. Treat each individual in a sensitive, caring way.
_____ 17. Experiment with new concepts and procedures.
_____ 18. Show empathy and concern in dealing with subordinates.

_____ 19. Seek to improve the workgroup's technical capacity.
_____ 20. Get access to people at higher levels.
_____ 21. Encourage participative decision making in the group.
_____ 22. Compare records, reports, and so on to detect discrepancies.
_____ 23. Solve scheduling problems in the unit.
_____ 24. Get the unit to meet expected goals.

_____ 25. Do problem solving in creative, clear ways.
_____ 26. Anticipate workflow problems, avoid crisis.
_____ 27. Check for errors and mistakes.
_____ 28. Persuasively sell new ideas to higher ups.
_____ 29. See that the unit delivers on stated goals.
_____ 30. Facilitate consensus building in the work unit.

_____ 31. Clarify the unit's priorities and direction.
_____ 32. Show concern for the needs of subordinates.
_____ 33. Maintain a "results" orientation in the unit.
_____ 34. Influence decisions made at higher levels.
_____ 35. Regularly clarify the objectives of the unit.
_____ 36. Bring a sense of order and coordination into the unit.

COMPUTATIONAL WORKSHEET FOR SELF-ASSESSMENT

The Facilitator

\# 9 _____
\# 12 _____
\# 14 _____
\# 21 _____
\# 30 _____

Total _____ / 5= _____

The Mentor

\# 10 _____
\# 16 _____
\# 18 _____
\# 32 _____

Total _____ / 4 = _____

The Innovator

\# 1 _____
\# 5 _____
\# 17 _____
\# 25 _____

Total _____ / 4 = _____

The Broker

\# 2 _____
\# 20 _____
\# 28 _____
\# 34 _____

Total _____ / 4 = _____

The Producer

\# 3 _____(R)
\# 13 _____
\# 19 _____
\# 29 _____
\# 33 _____

Total _____ / 5 = _____

The Director

\# 4 _____
\# 6 _____
\# 24 _____
\# 31 _____
\# 35 _____

Total _____ / 5 = _____

The Coordinator

\# 7 _____
\# 11 _____
\# 23 _____
\# 26 _____
\# 36 _____

Total _____ / 5 = _____

The Monitor

\# 8 _____
\# 15 _____
\# 22 _____
\# 27 _____

Total _____ / 4 = _____

COMPETING VALUES SELF ASSESSMENT: MANAGERIAL SKILLS

Listed below are some statements that describe managerial skills that are essential to each of the eight managerial roles. Indicate your feelings by using the scale below. Please place a number from 1 to 7 in the space beside each question.

Strongly Disagree 1   2   3   4   5   6   7 Strongly Agree

_____ 1. I like to "take charge" of situations that I am in.
_____ 2. I am an intensely motivated person.
_____ 3. In planning I know how to develop priorities.
_____ 4. I have a systematic approach for filing papers.
_____ 5. I have a clear understanding of who I am.

_____ 6. I am skilled in team building techniques.
_____ 7. My own personal coping strategies help me to adapt to change.
_____ 8. I know how to build personal power through the involvement of others.
_____ 9. When I have more than one goal, I set clear priorities.
_____ 10. I am skilled at motivating other people.

_____ 11. In organizing, I understand the division of labor principle.
_____ 12. In making logical organizational decisions, I can solve the problem of organizational conformity or "Group Think".
_____ 13. In communicating, I am very sensitive to feelings.
_____ 14. I know when to use participative decision making.
_____ 15. I think of myself as a creative person.

_____ 16. In negotiating, I know how to explore win-win outcomes.
_____ 17. The best way to get a job done is to do it yourself.
_____ 18. I always begin my day with a personal planning session.
_____ 19. I know the basic steps in building an organizational control system.
_____ 20. I feel comfortable in writing a business document.

_____ 21. I am able to coach others effectively.
_____ 22. I know how to create win-win situations in conflicts.
_____ 23. I can accurately assess the forces for and against change in a given situation.
_____ 24. I enjoy making oral presentations.
_____ 25. It is better to make a few mistakes by acting decisively than to sit around analyzing decisions.

_____ 26. I have a passionate commitment to the things I do.
_____ 27. I set deadlines when I plan.
_____ 28. In organizing my paperwork, I have a system that prevents me from forgetting where things are.
_____ 29. I have a clear set of values.
_____ 30. I can turn a collection of individuals into a smooth functioning team.

_____ 31. Planning successful change requires a good knowledge of how employees will react.
_____ 32. I know how to employ formal authority in an effective way.
_____ 33. I always have a clear set of objectives.

_____ 34. I can create high performance expectations in others.
_____ 35. I can recognize an organization designed by function.

_____ 36. In making logical organizational decisions, I can overcome the problem of ego involvement.
_____ 37. In conversations, I put people at ease.
_____ 38. I know how to employ participative decision making techniques.
_____ 39. I always try to look at old problems in new ways.
_____ 40. In negotiating, I know how to base the result on an objective standard.

_____ 41. I feel comfortable with the concept of delegation.
_____ 42. I always end the day with the feeling that I have accomplished at least one significant task.
_____ 43. In building organizational controls, I know how to design a performance appraisal system.
_____ 44. I know how to organize a business document.
_____ 45. I feel comfortable acting as an advisor to people.

_____ 46. I can manage tensions and get people to relax during a conflict.
_____ 47. I understand the principles of managing change.
_____ 48. I am an effective public speaker.
_____ 49. I can influence people through rational persuasion.
_____ 50. I am comfortable living with change.

_____ 51. I know how to turn a work group into a smooth functioning team.
_____ 52. I am very honest with myself.
_____ 53. I have a systematic format for taking notes in meetings.
_____ 54. I establish measurable objectives when I plan.
_____ 55. I love to feel challenged by the tasks I have to do.

_____ 56. I usually take initiative and act decisively.
_____ 57. Each day I have a well defined plan.
_____ 58. I often inspire people to do more than they are expected to do.
_____ 59. I can design a matrix organization.
_____ 60. In making logical organizational decisions, I can overcome the problem of stereotypic thinking.

_____ 61. During a conversation, I am in touch with the other's reactions.
_____ 62. I know which situations are inappropriate for participative decision making.
_____ 63. I would rather criticize than create new ideas. (R)
_____ 64. In negotiating, I know how to effectively acknowledge the existence of a conflict.
_____ 65. In preparing an oral presentation, I know how to get people's attention.

_____ 66. I know how to best involve people in designing organizational changes.
_____ 67. I know how to be tough but not offensive in a conflict situation.
_____ 68. I am able to mentor people, and help them grow and develop.
_____ 69. I am able to effectively criticize and improve my own first draft writing efforts.
_____ 70. I know how to manage resistance to the implementation of a management control system.

_____ 71. I always do the most important parts of my job during the time of day when I perform the best.

72. I understand and know how to apply the principles of effective delegation.
73. I know how to use reward to effectively influence others.
74. I adjust well to changing conditions.
75. I am a skilled group facilitator.

76. I recognize and work on my inconsistencies and hypocrisies.
77. I am skilled in managing paperwork.
78. When I do planning, I develop bench marks to measure progress.
79. I am driven by a need for continuous improvement in what I do.
80. I am comfortable moving into a situation and taking over.

81. In negotiating, I know how to keep the discussion issue-oriented.
82. I like to explore new ideas.
83. I feel comfortable involving people in group decisions.
84. I am very sensitive to nonverbal messages in a conversation.
85. In making logical organizational decisions, I can analyze the structure of the arguments that are presented.

86. I understand the advantages of organizing by divisional form.
87. I am skilled in getting the best out of people.
88. I always seek clear feedback about how I am doing.
89. I understand and know how to apply the principles of effective delegation.
90. In making an oral presentation, I know how to get people's attention.

91. I am skilled at facilitating organizational change.
92. I know how to keep a conflict situation moving towards a productive situation.
93. People trust me and come to me for advice.
94. Things that I write are easily understood.
95. I understand the characteristics of successful control systems.

96. I know how to manage stress.
97. I am an action person, who likes to see immediate progress.
98. I am an unusually hard worker.
99. I can apply the principles of organizational design.
100. When it comes to paperwork, I am very well organized.

101. I work hard at being honest and sincere.
102. I know how to run a meeting in which everyone feels involved and influential in the decisions that are made.
103. My approach to change is "If it ain't broke, don't fix it." (R)
104. I am able to influence others through persuasion.
105. I always establish a specific set of challenging goals.

106. I can get others to excel in their work.
107. I understand the problems of logical decision making in organizations.
108. I effectively use empathy and reflective listening.
109. I try to treat any new problem as an opportunity.
110. I am very relaxed when I have to speak to a group of people.

111. I often come up with useful innovations.
112. I regularly use stress management techniques.
113. I know how to analyze the dynamics of an on-going organizational change process.

THE COMPETING VALUES SKILLS ASSESSMENT
LEADERSHIP ROLE PROFILE

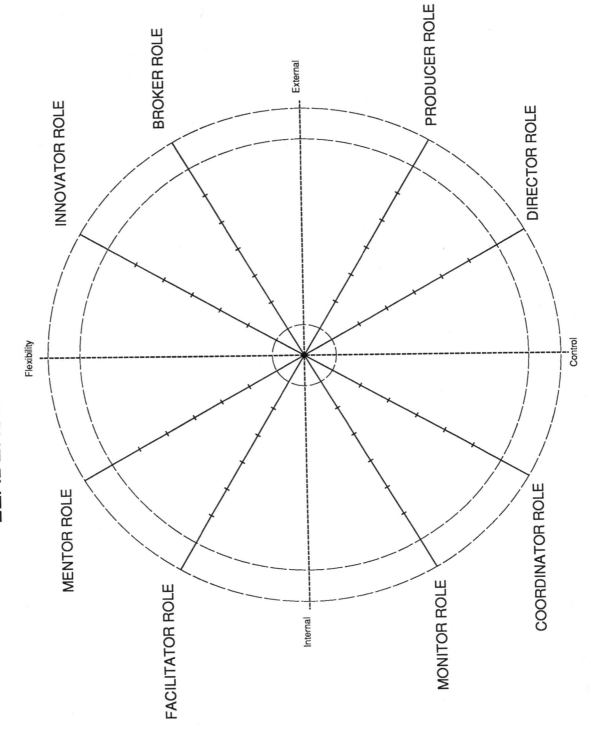

THE COMPETING VALUES SKILLS ASSESSMENT
SKILLS PROFILE

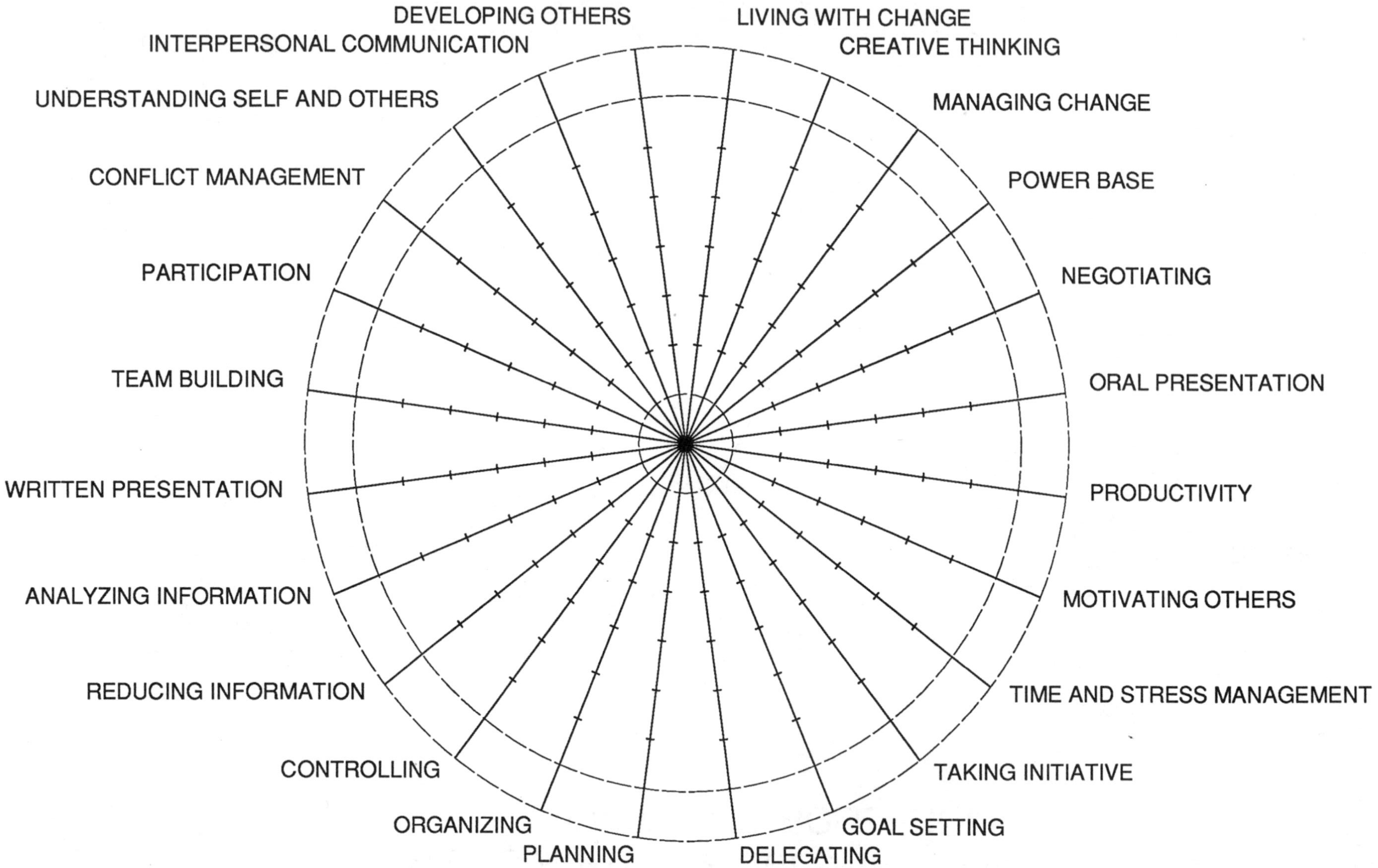

DEVELOPING OTHERS
LIVING WITH CHANGE
CREATIVE THINKING
MANAGING CHANGE
POWER BASE
NEGOTIATING
ORAL PRESENTATION
PRODUCTIVITY
MOTIVATING OTHERS
TIME AND STRESS MANAGEMENT
TAKING INITIATIVE
GOAL SETTING
DELEGATING
PLANNING
ORGANIZING
CONTROLLING
REDUCING INFORMATION
ANALYZING INFORMATION
WRITTEN PRESENTATION
TEAM BUILDING
PARTICIPATION
CONFLICT MANAGEMENT
UNDERSTANDING SELF AND OTHERS
INTERPERSONAL COMMUNICATION

DIRECTOR ROLE

Continually clarify the unit's purpose

Make the unit's role very clear

Regularly clarify the objective of the unit

Clarify the units priorities and direction

Get the unit to meet expected goals

TAKING INITIATIVE

I like to 'take charge' of situations that I am in

It is better to make a few mistakes by acting

decisively than to sit around analyzing decisions

I usually take initiative and act decisively

I am comfortable moving into a situation and taking over

I am an action person, who likes to see immediate progress

GOAL SETTING

When I have more than one goal, I set clear priorities

I always have a clear set of objectives

Each day I have a well defined plan

I always seek clear feedback about how I am doing

I always establish a specific set of challenging goals

DELEGATING

The best way to get a job done is to do it yourself

I feel comfortable with the concept of delegation

Delegating work frees up time to do more important things

I understand and know how to apply

the principles of effective delegation

I am skilled at delegation

PRODUCER ROLE

Ignore the need to achieve unit goals

Maintain a 'results' orientation in the unit

See that the unit delivers on stated goals

Push the unit to meet objectives

Seek to improve the workgroup's technical capacity

PRODUCTIVITY

I am an intensely motivated person

I have a passionate commitment to the things I do

I love to feel challenged by the tasks I have to do

I am driven by a need for continuous improvement in what I do

I am an unusually hard worker

MOTIVATING OTHERS

I am skilled in motivating other people

I can create high performance expectations in others

I often inspire people to do more than they are expected to do

I am skilled in getting the best out of people

I can get others to excel in their work

TIME AND STRESS MANAGEMENT

I always try to begin my day with a personal planning session

I always end the day with the feeling that I
have accomplished at least one significant task

I always do the most important parts of my
job during the time of day when I perform the best

I know how to manage stress

I regularly use stress management techniques

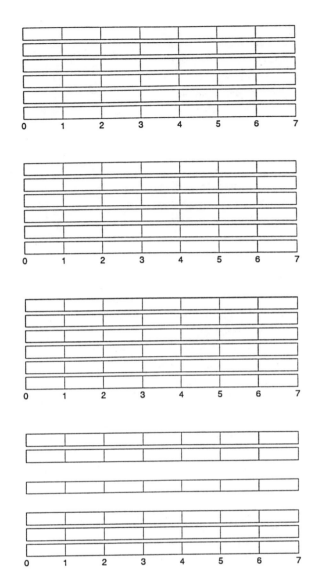

COORDINATOR ROLE

Maintain tight logistical control

Anticipate workflow problems, avoids crisis

Bring a sense of order and coordination into the unit

Solve scheduling problems in the unit

Maintain a highly coordinated, well organized unit

```
0    1    2    3    4    5    6    7
```

PLANNING

In planning, I know how to develop priorities

I set deadlines when I plan

I establish measurable objectives when I plan

When I do planning, I develop bench marks to measure progress

```
0    1    2    3    4    5    6    7
```

ORGANIZING

In organizing, I understand the division of labor principle

I can recognize an organization designed by function

I can design a matrix organization

I understand the advantages of organizing by divisional form

I can apply the principles of organizational design

```
0    1    2    3    4    5    6    7
```

CONTROLLING

I know the basic steps in building an organizational control system

In building organizational controls, I know
how to design a performance appraisal system

I know how to manage resistance to the
implementation of a management control system

I understand the characteristics of successful control systems

```
0    1    2    3    4    5    6    7
```

MONITOR ROLE

Monitor compliance with the rules

Compare records, reports, and so on to detect discrepancies

Check for errors and mistakes

Keep track of what goes on inside the unit

0 1 2 3 4 5 6 7

REDUCING INFORMATION

I have a systematic approach for filing papers

In organizing my paperwork, I have a system
that prevents me from forgetting where things are

I have a systematic format for taking notes in meetings

I am skilled in managing paperwork

When it comes to paperwork, I am very well organized

0 1 2 3 4 5 6 7

ANALYZING INFORMATION

In making logical organizational decisions, I can solve
the problem of organizational conformity or 'Group Think'

In making logical organizational decisions,
I can overcome the problem of ego involvement

In making logical organizational decisions, I
can overcome the problem of stereotypic thinking

In making logical organizational decisions, I can
analyze the structure of the arguments that are presented

I understand the problems of logical decision making in organizations

0 1 2 3 4 5 6 7

WRITTEN PRESENTATION

I feel comfortable in writing a business document

I know how to organize a business document

I am able to effectively criticize and
improve my own first draft writing efforts

Things that I write are easily understood

0 1 2 3 4 5 6 7

MENTOR ROLE

Listen to the personal problems of subordinates

Show empathy and concern in dealing with subordinates

Treat each individual in a sensitive, caring way

Show concern for the needs of subordinates

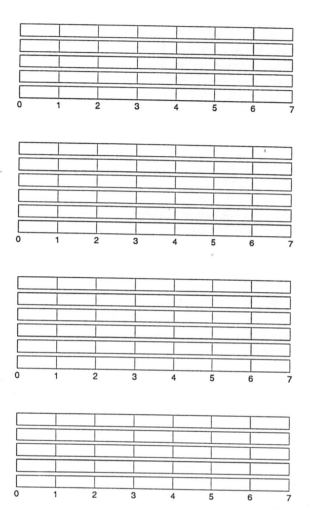

UNDERSTANDING SELF AND OTHERS

I have a clear image of who I am

I have a clear set of values

I am very honest with myself

I recognize and work on my inconsistencies and hypocrisies

I work hard at being honest and sincere

INTERPERSONAL COMMUNICATION

In communicating I am very sensitive to feelings

In conversations I put people at ease

During a conversation, I am in touch with the other's reactions

I am very sensitive to nonverbal messages in a conversation

I effectively use empathy and reflective listening

DEVELOPING OTHERS

I am able to coach others effectively

I feel comfortable acting as an advisor to people

I am able to mentor people, and to help them grow and develop

People trust me and come to me for advice

FACILITATOR ROLE

Facilitate consensus building in the work unit

Surface key differences among group

members, then works participatively to resolve them

Encourage participative decision making in the group

Hold open discussion of conflicting opinions in groups

Develops consensual resolution of openly expressed differences

TEAM BUILDING

I am skilled in team building techniques

I can turn a collection of individuals into a team

I know how to turn a work group into a smooth functioning team

I am a skilled group facilitator

PARTICIPATION

I know when to use participative decision making

I know how to employ participative decision making techniques

I know which situations are

inappropriate for participative decision making

I feel comfortable involving people in group decisions

I know how to run a meeting in which everyone feels

involved and influential in the decisions that are made

CONFLICT MANAGEMENT

I know how to create win-win situations in conflicts

I can manage tensions and get people to relax during a conflict

I know how to be tough but not offensive in a conflict situation

I know how to keep a conflict

situation moving towards a productive conclusion

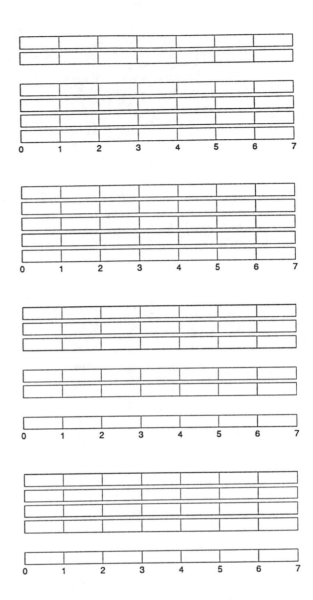

INNOVATOR ROLE

Come up with inventive ideas

Experiment with new concepts and procedures

Do problem solving in creative, clear ways

Search for innovations and potential improvements

```
0   1   2   3   4   5   6   7
```

LIVING WITH CHANGE

My own personal coping strategies help me to adapt to change

Planning successful changes requires a
good knowledge of how employees will react

I am comfortable living with change

I adjust well to changing conditions

My approach to change is 'If it ain't broke, don't fix it'

```
0   1   2   3   4   5   6   7
```

CREATIVE THINKING

I think of myself as a creative person

I always try to look at old problems in new ways

I would rather criticize than create new ideas

I like to explore new ideas

I try to treat any new problem as an opportunity

I often come up with useful innovations

```
0   1   2   3   4   5   6   7
```

MANAGING CHANGE

I can accurately assess the forces for
and against change in a given situation

I understand the principles of managing change

I know how to best involve people in designing organizational changes

I am skilled at facilitating organizational change

I know how to analyze the dynamics of
an on-going organizational change process

```
0   1   2   3   4   5   6   7
```

BROKER ROLE

Exert upward influence in the organization

Influence decisions made at higher levels

Get access to people at higher levels

Persuasively sell new ideas to higher-ups

```
0   1   2   3   4   5   6   7
```

POWER BASE

I know how to build personal power through the involvement of others

I know how to employ formal authority in an effective way

I can influence people through rational persuasion

I know how to use reward to effectively influence others

I am able to influence others through persuasion

```
0   1   2   3   4   5   6   7
```

NEGOTIATING

In negotiating, I know how to explore for win-win outcomes

In negotiating, I know how to base the result on an objective standard

In negotiating, I know how to
effectively acknowledge the existence of a conflict

In negotiating, I know how to keep the discussion issue-oriented

```
0   1   2   3   4   5   6   7
```

ORAL PRESENTATION

I enjoy making oral presentations

I am an effective public speaker

In preparing an oral presentation,
I know how to get people's attention

I am very relaxed when I have to speak to a group of people

```
0   1   2   3   4   5   6   7
```

The Director Role is the first role in the Rational Goal Model, and in many ways epitomizes the traditional posture of "manager as boss." The manager in the Director Role, clarifies goals and objectives, provides direction and instruction, delegates, and makes final decisions. In the words of one of the authors:

The whole notion of director is the old traditional role of "I'm the boss and I know best." That is in direct conflict with the biggest change in the workforce: the push for high involvement management. This new management manifests itself in self-directed work teams brought upon by the increasing educational and technological sophistication of the workforce. It is less frequently the case now that the boss knows more than the employees. The dilemma is this: organizations still have a need for the Director Role. How do you provide that in a workforce that does not want to be directed? How do you solve this dilemma?

Perhaps the solution to this dilemma is balance, and in the realization that the issue is: *how* to provide direction to a workforce that no longer wishes to be directed. The mentor role, located directly opposite the director role, can help provide this needed balance and skill.

Examination of the director role competencies reveals that they enjoy wide applicability, and are acknowledged as critical to personal achievement. Students often recognize the necessity of applying the competencies of the director role in their personal lives. Regardless of their situation in life, they often see themselves as needing to take initiative and set goals. Furthermore, most people find themselves having to ask others to do things, sometimes with mixed results. Improving one's ability to delegate is also seen as a life skill.

The competencies in the Director Role: The three competencies in this role and their corresponding topics in the learning activities are:

Competency #1: Taking Initiative

Topics: Taking initiative and being decisive
                         Directive decision style
                         Five steps for taking initiative
                         Keys to decisiveness

Competency #2: Goal Setting

Topics: Goal setting at different organizational levels
                         Strategic goal setting
                         Tactical goal setting
                   Lessons learned on goal setting research and practice
                   Using objectives as a management tool: MBO-type approaches
                         What Makes a Good MBO
                         S.M.A.R.T.
                         Writing an MBO

Competency #3: Delegating Effectively

Topics:
                          To delegate or not to delegate
                                Reasons for not delegating and counterarguments
                                Keys to effective delegation
                          Potential pitfalls of delegation

Conceptually, these are not the only competencies in this role. Other competencies have been identified as:

Logical problem solving
Effective uses of authority
The art of giving clear directions
Developing a vision
Setting priorities
Defining roles and expectations
Developing decision making skills

Which competencies to choose? We recognize that you, as the instructor, may not be able to cover all three competencies in your course. In order to assist in your decision of which ones to choose, the following questions were posed to the authors. You may not agree with the authors, but here are their opinions.

1. In teaching this course, if you could cover only ONE competency from this chapter, which one would that be and why?

One author noted: "Goal setting. This is the heart of the Director Role. While choosing a competency is a value judgement, its a very much needed and under-utilized skill."

Another author's response: "Delegation. This is a *key* management competency and cannot be left out of a management development text."

Still another author added: "Goal setting, because its not done very well and people who do it get a lot accomplished."

2. In teaching this course, if you could cover only TWO competencies from this chapter, which two would they be and why?

One author added delegation to goal setting, observing that "its the necessary next step in the process of directing. Setting goals is one thing; knowing how to appropriately use your own time and that of subordinates requires good skills in delegating."

Another author responded: "After delegating effectively, goal setting would be next. It is important for the director to plan - goal setting is defined as an organizational effectiveness criterion in the Competing Values Framework."

Still another author agreed with the first that after goal setting, delegation would be the second competencies because, again, " because its not done very well and people who do it get a lot accomplished."

3. If you had an additional 5 pages of space for each competency, what ideas and concepts would you wish to include?

Taking Initiative: Include more depth on the notion of decisiveness and the whole topic of decision making; add more on decision making.

Goal Setting: Add collaborative management by objectives (CMBO) as a separate topic; Discuss the "fit between strategic and tactical planning, and how MBO translates top-down or bottom-up planning across the levels."

Delegating Effectively: Add "more critical incidents on delegation, both successful and unsuccessful. This is a good lead in to the Producer Role." Also, add material on "deciding what should and should not be delegated; communication style needs in delegation and how they differ from/are similar to other communication styles."

The Director Role and current issues: As was noted earlier, the dilemma of the Director Role is how to direct a workforce that does not want to be directed. A related point regards managing a culturally diverse workforce. Directing will have to be seen as "individual-specific"; more than ever, it is clear that skills of judgment and discernment are necessary in directing different workers from varying backgrounds.

Some questions to consider in this chapter are:

1. Obviously the competencies in the Director Role are needed and necessary. It is important to consider, however, the possible consequences if the competencies are taken too far. What would it be like for the organization and for employees if managers carried the competencies of the Director Role to the extreme?

2. What organizational designs may rely less on the Director Role? Are there organizations that may need a more subtle emphasis than others? If so, what would be their characteristics?

A note from one of the authors:

"I see the Director Role as what many people typically think of as 'leadership'. It involves two additional competencies that are not well developed in the text. The first is "developing a vision" -- this is more than taking initiative; it is recognizing how to be a leader of followers. The second is "defining roles and expectations." Perhaps this is associated with delegating, but I see it as more - as setting policies and procedures. Again, these are somewhat associated with taking charge, but more concretely than in the case of creating a vision."

Assessment: Rowe Decision Style Inventory
Activity Flow Sheet

PURPOSE: The ability to take initiative is often associated with being directive in decision making. This activity helps students identify the extent to which they are comfortable with a directive decision making style. In this way they may be able to ascertain the extent to which they tend to take initiative.

KEY TOPICS: Taking initiative; keys to decisiveness.

TIME ESTIMATE: 30 minutes.

FORMAT: Individual activity followed by large group discussion.

SPECIAL NEEDS: None.

SEQUENCE: 1. Direct students to complete the inventory, as per the instructions on page 26.

2. Remind them to add their scores very carefully.

3. Have them record their scores in the boxes on page 28.

4. Give students information (see next pages) relating to the norms for each style, and assist them in locating themselves.

5. Conduct a large group discussion.

6. Summarize.

KEY POINTS: 1. Some of the behaviors involved in decisive decision making are reflected in the ability to take initiative.

2. If you are not naturally inclined to be directive and take initiative, you can learn to be more so. These tendencies are learned skills.

Assessment: Rowe Decision Style Inventory
Process Guide

PURPOSE: The purpose of this activity is to give students some basis to assess their ability to take initiative. While initiative is difficult to measure, it can be argued that a directive decision making style closely approximates the ability to take initiative. In addition to defining their style, students are able to assess their place on a continuum of norms associated with the style. With this information, they can assess the extent to which they are comfortable with the directive style. The inventory also enhances their understanding of the intricacies of the Director Role.

STEP 1. Direct students to complete the inventory, as per the instructions on page 26. Remind them that responses should reflect how **they** feel and what **they** prefer, not what they believe is the most correct or desirable.

STEP 2. Remind them to add their scores very carefully.

STEP 3. Have them record their scores in the boxes on page 28.

STEP 4. Give students information on previous pages relating to the norms for each style, and assist them in locating themselves.

STEP 5. Conduct a large group discussion. Some discussion questions may include:

   A. What is taking initiative? In what ways does the directive decision making style approach it? In what ways is the directive decision making style consistent and inconsistent with your view of taking initiative?

   B. How does one assess taking initiative? Why is it hard to measure?

   C How can you learn to be more directive, if you are not naturally inclined in that role?

   D. How does your Decision Style score correlate with the course assessment for chapter 1?

STEP 6. Summarize, using students' main ideas as well as the key points on the activity flow sheet.

INTERPRETING THE ROWE DECISION STYLE SURVEY

Excerpts taken from: Alan J. Rowe and Richard O. Mason,
Managing with Style: A Guide to Understanding, Assessing and Improving Decision Making.
San Francisco: Jossey Bass 1987, Chapter 3, pp. 37-53.

The Decision Style Inventory has been used by over 10,000 individuals, including presidents of companies, board chairs, nurses, architects, planners, etc. Face validity is high, as over 90% of the people who take the inventory agree with its findings.

Once students have their scores in each column, these scores can be compared with those of others who have completed the inventory. Column 1 represents the directive style, column 2 the analytical style, column 3 the conceptual style and column 4 the behavioral style. The typical score for each style are: directive: 75; analytical: 90; conceptual: 80; and behavioral: 55. Differences in respondents' scores from the typical scores can be explained by intensity, or style dominance. Using the bell shaped curve and standard deviations, extent of dominance can be ascertained. There are four levels of dominance:

1. Least preferred. This is the style seldom used, and identified by the score of more than 7 points (approximately one-half the standard deviation) below the average.

2. Backup. This is the style you would use if the occasion demanded, and identified by the score within the range of 7 points above or below the average.

3. Dominant. A person whose score is in this category will use this style frequently, as indicated by a score between 7-15 points above the average.

4. Very dominant. A person whose score is more than 15 points above the average would tend to use this style almost exclusively in most situations. Approximately 16% of the respondents have a very dominant style category in any of the four styles.

TYPICAL RANGE OF STYLE SCORES

	Least Preferred	Backup	Dominant	Very Dominant
Directive	20-67	68-81	82-89	90-160
Analytical	20-82	83-96	97-104	105-160
Conceptual	20-72	73-86	87-94	95-160
Behavioral	20-47	48-61	62-69	70-160

BRIEF DESCRIPTION OF THE BASIC STYLES

DIRECTIVE: Practical orientation with emphasis on the here and now. People with this style tend to use data that focus on specific facts and to prefer structure. They are action oriented, decisive, and look for speed, efficiency, and results. People with this style can be autocratic and exercise power and control. Their focus is short range, and they tend to have the drive and energy needed to accomplish difficult tasks. They also focus on problems internal to the organization, and may sometimes feel insecure and want status to protect their position.

Psychological aspects:

Focuses on: Tasks and technical problems
Considers: Facts, rules, and procedures
Acquires information: By sensing and using short reports with limited data
Evaluates information: Using intuition, experience, or rules
Complexity: Has a low tolerance for ambiguity and needs structure

Leadership Style:

Characteristics: Practical, matter of fact, authoritarian
Social orientation: Impersonal; needs power and status; forceful; dislikes committees and group
    discussions
Task orientation: Quick; action and results oriented
Motivation: Situations with measurable achievement potential, tangible rewards

Best organizational fit: Structured, goal-oriented, such as bureaucracies, or where power and authority are important

Major criticism: Too rigid, impersonal, simplistic, autocratic

ANALYTICAL: Tendency to over-analyze a situation or to always search for the best possible solution. People with this style often reach top posts in their companies, and while very technical in their outlook, they can often be autocratic.

Psychological aspects:

Focuses on: Tasks and technical problems involving a logical approach
Considers: Every aspect of a given problem
Acquires information: By careful analysis, using a large number of data
Evaluates information: Through abstract thinking, avoiding incomplete data
Complexity: High tolerance for ambiguity, innovative in solving problems

Leadership style:

Characteristics: Intellectual, ingenious, wants control
Social orientation: Impersonal, skilled in organizing facts, establishes controls, prefers limited
    control by others
Task orientation: Applies rigorous analysis, prepares elaborate, detailed plans
Motivation: Enjoys complex situations with variety and challenge, wants to be able to predict
    outcomes

Best organizational fit: Impersonal, planning, solving complex problems, science, engineering.

Major criticism: Too dogmatic, overcontrolling, impersonal, careful, abstract or mathematical; sometimes too slow

CONCEPTUAL: Characterized by creativity and a broad outlook, but may rely too much on intuition and feelings. Good at getting along with others, enjoys having discussions, and willing to compromise. Curious and open-minded, but independent and dislikes rules. Tend to be perfectionists, want many options, and to be concerned about the future. Creative problem solvers who easily visualize alternatives and consequences. Tend to closely associate with the organization, value praise, recognition, and independence. Prefer to loose control and willing to share power.

Psychological aspects:

Focuses on: People and broad aspects of a problem
Considers: Many options and future possibilities
Acquires information: By using intuition and discussion with others
Evaluates information: By integrating diverse cues to reach conclusions, applying judgment
Complexity: High tolerance for ambiguity; takes risks and is very creative

Leadership style:

Characteristic: Is insightful and enthusiastic
Social orientation: Very personal, shows concern for others' views, smooths over difficulties; is well liked.
Task orientation: Is adaptive and flexible, uses intuition, seeks new ideas
Motivation: Seeks recognition from others, wants independence, enjoys achieving personal goals

Best organizational fit: Loose, decentralized settings, open or organic organization

Major criticism: Is a dilettante; too idealistic, indecisive, imaginative, slow, difficult to control

BEHAVIORAL: Most people-oriented style of the four; likes being involved with people and exchanging views; good listener, supportive, receptive to suggestions, show warmth, uses persuasion, accepts loose control. Tends to focus on short-run problems. Action-oriented. Wants acceptance.

Psychological aspects:

Focuses on: People, social aspects of the work situation
Considers: Feelings, well-being of others
Acquires information: By sensing, listening, and interacting with others
Evaluates information: Using feelings; instincts
Complexity: Has low tolerance for ambiguity

Leadership style:

Characteristics: Sociable, friendly, supportive
Social orientation: Talent for building teams, encourages participation
Task orientation: Is action oriented, holds meetings

Motivation: Acceptance by peers, avoidance of conflict

Best organizational fit: Well-designed, people-oriented, collegial settings

Major criticism: Too concerned about others; too "wishy-washy," sensitive, can't make hard decisions, can't say no.

BASIC STYLE PATTERNS

Most people use a combination of the four styles, each in varying degrees. Composite scores are arrived at by summing the scores in varying combinations. Patterns of these styles have been identified and related to career interests. These are illustrated by the table below:

PATTERN	SCORE	TYPICAL OF
Left brain (analytical + directive)	165 or higher	Science, finance, law
Right brain (conceptual + behavioral)	135 or higher	Psychology, teachers, artists
Idea orientation (analytical + conceptual)	170 or higher	Senior executives, leaders
Action orientation (directive + behavioral)	130 or higher	Supervisors, sales, athletes
Executive (conceptual + directive)	155 or higher	Entrepreneurs, crossover executives
Staff (analytical + behavioral)	145 or higher	Technical managers
Middle management (directive + analytical + conceptual)	245 or higher	Flexible management style

**Analysis: The Case of the Eccentric Programmer
Activity Flow Sheet**

PURPOSE: This activity allows students to analyze a situation and identify the five steps for taking initiative.

KEY TOPICS: The five steps for taking initiative and the need for balance.

TIME ESTIMATE: 30 minutes.

FORMAT: Small groups of 4-6 students, followed by large group discussion.

SPECIAL NEEDS: None.

SEQUENCE: 1. Divide students into small groups.

                    2. Direct them to read the case and respond to the discussion questions.

                    3. Ask them to identify each character's decision style.

                    4. Have the groups report their findings.

                    5. Conduct a large group discussion.

                    6. Summarize.

VARIATIONS: 1. Assign students to read the case and respond to the questions as homework, and then in class discuss their findings in small groups, and report to the class.

                    2. Have students read the case and respond individually (as homework or in class), proceeding directly to the large group discussion.

KEY POINTS: 1. The three major characters can be classified according to the Rowe inventory.

                    2. An overemphasis on the values of task focus and tough-mindedness (Sid Young's behavior), or an under-emphasis in task focus (Wilfred Nortz's behavior) can be troublesome.

                    3. When the five steps are overemphasized, they will not always lead to success.

                    4. Note the need for balance. Just carrying out the 5 steps for taking initiative is not enough. The manager needs to take into account individual styles and other situational aspects.

Analysis: The Case of the Eccentric Programmer
Process Guide

PURPOSE: In this activity students analyze a situation and identify the five steps for taking initiative. In addition they can classify the three major characters to Rowe's Decision Style Inventory: Directive, Analytical, Conceptual, and Behavioral. This affords students the opportunity to recognize those styles, and to discern the need for balance.

STEP 1. Divide students into small groups.

STEP 2. Direct them to read the case and respond to the discussion questions on page 32. (If you prefer, this step could precede Step 1 as an individual activity.)

STEP 3. Ask them to identify which decision style is exemplified by each of the major characters in the case. The classifications are:

> Fred Wilson: Behavioral
> Sid Young: Directive
> Wilfred Nortz: Analytical

STEP 4. Have the groups report their findings, summarizing their points on the blackboard.

STEP 5. Conduct a large group discussion, responding to the questions in the text. Some suggestions for additional questions include:

A. How would a conceptual decision maker behave in any of the roles?

B. Where is it advantageous for Sid Young to exhibit his directive qualities?

C. How are each of the five steps for taking initiative illustrated? How are some overemphasized?

D. How does Sid Young overemphasize the values of task focus and tough-mindedness? How does this cause difficulty?

E. How does Wilfred Nortz get into difficulty by not being task focused enough? He tends to be more concerned with a perfectly current analytical solution than with getting the job done on time. How does this cause difficulty?

F. How does Fred Wilson's style affect the situation?

STEP 6. Summarize by having the class identify directive characteristics, and the need for balance.

**Practice: Role Play the Case of the Eccentric Programmer
Activity Flow Sheet**

PURPOSE: This activity permits students to explore the decision styles used by the characters in the Case of the Eccentric Programmer, and to practice the five steps to taking initiative.

KEY TOPICS: The five steps for taking initiative and the 11 keys to decisiveness.

TIME ESTIMATE: 35 minutes for 2 iterations of the role play.

FORMAT: Fishbowl role play in class and large group discussion.

SPECIAL NEEDS: None.

SEQUENCE: 1. Introduce the activity.

2. Designate 2 students to play the part of Nortz, and 2 to play Young.

3. Divide rest of class into groups of 4-5 to play the part of Fred Wilson.

4. Set up fishbowl exercise using one of the 2 students designed to play each role of Nortz and Young

5. Ask for volunteers from among the groups to play Fred Wilson.

6. Do second iteration of the role play using the second student to play Nortz and Young.

7. Summarize by comparing outcomes.

VARIATION: This activity can be conducted in small groups rather than using the fishbowl technique.

KEY POINTS: 1. This activity permits students to experience many of the key points of the analysis activity. See Activity Flow Sheet for that activity.

2. It can be noted that this case is an example of commonplace managerial situation of a conflict between two employees, one of whom supervises the other.

3. In playing the roles, students may wish to note the extent to which their role performance is affected by their own decision style (as per their scores on the Rowe Decision Style Inventory)

Practice: Role Play the Case of the Eccentric Programmer
Process Guide

PURPOSE: This activity permits students to explore the decision styles used by the characters in the Case of the Eccentric Programmer, and to practice the five steps to taking initiative. They also focus on the 11 keys to decisiveness. The objective is to arrive at different outcomes of the case.

STEP 1. Introduce the activity by directing students to read the instructions in the text.

STEP 2. Designate 2 students to play the part of Wilfred Nortz, and 2 to play Sid Young. [NOTE: female students playing these roles are invited to change the names of the characters. For instance, Wilfred can be Wilma and Sid could be Shirley.]

STEP 3. Divide rest of class into groups of 4-5 to play the part of Fred Wilson. [Again, Fred could become Florence.]

STEP 4. Set up fishbowl exercise using one of the 2 students designed to play each role of Nortz and Young. Give people 5-10 minutes to get into their roles.

STEP 5. Ask for volunteers from among the groups to play Fred Wilson.

STEP 6. Do second iteration of the role play using the second student to play Nortz and Young.

STEP 7. Summarize by comparing outcomes. It is also important to explore with students how they feel about how the role play went and why. Additional discussion questions may include:

A. What problem do each of the three people have and how do they differ? What do you think is the real problem between Nortz and Young?

B. In what ways do the 11 keys to decisiveness help Fred Wilson?

C. How can Fred Wilson advance balance in the styles of the other roles?

Application: Interviewing a Decisive Person
Activity Flow Sheet

PURPOSE: This activity allows students to explore the director role in two ways: by positing interview questions to a decision maker and by conducting the actual interview.

KEY TOPICS: 11 keys to decisiveness.

TIME ESTIMATE: In class set up time: 10 minutes; outside of class: 30 minutes to frame the questions and 1 hour for the interview; in class follow up discussion: 20 minutes.

FORMAT: An individual written homework assignment followed by large group discussion.

SPECIAL NEEDS: A decisive person to interview.

SEQUENCE: 1. Direct students to read the instructions on page 32 of the text.

                      2. Have them identify three decisive individuals.

                      3. Have students write out a few paragraphs on these individuals.

                      4. Instruct students to write out an interview schedule.

                      5. Ask students to write a short paper regarding their experience.

                      6. Conduct a large group discussion and summarize.

VARIATION: Students may be divided into groups for framing the questions. Besides having the advantage of refining their questions, they can more easily compare their interview findings.

KEY POINTS: 1. While important, decisiveness is not the only key to success in one's endeavors. One may appear decisive but be making premature decisions. Decisiveness balanced with deliberate reflection is optimal.

                      2. Appearing decisive may be a function of one's decision making style, rather than one's tendencies to make good decisions quickly.

                      3. We may appear more decisive to others than we actually feel.

Application: Interviewing a Decisive Person
Process Guide

PURPOSE: This activity allows students to explore the Director role in two ways: by positing interview questions to a decisive person and by conducting the actual interview. They may also refine their views of decisiveness by comparing the information from the interview with their initial impressions of the person.

STEP 1. Introduce the activity by directing students to read the instructions on page 32 of the text.

STEP 2. Have them identify three individuals whom they consider to be decisive, and to write a short paragraph on why they consider these individuals to be decisive. Hopefully students will be able to interview one of them within a few days of being given this assignment.

STEP 3. Once the interview has been scheduled, direct students to expand their written paragraph on the individual's decisiveness.

STEP 4. Instruct students to write out an interview schedule, based on their written description of the person as well as on the keys to decisiveness and taking initiative.

STEP 5. After the interview is completed, ask students to define ways in which the interview supported their impression of the individual as decisive, and ways in which the interview may have refined their views.

STEP 6. Conduct a discussion in class where students share what they have learned from the interviews, and summarize. Some possible questions may include:

   A. Did you use the keys to decisiveness in selecting the person to interview? If so, which ones and how?

   B. What did you glean from the interview in terms of why and how this person is decisive?

Assessment: Personal and Organizational Goal Setting
Activity Flow Sheet

PURPOSE: This activity introduces the learning section by helping students to consider goal setting as it relates to their lives as students and in the workplace.

KEY TOPICS: Goal setting.

TIME ESTIMATE: 10-15 minutes.

FORMAT: An individual activity, this assessment can be conducted in class, as an introduction to the learning activity, or as homework; followed by large group discussion.

SPECIAL NEEDS:.   None.

SEQUENCE: 1. Introduce the activity by having students read the directions.

                    2. Direct students to completing and interpret the instrument.

                    3. Conduct a large group discussion and summarize.

VARIATION: After individually completing the questionnaire, class members can be placed into 4-5 person groups to discuss their interpretations.

KEY POINTS: 1. Goal setting is not only an important skill for managers in organizations, but for people in their personal lives, as well.

                    2. Failure to set goals can result in undesirable consequences.

                    3. There are organizational sources of resistance to goals setting, just as there are individual sources of resistance to goal setting.

Assessment: Personal and Organizational Goal Setting
Process Guide

PURPOSE: This activity introduces the learning section by helping students to consider goal setting as it relates to their lives as students and in the workplace. Further, this assessment helps them to think about goal setting as a relevant skill to enhance their personal lives, as well.

STEP 1. Introduce the activity by having students read the directions on page 33 of the text. Remind them not to read the interpretation, beginning at the bottom of the page, until after they have completed the questionnaire.

> **NOTE:** The section of the questionnaire entitled "At Work" can be completed by students who have not had any work experience but who have participated in church, community, or other volunteer organizations.

STEP 2. After completing the instrument, have them read the interpretation on pages 32-34.

STEP 3. Discuss and summarize as a lead into the discussion of the learning section. Some suggested discussion questions are:

A. Is goal setting important in one's personal life? Why or why not?

B. What are some sources of resistance to goal setting that individuals may experience?

C. What are some of the psychological benefits to goal setting that you can identify?

D. What are some of the consequences in organizations of failing to adequately set goals?

Analysis: MBO Is Not For Me
Activity Flow Sheet

PURPOSE: This activity allows students to analyze a work situation where S.M.A.R.T. objectives, planning, and MBO could be developed more effectively.

KEY TOPICS: MBO, S.M.A.R.T objectives.

TIME ESTIMATE: 45 minutes.

FORMAT: Individual activity, work in 4-5 person groups, followed by large group discussion.

SPECIAL NEEDS: None.

SEQUENCE: 1. Introduce the activity.

2. Divide students into groups to discuss the questions.

3. Have students report back to the large group.

4. Conduct a large group discussion and summarize.

VARIATION: Step 1 may be completed as homework.

KEY POINTS: 1. MBO is applicable to many aspects of work.

2. MBO is a valuable tool when used appropriately.

3. S.M.A.R.T. objectives are central to MBO.

4. Performance-based planning and evaluation are valuable tools.

Analysis: MBO Is Not For Me
Process Guide

PURPOSE: MBO is often used by top level management. As a result, many lower-level managers feel that MBO does not apply to them. This activity allows students to analyze a work situation where S.M.A.R.T. objectives, planning, and MBO could be developed more effectively.

STEP 1. Introduce the activity by directing students to read the case individually and respond in writing to the questions at the end on page 43.

STEP 2. Divide students get into 4-5 person groups to discuss their responses to the questions. Someone should be designated as a reporter for the group.

STEP 3. Have the groups report back to the class what they discussed.

STEP 4. Conduct a large group discussion. Summarize, using the main points of the groups and the key points on the activity flow sheet. Some additional discussion questions may include:

A. What do you think of Don's objectives?

B. Is an MBO program applicable to Don's position? Why or why not?

C. How might Don start an MBO program in his work unit?

D. How might Don benefit from using S.M.A.R.T.?

Practice: Write Your Own MBO
Activity Flow Sheet

PURPOSE: This activity permits students to practice writing MBO's that may be relevant and meaningful in their own lives.

KEY TOPICS: Writing an MBO.

TIME ESTIMATE: 20-30 minutes.

FORMAT: Individual activity followed by large group discussion.

SPECIAL NEEDS: None.

SEQUENCE: 1. Review with students the steps to writing an MBO.

         2. Direct them to read the instructions for the activity.

         3. Walk them through the first goal of becoming a better manager.

         4. Allow 15-20 minutes for them to complete the activity.

         5. Discuss and summarize.

VARIATION: If students seem fairly comfortable with writing MBO's, then this activity can proceed as an individual in class or homework activity. However, if you sense that some of them may need some assistance, the could be placed into small groups for Step 3, and report back to the class.

KEY POINTS: 1. MBO is a managerial technique which is applicable to many aspects of life.

         2. Notice that the way in which the goals are stated can be psychologically frustrating. We may want to be a more supportive friend, and may berate ourselves for not being more supportive, but unless we are able to articulate *how* to become more supportive, we can be doomed to a cycle of negative feelings about ourselves.

         3. Positive benefits that accrue from using MBO are numerous, and include analyzing a situation, breaking it down into manageable components, and feeling a sense of improvement.

         4. It is important to recognize personal sources of resistance to MBO's in order to deal with those issues and to defuse that resistance.

Practice: Write Your Own MBO
Process Guide

PURPOSE: This activity permits students to practice writing MBO's that may be relevant and meaningful in their own lives. Such practice in personal life increases the probability that MBO's will be utilized as managerial competency.

STEP 1. Review with students the steps to writing an MBO. Refer them to sections on page 40 of the text which they may find helpful.

STEP 2. Direct them to read the instructions for the activity on page 43.

STEP 3. Walk them through the first goal to be a better manager. Note that being "a better manager" is way too vague. Take S.M.A.R.T. and apply:

    1. Be more **SPECIFIC**. Determine to be better at given managerial roles (Director, Innovator, etc.) rather than a better manager.

    2. **MEASURE.** How would you make this measurable? One possibility is to use a peer feedback process. Ask three people you work with to tell you how you're doing in each of the roles.

    3. **ASSIGNABLE** is next but this goal cannot be assigned because this is a personal improvement goal.

    4. Use **REALISTIC** by selecting one competency from each role to improve on.

    5. Use **TIME** to set a specific number of months to expect improvement.

STEP 4. Allow 15-20 minutes for them to complete the activity.

STEP 5. Discuss as a large group and summarize. You may want to ask for volunteers to share one of their MBO's, and allow the class to respond. Possible discussion questions include:

    A. Compare your feelings about your likelihood of achieving each goal, without the MBO and with the MBO. Is there a difference? How and why?

    B. Describe any resistance to writing your MBO's which you may have experienced.

    C. What other aspects of your life might you find MBO's helpful?

Application: Setting Your Goals
Activity Flow Sheet

PURPOSE: This activity affords students the opportunity to apply the competency of
                     goal setting using specific action plans.

KEY TOPICS: Goal setting; S.M.A.R.T.

TIME ESTIMATE: 30 minutes.

FORMAT: This is an individual homework activity followed by large group
                     discussion.

SPECIAL NEEDS: The Implementation Plan Worksheet (follows process guide).

SEQUENCE: 1. Ask students to select an important goal.

                     2. Hand out the worksheets; instruct students to read the directions.

                     3. Ask for volunteers to share their action plans.

                     4. Conduct a large group discussion.

                     5. Summarize.

VARIATION: This activity may be completed in class.

KEY POINTS: 1. Goal setting and planning are critical to implementation plans.

                     2. Using S.M.A.R.T. helps make goals seem more attainable.

Application: Setting Your Goals
Process Guide

PURPOSE: This activity affords students the opportunity to examine an important goal, applying the competency of goal setting. They are directed to translate their goals into specific action plans.

STEP 1. Introduce the activity by asking students to choose an important goal which they consider to be troublesome, overwhelming, and/or difficult. This should be a goal which they have experienced difficulty in handling.

STEP 2. Hand out the worksheets and have students read the directions on pages 43-44 of the text. Ask students if they have any questions about this activity.

STEP 3. Ask for volunteers to share their action plans. Encourage them to share their feelings about the process, and how they were able to overcome any resistance to completing the assignment.

STEP 4. After completion, discuss as a large group. Ask students how they feel about their plans. In what ways does their goal seem more attainable now?

STEP 5. Summarize, using their major points, as well as the key points on the activity flow sheet.

IMPLEMENTATION PLAN WORKSHEET

Choose a goal from your schoolwork, job, or personal life that you consider complex, difficult, troublesome, or overwhelming. Develop an Implementation Plan. Include the following:

Today's date: _____

My goal is: _____

I. S.M.A.R.T. Objectives:

II. Outside factors which might affect the objective:

III. Steps to Achieve Goal: By When?

     1.

     2.

     3.

     4.

     5.

     6.

     7.

     8.

     9.

IV. Criteria for Evaluating Results:

1. A **GOOD** result would be:

2. A **SATISFACTORY** result would be:

3. A **POOR** result would be:

V. Other comments about your plan:

Assessment: To Delegate or Not To Delegate
Activity Flow Sheet

PURPOSE: This activity provides students with the opportunity to assess their beliefs and assumptions about delegation.

KEY POINTS: Reasons for not delegating and counter-arguments.

TIME ESTIMATE: 20 minutes.

FORMAT: Individual activity followed by large group discussion.

SPECIAL NEEDS: None.

SEQUENCE:

1. Introduce the activity.

2. Have students complete the assessment.

3. Conduct a large group discussion.

4. Summarize.

VARIATION: Step #2 may be assigned as homework.

KEY POINTS:

1. There are major "myths" regarding delegation. These myths include:
   - Delegation takes too much time
   - Delegation lessens a manager's control
   - Delegation produces inferior work

2. Delegation is related to goal setting.

3. Regarding delegation, there are parallels between the manager-employee relationship and the teacher-student relationship.

**Assessment: To Delegate or Not To Delegate
Process Guide**

PURPOSE: This activity provides students with the opportunity to assess their beliefs and assumptions about delegation, and provides a lead into a discussion of the reasons for not delegating and the counter-arguments.

STEP 1. Introduce the activity by referring students to page 44 of the text.

> **NOTE:** Students should be reminded that there are no right or wrong answers to the assessment; it functions to provide a basis for discussing assumptions regarding delegation.

STEP 2. Have students complete the activity.

STEP 3. Conduct a large group discussion based on responses to the activity. Address the major myths of delegation:

- Delegation takes too much time
- Delegation lessens a manager's control
- Delegation produces inferior work

Additional discussion questions may include:

A. What experiences have you had in delegating?

B. What skills do you think are important to delegating effectively?

C. Recall instances when you have been delegated **to**. In your experience, what factors made the difference between a successful delegation and an unsuccessful delegation?

D. What problems have you faced in trying to delegate?

E. What are characteristics on individuals whom you consider to be successful delegators?

STEP 4. Summarize, using students' main points as well as they key points on the activity flow sheet.

Analysis: The Storm Window Assignment
Activity Flow Sheet

PURPOSE: This activity allows students to analyze a work situation in terms of the eight keys to effective delegation.

KEY TOPICS: Eight keys of effective delegation.

TIME ESTIMATE: 20 minutes.

FORMAT: Individual activity followed by large group discussion.

SPECIAL NEEDS: None.

SEQUENCE:
1. Instruct students to read the case.

2. Direct them to respond in writing to the discussion questions.

3. Conduct a large group discussion.

4. Summarize.

VARIATIONS:
1. Steps #1 and #2 can be completed as homework.

2. This activity can be conducted with small groups by having students compare their responses with one another in between .steps 2. and 3. Keep in mind, however, that this case forms the basis for the practice activity, which is conducted in small groups.

KEY POINTS:
1. This case illustrates delegation which was unsuccessful.

2. Fairness was an issue, which George could have used to change the rules.

3. Jack had understandable reasons for not wanting to admit that the irritating remarks of his co-workers had gotten the best of him.

4. The situation escalated into a power play on George's part.

SPECIAL NOTE: **This activity forms the basis of the practice activity which follows, entitled: "Improvising a Delegation Problem."**

Analysis: The Storm Window Assignment
Process Guide

PURPOSE: This activity allows students to analyze a work situation in terms of the eight keys to effective delegation. This case is a classic example of unsuccessful delegation which escalates into a power play on the part of the boss. Students have the opportunity to analyze the situation and determine how the boss could have handled things differently.

STEP 1. Have students read the case beginning on page 48. Refer them to the eight keys to effective delegation on page 47. Remind them to put themselves in the role of George Brown as they are reading the case.

STEP 2. Direct them to respond in writing to the discussion questions on page 51.

STEP 3. Conduct a large group discussion by asking students to share their responses to the discussion questions. Additional questions might include:

A. What are possible reasons Jack may have had for not wanting to do the windows again?

B. At what point did George's handling of the situation become a power play?

C. How could George have used fairness as an issue to resolve the situation?

STEP 4. Summarize, using the major points made by students, as well as the key points on the activity flow sheet.

Practice: Improvising a Delegation Problem
Activity Flow Sheet

PURPOSE: This activity permits students to explore the delegation style of George Brown in the previous activity and arrive at a different outcome.

KEY TOPICS: Effective delegation.

TIME ESTIMATE: 30 minutes.

FORMAT: 4-5 person groups followed by large groups discussion.

SPECIAL NEEDS: Students need their responses to the previous analysis activity, "The Storm Window Assignment".

SEQUENCE:
1. Introduce the activity.

2. Divide the class into 4-5 person groups.

3. Assign roles.

4. Have players brainstorm how they would carry out their roles.

5. Conduct a large group discussion and summarize.

VARIATION: If desired, one group could be selected to play their roles in a fishbowl format.

KEY POINTS:
1. Minor changes in George's handling of the conversation could eventuate in a happy outcome.

2. Special efforts to recognize the importance of the assignment could also change the outcome.

3. Students are likely to feel differently towards George as they play him handling this situation fairly.

Practice: Improvising a Delegation Problem
Process Guide

PURPOSE: This activity permits students to explore the delegation style of George Brown in the previous analysis case entitled "The Storm Window Assignment." The objective is to arrive at a different outcome than in the case, using the eight keys to effective delegation.

> **NOTE:** Students need their responses to the previous analysis activity, "The Storm Window Assignment".

STEP 1. Introduce the activity by referring to the instructions on page 51, and by reminding students of the conclusions from their discussion of the analysis activity.

STEP 2. Divide the class into groups of 4-5.

STEP 3. Assign 1-2 students in each group to play the role of Jack, and the others to play the role of George. [NOTE: female students may wish to change the names from George to Georgia, and from Jack to Jackie.]

STEP 4. Have each subset of players brainstorm how they would carry out their respective roles.

STEP 5. After the role plays, conduct a large group discussion to summarize. Possible additional questions include:

A. What minor changes in George's handling of the conversation could eventuate in a happy outcome?

B. What could have been done to elevate the status of the assignment? Would this be desirable? Why or why not?

C. Do you feel differently towards George now, that you have played him handling this situation in a positive manner? What accounts for any change in feelings which you might be experiencing?

Application: Interviewing a Delegator
Activity Flow Sheet

PURPOSE: This activity allows students to explore the delegator competency by conducting an interview of someone who delegates.

KEY TOPICS: Effective delegation.

TIME ESTIMATE: In class set up time: 10 minutes; outside of class: 45 minutes for the interview; follow-up discussion in class: 20 minutes.

FORMAT: Individual activity followed by large group discussion.

SPECIAL NEEDS: A delegator to interview.

SEQUENCE:
1. Direct students to read the instructions.

2. Have them identify an individual to interview.

3. Instruct students to write out an interview schedule.

4. Ask students to report their findings to the class.

5. Summarize.

VARIATION: Students may be divided into groups for comparing their findings, prior to the large group discussion.

KEY POINTS:
1. Everyone delegates to some extent.

2. This interview encourages the interviewee to delegate and places the student in the position of assisting in the planning of the delegation.

3. The eight keys to delegation have wide applicability.

Application: Interviewing a Delegator
Process Guide

PURPOSE: This activity allows students to explore the delegator competency by conducting an interview of someone who delegates. Students in the interview are in the position of encouraging the interviewee to delegate and assist in the planning.

STEP 1. Introduce the activity by directing students to read the instructions on page 52 of the text.

STEP 2. Have them identify someone to interview. Note that people in all sorts of roles delegate. Effective delegation can be regarded as a life skill. You may need to help them identify someone to interview. Indicate that the interview must be conducted by a certain date.

STEP 3. Instruct students to write out an interview schedule, as per the instructions in the book.

STEP 4. Conduct a discussion in class where students share what they have learned from the interviews, and summarize. Addition questions might include:

   A. Did you notice any resistance to delegation on the part of the person you interviewed? If so, what were the sources of the resistance and how did you handle it?

   B. What are your feelings about delegation now, as compared with when you took the assessment? To what do you attribute any change?

The Producer Role is the second role in the Rational Goal Model. The manager in this role is described as hard working, personally productive, goes beyond what is expected, meets commitments, stimulates productivity from others, and expects hard work.

The competencies involved in this role are readily recognized by students as being significant in their lives. Many students wrestle with personal motivation, as well as time and stress management issues. As such they will find the material in this chapter to be immediately helpful as well as revealing.

The importance of human motivation is a clear emphasis in this role. The dilemma for the manager is balancing the needs of the organization with the needs of the individual. This role is clear, however, in the belief that employee motivation is a first step toward increasing productivity, and that successful organizational reward systems seek to assess the needs of individuals and to meet them.

The competencies in the Producer Role: The three competencies in this role and their corresponding topics in the learning activities are:

Competency #1: Personal Productivity and Motivation

Topics: Personal Peak Performance
                                        Commitment
                                        Challenge
                                        Purpose
                                        Control
                                        Transcendence
                                        Balance

Competency #2: Motivating Others

Topics: Applying motivation theory
                                Guide for applying Expectancy Theory
                                        Tie effort to performance
                                        Link performance to outcomes
                                        Understand valences for desired employee outcomes
                                Be a positive Pygmalion

Competency #3: Time and Stress Management

Topics: The reality of time and stress management
                                The physiological consequences of stress
                                Negative and positive sources of stress
                                Oncken's multidimensional model of time and stress management

Conceptually, these are not the only competencies in this role. Other competencies have been identified as:

> Personal goal clarification
> Empowering others
> Project/program management
> Personal career planning
> Coping with mistakes, failure, and other personal crises
> Doing the tasks you would rather avoid
> Handling conflicting expectations

Which competencies to choose? It is unlikely that you will be able to cover all three competencies in your course. In order to assist in your decision of which ones to choose, the following questions were posed to the authors:

1. In teaching this course, if you could cover only ONE competency from this chapter, which one would that be and why?

One author responded: "I would do all and not cut out any of these competencies. Each one is vital."

Another author said: "Motivating others. Without the ability to do this, the manager is not going to be effective. Motivating others is how the manager gets help in accomplishing the work."

Still another author responded: "Time and stress management. You cannot be productive if you cannot handle stress."

2. In teaching this course, if you could only TWO competencies from this chapter, which two would they be and why?

One author said: "Personal productivity and motivation. Note that the ordering of the three competencies is logical. Understand yourself, and then understand motivational situations of subordinates.

Another author said: "Personal productivity and motivation. I see this as an extension of stress management."

Regarding the competency of motivating others, one author had this observation: "It is difficult for people to take the specific steps in this competency. We tend to make judgments regarding what motivates others based on what we prefer, and this is flawed."

3. If you had an additional 5 pages of space for each competency, what ideas and concepts would you wish to include?

Personal Productivity and Motivation: More on how to achieve peak performance, e.g., becoming more aware of mental and physical health (and the care they need), and discovering how to make changes in your life to increase your own motivation.

Motivating Others: Overview of motivation theories other than expectancy theory; content vs. process theories.

Time and Stress Management: More on the physiological dimensions of stress management, such as diet, exercise, and relaxation. Also, assertive communication skills as a stress management technique.

The Producer Role and current issues: The Producer Role seems to epitomize "life in the fast lane" for corporate America. Yet due to the increasing numbers of women in the workplace, there is an increasing tendency for firms to recognize and accommodate to family issues. If parents are worried about proper day-care for their children, or the care of an elderly family member, how productive can they be at work?

Furthermore, there is an increasing interest in the health and fitness levels of employees. Some firms offer aerobics programs and wellness centers at work, providing opportunities for employees to take "fitness breaks" from their desks. There seems to be a growing recognition that corporate attention to employee stress and health has payoffs in lower absenteeism and turnover rates.

Some questions to consider in this chapter are:

1. Obviously the competencies in the Producer Role are necessary. It is important to consider, however, the possible consequences for the organization if the competencies are not balanced. What would it be like for the organization and for employees if managers carried the competencies of the Producer Role to the extreme?

2. How are organizational reward systems related to employee motivation?

A note from one of the authors:

"There is a paradox between time and stress management. Time management is often presented as how to fit more into a day, which is quite the opposite of the focus of stress management. There is a need to focus on the balance between doing more, achieving peak performance, and knowing how/when to relax."

Assessment: Do You Produce?
Activity Flow Sheet

PURPOSE: This activity asks students to reflect on a personal experience, identifying their underlying motivators.

KEY TOPICS: Personal peak performance.

TIME ESTIMATE: 15-20 minutes.

FORMAT: Individual activity followed by large group discussion.

SPECIAL NEEDS: None.

SEQUENCE: 1. Introduce the activity.

                      2. Instruct them to write the paragraph and list their contributing factors..

                      3. Conduct a large group discussion.

                      4. Summarize.

VARIATION: 1. Step #2 can be completed as homework.

                      2. In step #4 nominal group technique could be used to elicit one point from each class member in turn, allowing everyone to participate.

KEY POINTS: 1. Contributing factors may be under one's personal and direct control, or they may be related to external factors.

                      2. It is important to determine what we can control and what we cannot control.

                      3. While we may not be able to control external factors, we do control our response to those factors.

                      4. Making the choice to have a positive perception of external factors may be a source of empowerment in our motivation and productivity level.

SPECIAL NOTE: The results of this activity are required in order to complete the analysis activity which follows.

Assessment: Do You Produce?
Process Guide

PURPOSE: This activity asks students to reflect on a personal experience. In their reflection they are able to identify factors which were under their direct and personal control, and factors which were external and beyond their control. As they separate the two types of factors, they have the opportunity to identify and dissect their underlying motivators and sources of personal empowerment.

STEP 1: Introduce the activity by directing students to read the instructions on page 54-55. Remind them that for best results, write the paragraph before reading the interpretation on page 55 or any part of the learning section.

STEP 2: After they have finished with the paragraph, instruct them to list their contributing factors and compare them with those discussed in the learning section.

STEP 3: Conduct a large group discussion. Ask students to share with the class insights they gained from the assessment, perhaps listing factors which were found to enhance their motivation levels. Additional discussion questions may include:

A. What examples can you given from personal experience or from the book of the conscious choice to control the interpretation of an external - or uncontrollable - factors?

B. Which of the identified conditions that stimulate personal peak performance enhance a positive interpretation of external events?

C. What can organizations and firms do to create a favorable climate for the developing of these conditions which stimulate personal peak performance?

STEP 4: Summarize the major points of the discussion.

Analysis: What Motivates You?
Activity Flow Sheet

PURPOSE: Like the assessment, this activity allows students to reflect on a personal experience and identify their underlying motivators. In addition students are permitted to work in small groups and comparing their contributing motiving factors with each other.

KEY TOPICS: Personal peak performance.

TIME ESTIMATE: 15-20 minutes.

FORMAT: 4-5 person groups followed by large group discussion.

SPECIAL NEEDS: Students need their responses to the previous assessment activity.

SEQUENCE: 1. Instruct class members to form 4-5 person groups.

                     2. Direct them to answer the 3 questions in the instructions.

                     3. Have each group share its findings with the class.

                     4. Conduct a large group discussion and summarize.

KEY POINTS: Mirroring those in the assessment activity, the key points include:

                     1. Contributing factors may be under one's personal and direct control, or they may be related to external factors.

                     2. It is important to determine what we can control and what we cannot control.

                     3. While we may not be able to control external factors, we do control our response to those factors.

                     4. Making the choice to have a positive perception of external factors may be a source of empowerment in our motivation and productivity level.

Analysis: What Motivates You?
Process Guide

PURPOSE: Like the assessment, this activity asks students to participate in action inquiry by allowing them to look back on a personal experience and identify their underlying motivators. In addition students are permitted to work in small groups and comparing their contributing motiving factors with each other.

STEP 1: Instruct class members to form small groups of 4-5 individuals each. Parts 1 and 2 of this **Instructional Guide** provides some discussion regarding methods for forming these groups.

STEP 2: Using their written work from the assessment activity, direct them to answer the 3 questions in the instructions on page 59.

STEP 3: In the large group, ask each group to share its findings with the class. Two suggestions for this include:

A. Give each group 5 minutes to report to the class.

B. Allow each group could present one point in turn, in an effort to insure that each group has an equal chance of participating.

As the responses are given, press the class to identify which one are under the direct control of the individuals.

STEP 4: Conduct a large group discussion and summarize, using students' main points.

Practice: "Feeling Dead Ended"
Activity Flow Sheet

PURPOSE:	This activity permits students to practice analyzing motivational levels in a work situation, applying techniques to managing the situation, and identifying preventative measures that might have been taken.
KEY TOPICS:	Personal peak performance.
TIME ESTIMATE:	30 minutes.
FORMAT:	4-5 person groups followed by large group discussion.
SPECIAL NEEDS:	None.
SEQUENCE:	1. Introduce the activity.
	2. Divide the class into groups of 4-5 students each.
	3. A spokesperson should be chosen from each group.
	4. Conduct a large group discussion.
	5. Ask individuals to share their answers to question 7.
	6. Summarize.
VARIATION:	The individual work in step one may be assigned as homework.
KEY POINTS:	1. In order to suggest ways to boost employees' motivation and enthusiasm, one must understand their situation from their point of view.
	2. Understanding the situation in this case is assisted by isolating issues and reconnecting them in a meaningful manner.

Practice: "Feeling Dead Ended"
Process Guide

PURPOSE: This activity permits students to practice analyzing motivational levels in a work situation, applying techniques to managing the situation, and identifying preventative measures that might have been taken. They have the opportunity to describe an employee's motivational level and how she got to this point, and practice the skills necessary to help the employee.

STEP 1: Introduce the activity by referring to the instructions on page 59 of the text. Direct them to read the case and respond to the questions on the bottom of page 60. This should be done individually.

STEP 2: Divide the class into small groups of 4-5 with the instructions that they compare their individual answers with each other.

STEP 3: A spokesperson should be chosen to report to the class their group's collective response to questions 2, 4, and 6.

STEP 4: Conduct a large group discussion based on the response of the groups to questions 2, 4, and 6. Process answers to questions 4 and 6 in as much detail as possible.

STEP 5: Ask individuals to share their answers to question 7. Noting that this is a public sector example, you may wish to discuss similarities in business firms, public agencies, and other hierarchical organizations (churches, etc.) as structured systems. The universality of the dynamics involved in this case can be acknowledged.

STEP 6: Summarize the discussion using students' main points as well as the key points on the activity flow sheet.

**Application: Creating Your Own Strategy for
Increasing Personal Motivation and Productivity
Activity Flow Sheet**

PURPOSE: This activity permits students to create their own strategy, or action plan, for increasing personal motivation. The activity, building upon the previous activities, encourages students to assume increased control over their motivation level by taking specific steps.

KEY TOPICS: Personal motivation and peak performance.

TIME ESTIMATE: 45 minutes.

FORMAT: Individual activity, work in 4-5 person groups, followed by large group discussion.

SPECIAL NEEDS: None.

SEQUENCE: 1. Introduce the activity; have students write their responses to each question.

                    2. Point out the introspective nature of this activity.

                    3. Divide the class into 4-5 person groups.

                    4. Conduct a large group discussion.

                    5. Summarize.

VARIATION: Students' individual written responses to the questions may be assigned as homework.

KEY POINTS: 1. This activity allows students to plan for their short-range future, based on what they have determined about their personal motivation.

                    2. Discussion key points in groups helps to affirm individual efforts and to establish that many blocks and hindrances are shared.

                    3. Mastering the skill of creating such action plans has the potential for long-term benefit.

Application: Creating Your Own Strategy for
Increasing Personal Motivation and Productivity
Process Guide

PURPOSE: This activity permits students to create their own strategy, or action plan, for increasing personal motivation. The activity, building upon the previous activities, encourages students to assume increased control over their motivation level by taking specific steps. Students are able to determine their motivation level in such a way as to increase their personal effectiveness.

STEP 1: Direct students to the activity on page 61, with the instruction to complete each question in writing. Allow 20 minutes for this, if done in class.

STEP 2: Point out the introspective nature of this activity, and that their honest reflections will benefit their emergent strategy.

STEP 3: Divide the class into groups, asking them to discuss their responses to questions 1, 4, and 5. Suggest that, if needed, they ask for help from group members, especially for responses to questions 4 and 5.

STEP 4: Conduct a large group discussion, asking for volunteers to share their action plans.

STEP 5: Summarize. Point out that such action planning is a valuable life skill, and that the key to making this work is for them to analyze their motivation level on a periodic basis, and adjust their plans based on their needs and wants.

**Assessment: Your Motivating Potential
Activity Flow Sheet**

PURPOSE:	This activity illustrates the issue of motivation within organizational settings; students are allowed to wrestle with the role of the manager in motivating others.
KEY TOPICS:	Motivating others in organizational settings.
TIME ESTIMATE:	30 minutes.
FORMAT:	Individual activity, work in 4-5 person groups, followed by large group discussion.
SPECIAL NEEDS:	None.

SEQUENCE:

1. Introduce the activity.

2. Have students complete the scale.

3. Place class members 4-5 person groups.

4. Conduct a large group discussion and summarize.

VARIATION:　Step #2 may be completed as homework.

KEY POINTS:

1. Wide differences between importance of employee needs and opportunities to fill them is a formula for low employee motivation.

2. Organizational effectiveness and efficiency are enhanced when employees are motivated to perform.

3. Organizational design may sometimes counter appropriate sensitivity to employee needs.

4. Managers may find themselves in the position of balancing the needs of the organization with the needs of the employees.

5. Organizations and employees stand to benefit when attention is given to meeting the needs of employees.

Assessment: Your Motivating Potential
Process Guide

PURPOSE: This activity illustrates the issue of motivation within organizational settings by noting the differences between the importance of identified needs, and the opportunity of individuals to pursue those needs. In completing this assessment, students wrestle with the role of the manager in motivating others. If a need is very important and yet there is little opportunity to fill that need, what can a manager do to reduce the difference?

STEP 1: Introduce this activity by asking students to draw on any work experiences in organizations, or other organizational experiences, to assess the needs of employees.

STEP 2: Have students complete the scale, as per the instructions on page 61.

STEP 3: Place class members in groups of 4-5 students each, with the charge of accounting for the differences in importance and opportunity and what they, as managers, would do to minimize that difference. Refer to questions on page 62.

STEP 4: Conduct a large group discussion and summarize. Additional discussion questions may include:

A. Recall a time when you were in an organization as an employee or as an individual with little power. Did you experience conflict when your needs were not being met? What were your feelings at the time?

B. In times of such conflict, individuals may feel initially that something is wrong with them rather than with the organization's policies, procedures, etc. How can managers affirm individual employees without operating in a counterproductive fashion within the organization?

Analysis: The Case of Michael Simpson
Activity Flow Sheet

PURPOSE: The purpose of this activity is to allow students to analyze a relatively common motivational dilemma in terms of expectancy theory.

KEY TOPICS: Expectancy theory.

TIME ESTIMATE: 40 minutes.

FORMAT: Individual activity, work in 4-5 person groups, followed by large group discussion.

SPECIAL NEEDS: None.

SEQUENCE: 1. Direct students to read the case and respond to the questions

2. Place class members into 4-5 person groups.

3. Conduct a large group discussion.

4. Summarize.

VARIATIONS: Step #1 can be completed as homework.

KEY POINTS: 1. Michael Simpson is confronted with this dilemma: after discovering that he is receiving $2000 less in salary than a newly hired MBA student, does he take a different job in a different company for more money? Or does he stay because every other aspect of his job is exactly the way he wants it, namely opportunity for challenge, responsibility, receiving the toughest assignments, and having a relatively fast career track?

2. An expectancy theory perspective would provide valuable assistance to Simpson in making an informed decision.

3. Simpson needs to consider the multiple outcomes that he gets from his job and the relative importance (i.e. valences) that are attached.

4. Recognize the emotion and put it aside and consider what is important among the tradeoffs.

Analysis: The Case of Michael Simpson
Process Guide

PURPOSE: The purpose of this activity is to allow students to analyze a relatively common motivational dilemma in terms of expectancy theory. Students should conclude that without an expectancy theory perspective, it is impossible for Simpson to make an informed decision.

STEP 1: Direct students to read the case of Michael Simpson and respond in writing to the three questions on page 69. Allow approximately 20 minutes for this.

STEP 2: Place class members into small groups of 4-5 students each, to discuss their responses to the three questions and to develop a group response to each question.

STEP 3: Conduct a large group discussion, asking each group to report the key points of their discussions. Additional discussion questions might include:

A. Expectancy theory suggests that Michael Simpson put aside the emotional components of his situation, allowing him to focus on the rational benefits from his job. How realistic is this suggestion?

B. In what ways does Michael Simpson feel downgraded in his position, in terms of his value and worth to the company?

C. How can a manager effectively respond to the emotional component of Michael Simpson's situation?

STEP 4: Summarize, using students main ideas as well as the key points on the activity flow sheet.

**Practice: The Same Old Job
Activity Flow Sheet**

PURPOSE:

This activity allows students to practice skills in determining motivation needs and identifying conflict sources that interfere with motivation.

KEY TOPICS:

Applying expectancy theory.

TIME ESTIMATE:

25 minutes.

FORMAT:

4-5 person group work followed by large group discussion.

SPECIAL NEEDS:

None.

SEQUENCE:

1. Direct students to read the case and answer the questions.

2. Place class members into small groups of 4-5 students each.

3. Conduct a large group discussion.

4. Summarize.

VARIATIONS:

1. Step #1 may be completed as homework.

2. In order to shorten the process, you may assign each group to discuss one of the questions rather than all 6.

KEY POINTS:

1. Turning to the list of needs in the assessment activity, Helen Ames seems to be experiencing a high opportunity for the fulfillment of some of those needs, but low opportunity for the fulfillment of others.

2. Sometimes the syndrome that Helen Ames is experiencing is temporary and may be related to other factors, such as a situation in her personal life. Perhaps it was even triggered by a thoughtless remark from a co-worker. However, it may also be indicative of a more lasting assessment of her job satisfaction.

Practice: The Same Old Job
Process Guide

PURPOSE: This activity allows students to practice skills in determining motivation needs, draw out factors that motivate and/or detract from motivation, and identify conflict sources that interfere with motivation.

STEP 1: Direct students to individually read the case on page 69-70, and to respond in writing to the questions on page 70.

STEP 2: Place class members into small groups of 4-5 students each, to discuss their responses to the questions and to develop a group response to each question.

STEP 3: Conduct a large group discussion with each group reporting to the class. Due to the large number of questions, assign the first group to report their findings on question #1. Permit the class to react. Then the second group take question #2 and so forth.

Additional discussion questions may include:

A. As you review the assessment scale on pages 61-62, which of Helen's needs do you think are being met and which are not?

B. What alternative explanations can you think of for her feelings at this time?

C. How might the reward systems of Helen Ames' workplace be redesigned to prevent such feelings as Helen is experiencing?

STEP 4: Summarize by using students' main ideas and the key points from the activity flow sheet.

Application: Understanding Organizational Reward Systems
Activity Flow Sheet

PURPOSE:

This activity permits students to apply what they have learned about individual motivation to organizational reward systems. Hopefully as they pursue their own career goals, this skill will enable them to better assess the fit between the organization they may consider working for, and their own motivational needs.

KEY TOPICS:

Expectancy theory and organizational reward systems.

TIME ESTIMATE:

In class set up time: 10 minutes; outside of class: 2 hours for the interviews; in class follow up discussion: 20 minutes.

FORMAT:

Individual activity followed by large group discussion.

SPECIAL NEEDS:

Three potential employers to interview.

SEQUENCE:

1. Introduce the activity.

2. Refer students to the directions on pages 70-71.

3. Have students select three employers to interview.

4. After the interviews are completed, allow time for students to discuss briefly their interviews in class.

5. Conduct a large group discussion and summarize.

KEY POINTS:

1. Expectancy theory and one's own motivational profile can be used to determine which organizations would pose the best fit for a potential employee.

2. Organizational reward systems vary widely, often reflecting different constraints as well as different assumptions about employee motivation.

**Application: Understanding Organizational Reward Systems
Process Guide**

PURPOSE: This activity permits students to apply what they have learned about individual motivation to organizational reward systems. Hopefully as they pursue their own career goals, this skill will enable them to better assess the fit between the organization they may consider working for, and their own motivational needs. Like the other interview activities, this one functions to assist students in practicing interviewing skills as well as making contacts with the business community.

STEP 1: Introduce students to this assignment by noting the role of organizational reward systems in meeting the motivational needs of employees.

STEP 2: Refer students to the directions on pages 70-71. Note that the interview schedule is provided. If they do not have potential employers yet, just suggest that they interview three employers.

STEP 3: Have students select three employers to interview. You may need to assist them in this task. Clarify that the interviews must be conducted by a certain date.

STEP 4: After their interviews are completed, permit them to briefly discuss their interviews in class.

STEP 5. Conduct a large group discussion and summarize, using students' major points from their experiences.

Assessment: Social Readjustment Rating Scale
Activity Flow Sheet

PURPOSE: This activity permits students to assess the (very approximate) stress levels in their lives by responding to a classic instrument in stress management research.

KEY TOPICS: Stress management.

TIME ESTIMATE: 20 minutes.

FORMAT: Individual activity followed by large group discussion.

SPECIAL NEEDS: None.

SEQUENCE: 1. Introduce the activity by having students read the directions on page 71.

2. Direct students to add and record their scores and to respond in writing to the interpretation questions on page 72.

3. Conduct a large group discussion, asking students to volunteer their observations regarding the scale.

4. Present interpretation of scores (see process guide).

5. Conduct a large group discussion and summarize.

VARIATIONS: 1. This scale may be completed as homework, with steps #3-#5 being completed during the next class.

2. Students can complete this scale for each of the past 5 calendar years, and compare their total annual scores. See process guide, step #2.

KEY POINTS: 1. While we may expect negative life events to be stressful, positive life events may generate their own stresses, as well.

2. Sometimes we tend to think of stress levels as related to our inabilities to manage time or to lack of psychological strength. It is important to note that normal life events often trigger stress.

3. While we cannot often control some of the major life events that happen to us, we can take action to mitigate any consequent negative effects.

Assessment: Social Readjustment Rating Scale
Process Guide

PURPOSE: This activity permits students to assess the (very approximate) stress levels in their lives by responding to a classic instrument in stress management research. Not only does this personalize the discussion regarding stress, but it helps students to understand that even positive life events can be stressful.

STEP 1: Introduce the activity by having students read the directions on page 71.

STEP 2: Direct students to add and record their scores and to respond in writing to the interpretation questions on page 72. As a variation, ask them to also complete the scale for the past 5 years (eg.: 1989, 1988, 1987, 1986, 1985) and to compare their scores for the various years. In this manner they may be able to identify a year that was unusually stressful for them. They may also note any health problems which may have emerged after a high stress level year.

STEP 3: Present an interpretation to the scale. It is important to emphasize that these figures are *very tentative*, but in general:

Under 100 = very low stress level
100-199 = typical stress level
200-299 = moderately high stress level
over 300 = very high stress level

STEP 4: Conduct a large group discussion, asking students to volunteer their observations regarding the scale.

Additional questions may include:

A. Would you make any changes to any items on the scale? Are there any additional life events that you would add to the scale? If so, what are they?

(**NOTE:** Some current research suggests that one of the major stressors for adults is the decision to place a parent in a nursing home.)

B. Would you change any point values of events in order to more accurately reflect comparative stress levels? If so, what would you change?

C. Are there any personality traits which, in your judgment, would make some of these events more stressful for some individuals than for other people? If so, what can you identify?

D. Since life events trigger stress, how can we gain control of our stress levels?

STEP 5: Summarize the discussion, using the key points from the activity flow sheet, and the main ideas which students generate.

Analysis: Job Stress
Activity Flow Sheet

PURPOSE:	The purpose of this activity is to demonstrate typical stressors in the workplace setting by having students respond to a comprehensive list.
KEY TOPICS:	Job stressors.
TIME ESTIMATE:	40 minutes.
FORMAT:	Individual activity followed by work in 4-5 person groups and large group discussion.
SPECIAL NEEDS:	None.

SEQUENCE:

1. Direct students to read and complete the activity.

2. Explain the context of the activity.

3. Divide the class members 4-5 person groups.

4. Conduct a large group discussion

5. Summarize.

KEY POINTS:

1. In general most people feel that the less control they have in a situation, the more of a stressor it is.

2. There are multiple coping mechanisms for individuals to draw on.

3. There may be particular classes of stressors that most people deal with in the same way.

4. Often what seems like a big stressor to us is commonplace to many people. Such realizations help us to avoid attributing our stresses in life to any personal deficiencies.

Analysis: Job Stress
Process Guide

PURPOSE: The purpose of this activity is to permit students to respond to a comprehensive list of typical stressors in the workplace setting. In so doing they identify their level of control over the stressor and their coping mechanisms.

STEP 1: Direct students to read and complete the activity on pages 77-78.

STEP 2: Note that the context of the activity is job-related. If currently not employed, ask students to reflect on a time of any previous employment in order to complete the activity.

STEP 3: Divided the class members into groups of 4-5 students each. Have group members compare their responses, and draw one conclusion on which each of them agree.

STEP 4: Conduct a large group discussion, eliciting the one conclusion from each group. Additional discussion questions may include:

A. To what extent is stress level related to level of control over the situation?

B. To what extent to stress management strategies allow a measure of control?

C. What interest do organizations and firms have in helping employees cope with stress?

STEP 5: Summarize, using students' main ideas and the key points from the activity flow sheet.

**Practice: Wasting Time
Activity Flow Sheet**

PURPOSE: The purpose of this activity is to allow students to practice identifying time wasters on the job, and determine strategies for controlling them.

KEY TOPICS: Time management strategies

TIME ESTIMATE: 45 minutes.

FORMAT: Individual activity and small group discussion, followed by large group discussion.

SPECIAL NEEDS: None.

SEQUENCE: 1. Direct students to read the case and instructions on page 78-80 of the text.

                  2. Divide class members 4-5 person groups.

                  3. Conduct a large group discussion.

                  4. Summarize.

VARIATION: Step #1 may be completed as homework, followed by group discussion the next class session.

KEY POINTS: 1. No one is a perfect user of time.

                  2. Sometimes assertive communication skills are necessary in order to minimize time waste.

                  3. In order to manage one's time, one must determine one's willingness to handle time wasters, and not merely to use them as excuses.

Practice: Wasting Time
Process Guide

PURPOSE: The purpose of this activity is to allow students to practice identifying time wasters on the job, and determine strategies for controlling them.

STEP 1: Direct students to read the case of Frank Fernandez on page 78-80 of the text, and to respond in writing to the questions on page 80.

STEP 2: Divide class members into small groups of 4-5 students each. Ask group members to discuss the questions and be prepared to present a composite list of responses to the three questions on page 80.

STEP 3: Conduct a large group discussion based on the responses of the small groups. Additional discussion questions may include:

    A. Most of us can improve our time management techniques. Did any student see themselves in Frank Fernandez? If so, in what way? Explain.

    B. What positive function do time wasters serve, in terms of providing us with excuses for procrastination?

    C. What are some strategies that can reduce the number of interruptions?

STEP 4: Summarize, using students' main ideas and the key points from the activity flow sheet.

Application: Improving Your Time and Stress Management
Activity Flow Sheet

PURPOSE: This activity allows students to apply time management techniques in order to develop their own personal time and stress reduction program.

TIME ESTIMATE: 45 minutes.

FORMAT: Individual activity for questions 1, 2, and 3; 4-5 person groups for question 4, followed by large group discussion.

SPECIAL NEEDS: None.

SEQUENCE:
1. Direct students to read and complete the assignment.

2. Note that this activity is a valuable life skill.

3. Place class members into 4-5 person groups.

4. Conduct a large group discussion and summarize.

VARIATION: Step #1 may be completed as homework, followed by small group discussion the next class session.

KEY POINTS:
1. Developing strategies for time management inherently reduces our stress level - even before the strategies are implemented.

2. Effective strategies assume and find measures of control over situations and events.

3. Note that some strategies may require more effective communication skills. See chapter 6, the Mentor Role.

Application: Improving Your Time and Stress Management
Process Guide

PURPOSE: This activity allows students to apply time management techniques in order
to develop their own personal time and stress reduction program.

STEP 1: Direct students to read the assignment on page 80, and to respond to questions
1, 2, and 3 in writing.

STEP 2: Note that this activity is a valuable life skill. Encourage students to practice it
periodically.

STEP 3: Place class members into small groups of 4-5 students each in order to discuss
their responses to the questions. Encourage students to ask their group
members for assistance in developing solutions and strategies.

STEP 4: Conduct a large group discussion. Summarize, using students' main ideas and
the key points from the activity flow sheet.

The Coordinator Role, along with the Monitor Role, comprises the Internal Process Model of the Competing Values Framework. As such this managerial role is often associated with the organization as a closed system, with attention to detail and documentation, and with tracking activity and performance. The manager as coordinator is responsible for operational planning, organizing and maintaining the workflow, trouble shooting, controlling resources, providing procedural advice, advancing rule observance, and enforcing compliance to standards.

While the coordinator role competencies may appear rather ordinary and unexciting to some, they have formed the basis for the concept of management for decades. These competencies may not be the current focus of most trade books and magazines, but they are essential to organizational and managerial functioning. In the words of one of the authors, "Central to the coordinator role is the need to make sure that the right people are in the right place at the right time to do the right work."

The competencies of the coordinator role are also important in our personal lives. Most people realize that budgeting and controlling their financial resources, planning their futures, and organizing their homes provide for a level of predictability in life which enhances personal freedom. Failure to apply these competencies may lead to unpleasant surprises, such as returned checks from the bank.

While paradox is reflected to some extent in each of the competencies, the competency of control raises a basic paradox. On the one hand organization need control systems; they need to control the behaviors of individuals within those organizations. On the other hand, individuals need some autonomy and to experience a measure of control in their lives. To add to this mixture, some controls are deemed necessary for human freedom. Paradoxically, anarchy is not characteristic of a society where individual freedom is maximized.

It is important for students to understand the human side of control. The basic dilemma here is between the organization's need for some measures of control and employees' or human needs for some measure of autonomy and control over their own situations. Students need to understand both sides of this argument and to find solutions that address both sets of concerns.

The competencies of the Coordinator Role: The three competencies in this role and their corresponding topics in the learning activities are:

Competency #1: Planning

Topics: Operational planning
                        Establishing standards and priorities
                        Planning and scheduling tools
                              Statement of work
                              Task relationship diagrams
                              Gantt charts
                              PERT and CPM

Competency #2: Organizing

Topics:
            Efficiency as an organizing principle
            Division of labor and specialization
            Designing organizations through departmentation
                Lines of authority
                Unity of command principle
                Scalar principle
                Span of control
                Tall versus flat organizations
            Conflicts among organizing principles
            Designing subsystems
                Environment and technology
            Differentiation and integration
            Designing jobs and job design strategies
                Objective and subjective job characteristics
                Job design strategies
            Allocating jobs across the work unit
                Responsibility charting

Competency #3: Controlling

Topics:
            The basis of control
                Identifying critical control points
                    Feedforward, concurrent, and feedback systems
            Examples of organizational control systems
                Performance appraisal systems
                Financial control systems
                Information systems
            Human reactions to control
            Guidelines for establishing effective control systems

Conceptually the coordinator role is not limited to these competencies. Other competencies have been identified as:

        Coordinating work group activities
        Keys to rule enforcement
        Buffering your core technology
        When to conform, when to question
        Scheduling job rotations for employees
        Making physical arrangements for meetings
        Overseeing maintenance of buildings, structures, and/or
           equipment

Which competencies to choose? As with the other roles, you may not be able to cover all three competencies in your course. In an effort to assist in your decision of which ones to choose, the following questions were posed to the authors:

1. **In teaching this course, if you could cover only ONE competency from this chapter, which one would that be and why?**

One author choose planning, while another author choose organizing. This second author reasoned that of the three competencies, organizing is the most central to the coordinator role.

2. **In teaching this course, if you could cover only TWO competencies from this chapter, which two would they be and why?**

To the first choice of planning, one author added organizing, due to the design features in this concept. To the first choice of organizing, another author added the competency of control, seeing it as closer to coordination than planning.

3. **If you had an additional 5 pages of space for each COMPETENCY, what ideas and concepts would you wish to include?**

Planning: More on different types of plans: production, financial, personnel, facility, and workforce planning. Also, the importance of planning in the control cycle.

Organizing: More on the influence of technology on organizational design and the influence of the external environment on organizational design. Managers need to recognize that they cannot simply design organizations based on personal preference without attention to these factors.

Controlling: More focus on specific types of control systems: performance evaluation, financial systems, statistical control systems, etc.

The Coordinator Role and current issues: The competency of controlling poses basic ethical issues for the manager. To what extent are controls consistent with the ethical treatment of individuals? To what extent can ethics be used as a control mechanism? To what extent do organizational ethics provide for self-control on the parts of employees?

Additionally one could argue that technology and management are related. Certain abilities to control are determined by new computer technologies. Certainly management information systems are technology driven.

Some questions to consider in this chapter are:

1. How does a manager plan for change? How do organizations plan and organize to meet rapidly changing demands and conditions?

2. What is the distinction between controls and manipulation? Is the distinction important?

3. What are sources of individual resistance to controls in organizations?

4. What is the relationship between controls and productivity? Is this relationship different among diverse organizations (e.g. business firms, public agencies, charitable organizations, religious organizations, etc.)?

A note from one of the authors:

This chapter is not an attempt to fit an entire semester of a principles of management course into a single textbook chapter. We recognize that it could take an entire academic year--if not more--to cover in depth the material in and related to this chapter. In controlling, for instance, the issue is balance with the human side of controls. The use of computer delivery system case study gets at the human aspect of control.

Assessment: Planning a Reunion
Activity Flow Sheet

PURPOSE:	This activity demonstrates the need to plan complex tasks, and the tendency to neglect details.
KEY TOPICS:	Different levels of planning; task relationship diagrams.
TIME ESTIMATE:	45 minutes.
FORMAT:	Individual activity followed by large group discussion.
SPECIAL NEEDS:	None.
SEQUENCE:	1. Introduce the activity.
	2. Allow students 20 minutes to complete the activity.
	3. Ask for 5-7 volunteers to present their plans to the class.
	4. Conduct a large group discussion and summarize.
VARIATION:	This activity can be completed as homework, with the next class beginning with a discussion.
KEY POINTS:	1. Often tasks which appear to be simple need to be broken down into task components, planned, and coordinated.
	2. Operational planning involves translation of a big idea into detailed plans.
	3. It is easy to neglect some simple details.
SPECIAL NOTE:	**This activity forms the basis of the practice activity for this competency on page 94 of the text.**

Assessment: Planning a Reunion
Process Guide

PURPOSE: This activity demonstrates the need to plan complex tasks, and the tendency to neglect details. Coordination happens best when there are advance plans for "how things should happen". This could naturally lead into a discussion of strategic vs. tactical vs. operational levels of planning: differences in focus and time range. The emphasis here is on day-to-day scheduling and planning.

STEP #1: Introduce the activity by telling students that this activity will help them begin to focus on coordination by giving them an opportunity to plan and coordinate a social event. Explain that tasks and projects often appear easy to coordinate and complete, particularly if we do not closely analyze all of the needed components.

STEP #2: Allow students 20 minutes to complete the activity individually.

STEP #3: Ask for 5-7 volunteers to record their plans on the board and present to the class.

STEP #4: Conduct a large group discussion and summarize. While the questions in the text on page 86 may form the basis of this discussion, additional questions may include:

A. What about this activity surprised you?

B. Why do people tend to overlook some necessary details?

C. What were the first three things you did in planning this project?

D. Was your approach similar to or different from the way you usually approach tasks?

E. To what extent did you consider the resources you would need to complete this project?

F. Did you use any kind of schedule or time line? Why or why not?

G. Did you determine how to check your progress? Explain?

H. What are some of the differences associated with planning for events involving many people vs. events involving a small number of people?

Analysis: The Case of Jack Matteson
Activity Flow Sheet

PURPOSE: This activity permits students to analyze a situation of a manager who is experiencing problems due to neglect of basic planning principles.

KEY TOPICS: Operational planning; task relationship diagrams; Gantt charts; PERT/CPM.

TIME ESTIMATE: 30 minutes.

FORMAT: Individual activity, small group discussion, followed by large group discussion.

SPECIAL NEEDS: None.

SEQUENCE:
1. Introduce the activity.

2. Students individually read the case and respond to the questions.

3. Place students into 4-5 person groups.

4. Conduct a large group discussion and summarize.

VARIATIONS:
1. Step #2 could be completed as a homework assignment.

2. Eliminate step #3, proceeding directly from the individual activity to the large group discussion.

KEY POINTS:
1. Planning requires care and attention to detail.

2. Neglecting planning can result in major difficulties as far as the project is concerned, as well as a degree of undue stress and psychological distress.

3. The longer we let something go without attention to planning, the more difficult the situation often becomes. In order to get things back on track, we sometimes have to go back to the beginning.

Analysis: The Case of Jack Matteson
Process Guide

PURPOSE: This activity permits students to analyze a situation of a manager who is experiencing problems due to neglect of basic planning principles. The human tendency to over generalize from a simple lack of skill is highlighted. Matteson experiences considerable stress due to his fears that his dilemma is based in basic character flaws and/or job incompetency.

STEP #1:   Introduce the activity by referring students to the case and questions on pages 92-94. Tell them that they will be analyzing a situation where the manager has neglected to use planning skills in his work.

STEP #2:   Allow students 20 minutes to read the case and respond in writing to the questions on page 94.

STEP #3:   Place students into 4-5 person groups. Direct the groups to act as consulting teams to Jack, and to recommend a plan. Use question #3 as the model.

STEP #4:   Conduct a large group discussion based on the group reports and the questions on page 94. Summarize students' major points. Additional questions may include:

A. What were some of the psychological consequences of Jack's lack of planning skills? What assumptions (faulty) was he beginning to make about himself?

B. What were some of the time management consequences of Jack's lack of planning skills? It is frequently the case that once we don't plan, the process takes off in undesirable ways. In order to get things back on track, we sometimes have to go back to the beginning.

B. What were some of the cultural assumptions that led to Jack's neglect of planning skills? Note that unlike some other societies, in our society we do not tend to focus on the detailed preparation of an event; we tend only to celebrate the event, or the finished product. As an example of our preoccupation with the finished product and neglect of the process, some societies celebrate pregnancy, while American society tends to celebrate birth. Attention to the process, then, requires conscious effort.

Practice: Planning the Annual Office Picnic
Activity Flow Sheet

PURPOSE: This activity allows students to practice the operational planning concepts involved in the learning section, considering planning tools at their disposal and how they can use those tools.

KEY TOPICS: Task relationship diagrams; Gantt charts; PERT/CPM

TIME ESTIMATE: 30 minutes.

FORMAT: Individual activity followed by large group discussion.

SPECIAL NEEDS: This activity builds on the assessment activity on page 85-86. While completion of the assessment is not absolutely necessary, student ability to complete this practice activity is definitely enhanced by prior completion of the assessment. Also, for step #2 it might be helpful to have the use of an overhead projector and blank transparencies for students to write on.

SEQUENCE: 1. Introduce the activity.

2. Direct students to complete the activity and submit the memo.

3. Ask for volunteers to share their memos.

4. Conduct a large group discussion and summarize.

VARIATION: Have students complete the activity as a homework assignment. Commence the next class discussion with memos from volunteers.

KEY POINTS: 1. The planning competency incorporates a number of skills generic to many situations: social, job, project, and personal.

2. Careful planning has the effect of changing our perceptions of a task from overwhelming to manageable.

3. Life is easier when we plan, break down the task into component parts, and pay attention to the details.

Practice: Planning the Annual Office Picnic
Process Guide

PURPOSE: This activity allows students to practice the operational planning concepts involved in the learning section, considering detailed planning tools at their disposal and how they can use those tools.

STEP #1: Introduce the activity by directing students to the instructions on page 94. Have them refer to their written response to the assessment activity (Planning a Reunion) at the beginning of this competency. Suggest that they will be assisted by placing themselves in the role described by the instructions. This is their chance to identify and put planning tools to work.

STEP #2: Direct students to complete the activity and submit the memo. This may be assigned as homework. If so, be sure to specify a due date (the next class session, or later).

STEP #3: After their memos are completed, ask for volunteers to share their memos. They may wish to write them on the chalkboard, or if possible, write them on blank transparencies for use with an overhead projector. Another alternative - especially if this is homework - is to have the volunteers type their memos and photocopy them for class members.

STEP #4: Conduct a large group discussion comparing the memos and summarize. Use students' main ideas as well as the key points from the activity flow sheet. Additional discussion questions may include:

A. Did anything surprise you about completing this activity? Many students report that at first glance it seemed difficult and overwhelming, but once they got into it, it was easier than expected. A point here is that this response is not unusual with regards to planning.

B. Did you choose to use a task relationship diagram, a Gantt chart, or the PERT/CPM technique? What considerations did you bring to bear in making your choice?

C. What applications do you see for these skills in the future?

D. What are sources of individual resistance to planning?

Application: Getting in (Operational) Gear
Activity Flow Sheet

PURPOSE:	This activity gives students the opportunity to apply planning principles to a project with which they are involved.
KEY TOPICS:	Statement of work; task relationship diagram; Gantt chart; Pert/CPM.
TIME ESTIMATE:	45 minutes.
FORMAT:	Individual activity followed by large group discussion.
SPECIAL NEEDS:	None
SEQUENCE:	1. Introduce the activity.
	2. Discuss with the class what their choice of a project might be.
	3. Set a due date for the report.
	4. Conduct a large group discussion and summarize.
VARIATION:	Divide the class into 4-5 person teams. Instruct them to plan a project for completion by the end of the semester. The project might entail some service to the campus or the community, or a research project involving community businesses. After choosing the project, the teams submit reports, as per the instructions for the application activity.
KEY POINTS:	1. Planning is an essential competency for the completion of complex work.
	2. Planning tools are not unique to management in organizations. They are generic to many aspects of life and assist in planning a wide array of projects or activities.
	3. Planning is a valuable competency that applies to many aspects of life, and is not only a managerial skill in the career sense.

Application: Getting in (Operational) Gear
Process Guide

PURPOSE: This activity gives students the opportunity to apply planning principles to a project with which they are involved. This activity demonstrates to students the applicability of planning tools to projects and the value of such tools for their current effectiveness.

STEP #1: Introduce the activity by directing students to the instructions on page 94-95. Note that this activity represents a summation of the competency, essentially involving students in applying the key points of the learning section to improve their effectiveness in a personal project.

STEP #2: Discuss with the class what their choice of projects might be. Encourage them to select a project which currently is facing them.

STEP #3: Indicate that they are required to submit a final report of 2-3 pages, and set a date that the report is due.

STEP #4: On the day the final report is due, conduct a large group discussion and summarize. Discussion questions might include:

A. What surprised you about this activity?

B. How did applying planning tools to your project affect your attitude towards that project?

C. What would you surmise to be the relationship between the use of planning tools and one's tendency to procrastinate?

D. Someone has said that the act of starting a project takes 50% of the effort to complete it. While this statement may not have scientific validity, do you think it has some merit? How does the use of the planning competency apply to this statement?

E. What do you feel are the advantages of consistent, efficient planning?

Assessment: Analyzing Tasks
Activity Flow Sheet

PURPOSE:

In this assessment, students experience identifying three of their major tasks, breaking them down into components and steps.

KEY TOPICS:

Making complex structures simple through categories; coordination through structure.

TIME ESTIMATE:

30 minutes.

FORMAT:

Individual activity followed by large group discussion.

SPECIAL NEEDS:

None.

SEQUENCE:

1. Introduce the activity.

2. Have students complete the activity individually.

3. Ask for volunteers to share their responses.

4. Conduct a large group discussion and summarize.

VARIATIONS:

1. Step 2 may be completed as homework, with the next class session beginning with step 3.

2. After step 2, students may be placed in 4-5 person groups to discuss their responses with one another.

KEY POINTS:

1. Even mundane tasks have components and are amenable to analysis.

2. Task analysis skills are an important resource to the manager.

SPECIAL NOTE:

This activity forms the basis of the analysis activity for this competency on page 107 of the text.

Assessment: Analyzing Tasks
Process Guide

PURPOSE: In this assessment, students experience identifying three of their major tasks, breaking them down into components and steps. This activity demonstrates the value of analyzing tasks, no matter how routine, and in general serves as a relevant introduction to the competency of organizing.

STEP #1: Introduce the activity. Anticipate that the following distinctions may need to be made:

    A. A job (job description) includes functions or tasks.

    B. A task is a group of related activities directed towards a goal.

    C. Tasks may vary in complexity and may be performed by one person in a job or by many working on a joint project.

STEP #2: Have students complete the activity individually. Direct them to respond in writing to the interpretation questions on page 95.

STEP #3: Ask for volunteers to share their responses.

STEP #4: Conduct a large group discussion based on responses to the interpretation questions on page 95, as well as the responses of the volunteers. Summarize, using the key points from the activity flow sheet, as well as students' main ideas.

Analysis: What's My Job Design?
Activity Flow Sheet

PURPOSE: In this activity students analyze their own situation in terms of the principles of job design.

KEY TOPICS: Job design; objective and subjective job characteristics.

TIME ESTIMATE: 30 minutes.

FORMAT: Individual activity followed by large group discussion.

SPECIAL NEEDS: The results of their assessment activity for this competency: "Analyzing Tasks", page 95 of the text.

SEQUENCE: 1. Introduce the activity.

                         2. Direct students to work individually on the questions.

                         3. Ask for volunteers to share their responses.

                         4. Conduct large group discussion and summarize.

VARIATION: Step #2 may be assigned as homework, using step #3 to begin the next class session.

KEY POINTS: 1. Note the relevance of job design concepts when applied to our personal situations.

                         2. Note how coordination is provided through structure.

SPECIAL NOTE: **This activity forms the basis of the next activity: "Practice: Redesigning Jobs" on page 108 of the text.**

Analysis: What's My Job Design?
Process Guide

PURPOSE: In this activity students analyze their own situation in terms of the principles of job design. This allows students to utilize task analysis techniques and apply these skills to their own situation. This activity demonstrates the importance of objective and subjective job characteristics.

STEP #1: Introduce the activity by explaining the purpose. Explain to students that the competencies learned thus far are the building blocks for efficient and effective coordination.

STEP #2: Direct students to work individually on the questions.

STEP #3: Ask for volunteers to share their responses.

STEP #4: Conduct large group discussion and summarize. Highlight the importance of applying what they have learned. Summarize the major points which they made in the discussion.

Practice: Redesigning Jobs
Activity Flow Sheet

PURPOSE: In this activity students work with a partner to redesign a job.

KEY TOPICS: Matching people to jobs; job redesign

TIME ESTIMATE: 30 minutes.

FORMAT: Dyads followed by large group discussion.

SPECIAL NEEDS: Individual responses from the previous activity: "Analysis" What's My Job Design?" on page 107-108 of the text.

SEQUENCE: 1. Introduce the activity.

                     2. Divide class members into dyads. If the class is not even numbered, make a 3-person group.

                     3. Direct the groups to complete the activity on page 108 of the text.

                     4. Ask for volunteers to report their responses to the class.

                     5. Conduct a large group discussion and summarize.

VARIATIONS: 1. Step 3 may be completed as homework, with the next class session beginning with step 4.

                     2. Require a 2-3 page written report from the groups, detailing their responses to the activity.

KEY POINTS: 1. People and jobs can be successfully matched.

                     2. Matching people and jobs, taking into account their abilities and growth/development needs is a win-win situation for employees and the organization.

Practice: Redesigning Jobs
Process Guide

PURPOSE: In this activity students work with a partner to redesign a job. This is an empowering activity, as many times people think of themselves as having to "fit into" a job. This activity demonstrates that jobs can be redesigned for the benefit of employee and organization alike.

STEP #1: Introduce the activity. Direct students to the instructions on page 108 of the text. Explain that this activity permits them to build on the previous activity, and allows them to think about decisions involved in job redesign.

STEP #2: Divide class members into dyads. If the class is not even numbered, make a 3-person group. As a reminder: if possible, pair students who chose being a student as their job with students who chose a job in a work organization.

STEP #3: Direct the groups to complete the activity on page 108 of the text.

STEP #4: Ask for volunteers to report their responses to the class.

STEP #5: Conduct a large group discussion based on the groups' reports and on the questions posed in the activity. Summarize students' major points. Additional questions may include:

A. On what basis did you decide which job to redesign?

B. How did you feel about redesigning this job? Was it easier or harder than you anticipated?

3. What are some organizational sources of resistance to redesigning jobs?

4. What are some advantages to the organization of redesigning jobs? Advantages to employees?

5. Who should be involved in job redesign?

**Application: Identify the Organizational Structure
Activity Flow Sheet**

PURPOSE: This activity permits students to explore different organizational designs and structures. It also provides students with a valuable opportunity to make contact with organizations and analyze organizational charts.

KEY TOPICS: Organizational design; lines of authority; technology and organizations.

TIME ESTIMATE: In class set up time: 10 minutes; outside of class: 3 hours; in class follow up discussion: 20 minutes.

FORMAT: Individual activity followed by large group discussion.

SPECIAL NEEDS: Access to two organizations.

SEQUENCE: 1. Introduce the activity.

2. Direct students to choose two organizations to contact.

3. Assign a written report of their efforts, along with a deadline.

4. Conduct a large group discussion on the day their reports are due.

VARIATION: Permit them to work as 3-4 person teams.

KEY POINTS: 1. Organizations differ considerably according to structure, but most maintain common elements.

2. Organizational structure is not set but may be changed to adapt to a changing environment.

3. Sometimes the mission of the organization affects the structure.

Application: Identify the Organizational Structure
Process Guide

PURPOSE: This activity permits students to explore the designs and structures of two different organizations. In this activity students identify lines of authority and other elements of organizational design, associating structural design with the consequences for employees in the organizations. It also provides students with a valuable opportunity to make contact with organizations and to analyze organizational charts.

STEP #1: Introduce the activity by directing students to the instructions on page 108 of the text. Explain that in exploring organizational designs, they become able to appreciate the effect that structure has on the every-day operations of the organization.

STEP #2: Direct students to choose two organizations to contact. Discuss with the class various types of organizations locally that they may contact. Students may choose between a business firm, a state or local government agency, a non-profit organization, or a religious organization: all of which offer a rich variety in structures while maintaining common elements.

STEP #3: Assign a written report of their efforts, along with a deadline. The report should include the organizational charts and their conclusions.

STEP #4: Conduct a large group discussion on the day their reports are due. Additional questions may include:

A. How did your organizations differ in mission and purpose?

B. Did you find as many differences in design and structure as you expected?

C. Did anything about this assignment surprise you? If so, what?

D. What did your organizations have in common, as far as this activity is concerned?

Assessment: In and Out of Control
Activity Flow Sheet

PURPOSE:	This activity permits students to identify positive and negative aspects of control and to assess their responses to control in their lives.
KEY TOPICS:	Human reactions to control.
TIME ESTIMATE:	20 minutes.
FORMAT:	Individual activity followed by large group discussion.
SPECIAL NEEDS:	None.

SEQUENCE:

1. Introduce the activity.

2. Instruct students to write their lists and responses.

3. Make three lists on the chalkboard.

4. Conduct a large group discussion.

5. Summarize, leading into a discussion of the learning activity.

VARIATIONS:

1. Assign step 2 to be completed entirely as homework.

2. In between steps 2 and 3, break the class into 4-5 person groups to discuss their lists and their responses to the questions.

KEY POINTS:

1. Control has positive and negative aspects.

2. It is important to individuals to feel that they have some measure of control in their lives, to feel autonomous.

3. It is also important for organizations to exercise a measure of control over the individual within those organizations.

4. Managers often find themselves balancing these apparently contradictory needs.

Assessment: In and Out of Control
Process Guide

PURPOSE: This activity permits students to identify positive and negative aspects of control, explore the role of control in their lives, the various functions of control, and to assess their responses to control.

STEP #1: Introduce the activity by directing students to the instructions on page 109 of the text. Explain that this activity gives them an opportunity to explore the role of control in their lives, and their feelings about control.

STEP #2: Instruct students to write out their responses to the 5 questions in the activity.

STEP #3: Make three lists on the chalkboard which correspond to the 3 lists in the activity. Items on these lists are responses from students of what they wrote on their lists.

STEP #4: Conduct a large group discussion based on the 5 questions in the activity.

STEP #5: Summarize, leading into a discussion of the learning activity. Additional discussion questions may include:

A. Why is it important for organizations to maintain control?

B. Why do individuals react negatively to being controlled?

C. What are the implications of this tension for the manager?

D. How is the existence of controls related to individual freedom? Note that at first glance, it seems that the controls and freedom are opposites, yet it can be argued that the existence of controls in society is precisely what permits individual freedom. The fact that most drivers adhere to the rules of the road allows for all freedom and mobility. If most drivers insisted on regularly breaking the rules, driving on the wrong side of the interstates, etc., then their actions would limit the freedom of others to go places by car. On the other hand, of course, totalitarian societies, where individual freedoms are severely limited, are the epitome of control.

E. How is evaluation related to controls?

SPECIAL NOTE: These learning topics lend themselves to the use of an guest lecturer from a local firm, speaking with the class on the use of any control system. Perhaps someone from a human resources or a personnel department could address performance appraisal as a control system, or an auditor, an MIS person, or a quality control person could speak on their respective control systems.

Analysis: Computers, People, and the Delivery of Services
Activity Flow Sheet

PURPOSE: In this activity students analyze a case involving the institution of
                a control system, and the resistance that was encountered to that
                system.

KEY TOPICS: Information systems; human reactions to control; guidelines for
                establishing effective control systems.

TIME ESTIMATE: 50 minutes.

FORMAT: Individual activity, followed by large group discussion.

SPECIAL NEEDS: Optional: blank transparencies and overhead projector.

SEQUENCE: 1. Introduce the activity.

                2. Ask for volunteers to share their memos with the class.

                3. Compare the memos and discuss.

                4. Conduct a large group discussion based on responses to the
                memos and on the discussion questions on page 119.

                5. Summarize students' major points.

VARIATION: Assign the activity as homework. The next class session, place
                students into 4-5 person groups to discuss their responses to the
                questions and to generate a memo.

KEY POINTS: 1. One can expect resistance to control systems if they are not
                properly established.

                2. Employee/participant input is often essential to the
                establishment of an effective control system.

                3. Sometimes the real issues underlying resistance to control
                systems are difficult to uncover.

                4. Sometimes control systems are seen by management as
                productivity/efficiency systems, and by employees as loss of
                autonomy.

Analysis: Computers, People, and the Delivery of Services
Process Guide

PURPOSE: In this activity students analyze a case involving the institution of a control system, and the resistance that was encountered to that system. This activity demonstrates that often the real issues underlying resistance to control systems are seldom made explicit, and that following the guidelines for establishing effective control systems (pages 114-115 of text) can help to identify sources of resistance early in the process.

STEP #1: Introduce the activity by directing students to the instructions on page 115 of the text. Explain that they will be reading a case involving the employment of a new control system, and the resistance that was encountered to that system. Point out that, for best results, they should stop reading after each segment of the case and respond to the designated questions in writing before proceeding to the next segment. Note that at the end of the case, they will be required to rewrite a memo.

STEP #2: After completion of the activity, ask for volunteers to share their memos with the class. These may be written on blank transparencies and used with an overhead projector.

STEP #3: Compare the memos, asking students to place themselves in the roles of the recipients (the center directors) and share what their responses would be.

STEP #4: Conduct a large group discussion based on responses to the memos and on the discussion questions on page 119.

STEP #5: Summarize students' major points. Additional discussion questions may include:

A. In what ways did the Computer Center's efforts to establish a control system follow the guidelines on pages 114-115 of the text? When these guidelines were not followed, what were the consequences?

B. Why are the real issues underlying resistance to control systems sometimes difficult to discern? What organizational factors come into play? What group dynamics factors may sometimes operate?

C. How would you describe the "human side of control?" Why is it important?

Practice: Instituting a Control System
Activity Flow Sheet

PURPOSE:

This activity gives students an opportunity to redesign the information system discussed in the previous activity: "Computers, People, and the Delivery of Services".

KEY TOPICS:

Information systems, human reactions to control, guidelines for establishing effective control systems.

TIME ESTIMATE:

45 minutes.

FORMAT:

5-7 person groups, each playing a different role from the previous activity.

SPECIAL NEEDS:

Students may be assisted in this activity by their responses to the previous activity.

SEQUENCE:

1. Introduce the activity.

2. Place students into 5-7 person groups and assign roles.

3. Allow students 30 minutes to redesign the system.

4. Allow groups to present their designs, and conduct a large group discussion.

5. Summarize students' major points.

KEY POINTS:

1. It is possible to redesign information systems to maximize benefit to all concerned.

2. Effective information systems are more likely to be designed following the guidelines on pages 114-115.

3. Employee input is a valuable resource in the design of information systems that are both efficient and effective.

4. It does not occur to many people that organizational control systems can even be redesigned, or that they can participate in the effort. The realization that they can participate in redesign efforts is often very empowering.

Practice: Instituting a Control System
Process Guide

PURPOSE: This activity gives students an opportunity to redesign the information system discussed in the previous activity: "Computers, People, and the Delivery of Services" on pages 115-119 of the text. As such this activity provides valuable experience for students that people seldom have an opportunity to practice.

STEP #1: Introduce the activity by directing students to the instructions on page 119 of the text. Explain that they will draw on their responses to the analysis activity (pages 115-119 of the text) and redesign the information system.

STEP #2: Place students into 5-7 person groups and assign roles. As indicated in the instructions, in each group choose one person to play the role of Paul (or Paula) Powers, and one person to play the role of Brenda (or Brendon) Tybe. The other members of the groups should play the roles of center directors.

STEP #3: Allow students 30 minutes to redesign the system and to discuss the questions indicated on page 119.

STEP #4: Allow groups to present their designs, and conduct a large group discussion. Additional discussion questions may include:

A. The text makes the following point on page 110: "Implementing and maintaining organizational control systems are often considered to be one of the more uncomfortable jobs of the manager." Do you feel that the way in which you redesigned the information system in this activity had the potential of lessening that managerial discomfort? Why or why not?

B. Do you think that it is appropriate to have a control system for the United Way or other charitable organizations? Are there some organizations/ projects/ etc. for which controls are nonexistent or inappropriate? Why or why not?

C. It is argued that the most effective control systems are those which respect the individual's need for autonomy. Do you agree? Is it possible to design such a system?

STEP #5: Summarize, using students' main ideas as well as the key points from the activity flow sheet.

Application: Check Your Organizational Control
Activity Flow Sheet

PURPOSE: This activity permits students to apply what they have learned regarding control systems and to see how these concepts are expressed and implemented in organizations.

KEY TOPICS: Organizational control systems.

TIME ESTIMATE: In class set up time: 10 minutes; outside of class: 3 hours; in class follow up discussion: 20 minutes.

FORMAT: Individual activity followed by large group discussion.

SPECIAL NEEDS: Exposure to an organization. They may wish to choose one of the organizations they worked with in the previous application activity on page 108 of the text: "Identify the Organizational Structure."

SEQUENCE: 1. Introduce the activity.

2. If necessary, review control systems in organizations.

3. Set a date when the 3-5 page report is due.

4. Ask for volunteers to share their experience with the class.

5. Conduct a large group discussion.

6. Summarize.

VARIATION: Students may be assigned to work in teams to complete the activity, submitting a team report.

KEY POINTS: 1. Control systems are essential to organizations.

2. Organizational control systems vary widely in their effectiveness.

3. Organizational control systems, while seemingly static, are subject to change and revision.

Application: Check Your Organizational Control
Process Guide

PURPOSE:: This activity permits students to apply what they have learned regarding control systems and to see how these concepts are expressed and implemented in organizations. After choosing an organization, students identify the control systems and gauge their effectiveness.

STEP #1: Introduce the activity by directing students to the instructions on page 120 of the text. Explain that they will apply what they have learned to an organization. It may be necessary to assist them in choosing an organization.

STEP #2: If necessary, review control systems in organizations, using the college or university as an organization and identify various elements of the control system for students: program requirement, minimum grade point average, scheduled examinations, etc.

STEP #3: Set a date when the 3-5 page report is due.

STEP #4: On the day that the assignment is due, ask for volunteers to share their experience with the class.

STEP #5: Conduct a large group discussion by asking for examples of different control measures that they found. Additional discussion questions may include:

A. Why are control systems essential to organizations?

B. What are the most effective control system you know of?

C. How do control systems relate to ethics in organizations?

STEP #6: Summarize, using students' main ideas and the key points from the activity flow sheet.

To begin our discussion of the Monitor Role chapter, it is necessary to point out that the analysis activity of competency #3 (page 160 of the text) requires students to bring three samples of their writing to class. Students should be alerted to this possibility well in advance.

The Monitor Role, along with the Coordinator Role, comprises the Internal Process Model of the Competing Values Framework. While some organizations epitomize the monitoring process (such as the Internal Revenue Service), monitoring skills are necessary for managers in any organization. In this role, managers pay attention to details, collect, maintain, and disseminate routine information, monitor employee compliance to standards, do statistical and financial analyses, and write procedural material.

While some may not feel comfortable with the paper-intense, detail-focus of this role, the fact is, attention to this detail permits top functioning in the other roles. For instance, only if we know where we are and what we have, can we strengthen our positions as brokers and innovators. Thus, while monitor appears in the framework opposite of broker, the fact is they are complementary. Both roles collect information which is necessary for the organization. Monitor collects data from within with organization, and broker collects data from outside of the organization. It is apparent that effective monitoring is enabling to the proficient functioning of the other roles in the framework.

The competencies in the Monitor Role: The three competencies in this role and their corresponding topics in the learning activities are:

Competency #1: Reducing Information Overload

Topics: The TRAF system
                        Filing
                        Taking good notes
                        External monitoring

Competency #2: Analyzing Information with Critical Thinking

Topics: Evaluating routine information
                        Seeing things as we really are
                        Impediments to sound judgment
                                  Not Invented Here Syndrome
                                    Pattern hypnosis
                                    Denial
                                    Conformity, including groupthink
                                    Ego involvement
                                    Faulty or incomplete analysis

Flexibility and openness
Analyzing arguments
Claim
Grounds
Warrant

Competency #3: Presenting Information; Writing Effectively

Topics: Presenting information
Writing in the bureaucracy
Drawing a blank
Don't know how to begin
Target statement
Automatic writing
Finding the right words
The memo
Making your message accessible

Conceptually. these are not the only competencies in this role. Other competencies have
been identified as:

Monitoring the effectiveness of the work unit
Simple roads to quantitative analysis
The essentials of financial analysis
Keeping detailed records
Tracking and evaluating routine information
Monitoring employee performance
Receiving and organizing routine information

Which competencies to choose? We recognize that you may not be able to cover all
three competencies in your course. In order to assist in your decision of which
ones to choose, the following questions were posed to the authors.

**1. If you were teaching a course and could cover only ONE competency from each
chapter, which one would that be and why?**

One author noted: "Presenting information because this is the only place in the
book where writing is covered."

Another author echoed: "Presenting Information; Writing Effectively."

Still another author's view: "Reducing Information Overload because we are in an
information revolution. We need to know how to handle incoming information - a
management essential."

**2. If you were teaching a course and could cover only TWO competencies from each of
your chapters, which two would they be and why?**

One author noted: "In addition to Presenting Information, I would choose
Reducing Information Overload because managers are frequently deluged with
information."

Another author responded: "In addition to Presenting Information, I would choose Analyzing Information with Critical Thinking because the distinction between critical thinking and creative thinking (in Chapter 8) is consequential."

3. If you had an additional 5 pages of space for each COMPETENCY, what ideas and concepts would you wish to include?

Reducing Information Overload: More specific information on the current research in problem of information overload, and how people tend to drown in routine information. The case could be made more clearly that we do have a problem with information overload. Also, issues associated with information management in a computer environment. One problem that has been created by the automated office has been an increase in the paper available.

Analyzing Information with Critical Thinking: More on the sources of human error.

Presenting Information and Writing Effectively: More on polish and why it is a problem in business writing if you have mechanical and grammatical errors; how it hurts you because people judge you very harshly if you have some polish problems in your writing. Also, discussions on preparing functional documents.

Note: A tie exists between this competency and competency #3 in the Broker Role on effective oral presentations; these two complement one another.

The Monitor Role and current issues: The monitor role is related to issues surrounding globalization due to the increasing need to write for an international audience as well as collect information from an international audience. With regard to managing a culturally diverse workforce, some U. S. firms are now finding it necessary to write memos in a number of different languages. In addition, writing to document rather than to communicate has some ethical ramifications.

Some questions to consider in this chapter are:

1. Do bureaucracies demand the competencies of the monitor role more than, for instance, the innovator role? What is it about structure that might lead managers to define "good management" more in terms of monitor skills than in terms of innovator skills?

2. Managers in the monitor role track employee performance and compliance with the control systems of the organization. How do the competencies of the mentor role provide balance, and enable the manager to do a better job of managing?

3. What are some of the implications of writing to communicate and writing to document?

A note from one of the authors. One of the authors had these thoughts to share on various aspects of this chapter:

Shortly after finishing my Ph.D. in rhetoric, I wanted to go into organizations and help people write clearly and really communicate. Then I realized that many people who work in bureaucracies do not write to communicate; instead they write to document. Clear concise communication is often not the objective. This was a real surprise to me and a shock. Perhaps this may interest some students.

For a disturbing discussion on how writing is sometimes assessed by professional managers, see "An Analysis of Communication Efficiency" by James Suchin and Robert Colucci, *Management Communication Quarterly*, vol. 2 (4) May, 1989, pp. 454-481. Suchin and Colucci demonstrate that some managers do *not* value the clear, high impact, readable style we are trying to teach our students, but rate the obfuscated, bureaucratic style as more "professional and intelligent."

I would like to have included more material on monitoring the effectiveness of the work unit - the kinds of concepts found in the literature on Total Quality Management. For example, I recommend the simple, statistical analysis presented by W. Edwards Deming in his book, *Out of the Crisis*, published by the M.I.T. Center for Advanced Engineering Study (1976). Deming does not ignore service organizations in his discussion. I would also look at Masaaki Imai's book *Kaisen*, (Random House, 1986) for more material on how to monitor the performance of a work unit. Another book that is little known, but very helpful in this area, is William F. Gilbert's *Human Competence: Engineering Worthy Performance*. I especially like his chapter on "Information and Competence." His advice on assessing the performance (productivity) of a work unit, and on giving people feedback on their performance, is solid.

Assessment: Are You in Information Overload?
Activity Flow Sheet

PURPOSE: This activity is designed to help students assess how much
                  information they are being exposed to, and how they are sorting,
                  ignoring, or using that information.

KEY TOPICS: Many people feel deluged by it information; TRAF

TIME ESTIMATE: 15-20 minutes to respond to the questions and discuss.

FORMAT: Individual activity followed by a large group discussion in class.

SPECIAL NEEDS: None.

SEQUENCE: 1. Introduce the activity and have students individually complete
                  the questions.

                  2. Conduct large group discussion.

                  3. Summarize. As a lead into the learning activity, TRAF can be
                  presented as a proven strategy.

VARIATION: The questionnaire may be completed as homework, with the large
                  group discussion beginning at the next class session.

KEY POINTS: 1. The amount of information to which we are exposed will likely
                  increase instead of lessen.

                  2. Information overload is a problem common to many people,
                  managers and students alike.

                  3. There are systems and techniques which can handle
                  information.

Assessment: Are You in Information Overload?
Process Guide

PURPOSE: This activity is designed to help students assess how much information they are being exposed to, and how they are sorting, ignoring, or using that information. While the focus in this activity is on paper information, the principles in this chapter also help students to manage information they receive from non-paper sources: conversations over the telephone, information disseminated in meetings, and the vast array of verbal information. Students are asked to consider how they deal with incoming information, and what they do when they feel overwhelmed with information.

STEP 1: Introduce the activity on page 123 and have students individually complete the questions in writing.

STEP 2: Conduct large group discussion based on their responses, focusing on what strategies students presently use to handle information, barriers to using strategies, and the extent to which these strategies are useful. Additional discussion questions may include:

   A. How do you know if you are experiencing information overload?

   B. As you look to your future, do you expect the amount of information to which you are exposed to automatically increase or decease without any action on your part? Why?

   C. What causes the overload and how do you recover from it?

   D. What problems do you now have in handling information?

   E. What techniques and skills have you found helpful in handling routine information?

STEP 3: Summarize the major problems that students voiced in handling information. Note any skills that they may have found helpful in handling information. This discussion leads into the learning activity where TRAF can be presented as a proven strategy.

A NOTE FROM ONE OF THE AUTHORS: This section on dealing with information overload can be very stimulating and helpful to the class, or it can be deadly - depending upon how it is introduced and handled. For background information, I would suggest two books: *Information Anxiety* (see references) By Richard Saul Wurman, and *Organized To Be The Best* by Susan Silver (Adams Hall, 1989). Wurman's book is a provocative and creative discussion about the blessing and curse information is in our lives, and how we can cope with it. I've loaned my copy to many people, and they have been grateful for the help Wurman offers. I use Wurman when I teach sections on writing. He has great things to say about displaying and presenting information.

Silver's book is a fundamental, hands-on, how-to book on channeling and sorting mountains of paper. Both books are very practical and help students immensely.

I have found that there are always three or four "structure freaks" (I use the term with affection) in the class who are great resources on handling routine information. Recruit them to help teach the others. Have some students give presentations on filing and record keeping systems; on setting up files on their personal computers, or tricks and strategies for handling the information a college student often gets buried under.

The main point I make when I teach this stuff is that we have to find a match between our personality type and the organizing methods we use. A highly structured, compulsively organized person will do this stuff almost reflexively; others, like, me, will never be able to tolerate a system that requires too much maintenance and too much attention to detail. We must be realistic. I like some ambiguity and a little confusion in my life, but I don't like waking up in Pittsburg when I'm supposed to be in Chicago, or missing meetings, or forgetting my son's birthday.

Analysis:
Burke Jackson: Information Anxiety
Activity Flow Sheet

PURPOSE: This activity allows students to apply what they have learned in the learning activity, analyzing how a middle manager handles information.

KEY TOPICS: TRAF system, four steps in the control process, and barriers to using information management techniques. In addition: delegation and time management.

TIME ESTIMATE: 30 minutes.

FORMAT: Individual activity followed by large group discussion.

SPECIAL NEEDS: None.

SEQUENCE:
1. Introduce the activity.

2. Remind students of salient points.

3. Give assignment.

4. Direct students to respond in memo form.

VARIATIONS:
1. Assign as homework.

2. Form class members into groups of 4-5 students each to discuss the two questions in the text and to present in a large group discussion the combined responses of group members.

Note: keeping this as an individual activity has the advantage of providing valued practice in memo writing.

KEY POINTS:
1. This activity represents a case typical of mid-level managers and mistakes they make in using information.

2. The competencies in the Monitor Role suggest considerable attention to detail. However, note that Burke Jackson, who tinkers a lot with details, still has difficulty in the Monitor Role.

3. Burke Jackson under-utilizes two very important resources: his talented administrative assistant and his secretary.

Analysis:
Burke Jackson: Information Anxiety
Process Guide

PURPOSE: This case allows students to apply what they have learned in the learning activity, analyzing how a middle manager handles information. This case portrays typical difficulties in information management on the managerial level.

STEP 1: Introduce the activity by referring students to the case and instructions on page 131 of the text.

STEP 2: Remind students that managing information frequently is not done well, for a variety of reasons which Burke Jackson illustrates.

STEP 3: With reference to the questions on pages 132 and 133, ask students to detail as many distractions as they can find, and also as many suggestions for improvement as they can recommend.

STEP 4: Direct students to respond in writing in memo form and conduct a large group discussion. Additional points to be made in the discussion include:

A. What are the common difficulties portrayed by this case? Note: not keeping track of things, missing opportunities to get help from other people, ignoring the things which are most important and going after things of personal interest.

B. Why does Burke Jackson, a detail person, have difficulty with the Monitor Role? Note that Burke Jackson, who tinkers a lot with details, still has difficulty in the Monitor Role. The reason is, he is a technical specialist who lives emotionally and cognitively in the realm of technical details, but he does not exhibit the high overview frame of mind that a good manager has to have.

C. How does Burke under-utilize his secretary? Note that Jackson doesn't listen to his secretary. His secretary, like most secretaries, is a goldmine of information, support, and important psychological insights. Secretaries can provide information such as: what frame of mind the person is in who calls and asks for information, or wants you to come to a meeting, or go see him or her. Unfortunately, Burke fails to look more deeply at what Muriel has to say. She makes some effort but he dismisses it.

D. How did Jackson mishandle the meeting? Jackson fails to discriminate between the things that only he should be doing, and the things that he can delegate to other people. He is asked to have a representative at a meeting but instead he grabs his calendar and immediately commits another block of precious time.

Practice:
Christine Elm: Is There Safety in Numbers?
Activity Flow Sheet

PURPOSE: With this activity students practice making sense of routine
                    information, and distinguishing between raw data and information.

KEY TOPICS: External monitoring; Deming's points regarding monitoring work-
                    unit performance.

TIME ESTIMATE: 40 minutes.

FORMAT: Individual activity, small group work and large group discussion.

SPECIAL NEEDS: None.

SEQUENCE: 1. Introduce the activity.

                    2. Direct students to read the case and respond in writing to the
                    questions on page 135.

                    3. Divide class into 4-5 person groups..

                    4. Conduct a large group discussion and summarize.

VARIATION: Step #2 may be completed as homework, with the group
                    discussions being held during the following class session.

KEY POINTS: 1. The information that is available, that Christine gathers, is raw
                    data - not information.

                    2. Raw data must be sorted and categorized - or given meaning -
                    in order to be considered information.

                    3. Once data is categorized and made sense of, it is important to
                    look at it chronologically in order to gain a meaningful
                    perspective.

Practice:
Christine Elm: Is There Safety in Numbers?
Process Guide

PURPOSE: With this activity students practice making sense of routine information, and distinguishing between raw data and information.   They are also able to perceive the dimensions of external monitoring.

STEP 1: Introduce the activity by referring students to the directions and case on pages 133-135 of the text.

STEP 2: Direct students to read the case and respond in writing to the questions on page 135.

STEP 3: Divide class into small groups of 4-5 students each.   Have them discuss the questions and agree on a group response to them.

STEP 4: Conduct a large group discussion, summarizing the main points that the groups brought out.   Additional questions for discussion may include:

A. What is the difference between raw data and information?   In what ways can different information emerge from the same raw data?   Can you give examples of this?

B. Why was Stuart Reese so upset about the system?   What principles for handling information was he ignoring?   Note the following about Stuart Reese:

1. Once the information is categorized, it becomes clear that there is not an inordinate number of accidents taking place on the shop floor of this company.   The factory initiated some changes that made the shop floor safer: covering up cables, structural changes, passed tighter regulations on the wearing of hardhats, etc. After these changes, the number of accidents went down, and the factory pretty much stayed within a tight range from year to year. The system is "statistically stable" - in spite of the occasional flare ups that make Stuart so nervous.

2. Stuart's perceptions had more to do with timing, and with the fact that a couple of accidents have occurred close together.

3. Stuart is emotionally and socially invested in a the idea of having a safe workplace. Accidents are psychologically a very salient issue for Reese. It bothers him that shortly after a couple of significant accidents on his shop floor, he has to go give a presentation on safety in the workplace before a national group.

Application: Information Overload or Overdrive?
Activity Flow Sheet

PURPOSE:	This exercise has two tasks: Task 1 provides students with an opportunity to observe themselves as a monitor, and Task 2 directs students to activities which allow them to consider information management in organizations.
KEY TOPICS:	TRAF, filing, taking good notes, and external monitoring.
TIME ESTIMATE:	In class to set-up: 10 minutes; Outside of class: 3-4 hours; in-class followup discussion: 15-20 minutes.
FORMAT:	An individual activity which takes place over a 3 week time span, followed by large group discussion.
SPECIAL NEEDS:	None.

SEQUENCE:

1. Direct students to the instructions on pages 136-137 of the text.

2. A memo is submitted at the conclusion of the assignment.

3. Conduct a large group discussion.

VARIATIONS:

1. Both tasks are demanding, and students could be asked to choose one of the tasks, or be assigned to do one rather than complete both.

2. Students could be divided into teams to complete these tasks and write a team report in the form of a memo.

KEY POINTS:

1. There are common barriers to effective information management which nearly everyone experiences.

2. Managing information, like managing time, is a life skill, the mastery of which will result in great benefits.

Application: Information Overload or Overdrive?
Process Guide

PURPOSE: This exercise has two tasks. Task 1 provides students with an opportunity to observe themselves as a monitor, noting ways in which they assess, retrieve, sort and analyze information. Task 2 directs students to activities which allow them to consider information management in organizations. Students also receive additional practice in memo writing.

STEP 1: Direct students to the instructions on pages 136-137 of the text. Remind them that this is an opportunity for them to apply the main learning points of this competency.

STEP 2: Remind them to submit a memo detailing the results of this assignment. Specify a due date.

STEP 3: Conduct a large group discussion on the results of the assignment. Additional discussion questions may include:

    A. What were the most frequent barriers you encountered to reducing your information overload?

    B. Why do many people tend to believe that we need to acquire more information? How can you counter their arguments?

    C. What strategies did you practice for improving your situation?

    D. Is information overload acknowledged as important in organizations? Why or why not?

    E. What characteristics of organizational life mitigate against efforts to reduce information overload?

    F. What advantages did you notice in your efforts to reduce information overload?

Assessment: Who to Send for Training?
Activity Flow Sheet

PURPOSE: The purpose of this activity is to demonstrate how personal, complex, and subjective, these human/ managerial choices are. By assuming different roles, students understand that many times there is no right or wrong choice to make. This activity demonstrates that there is a need to establish a rationale for choices without hiding the emotional and personal values that are brought to the decisions.

KEY TOPICS: Illustrates the part of the learning section entitled: *Seeing Things As We Really Are*; also the six impediments to good judgment.

TIME ESTIMATE: 20-30 minutes.

FORMAT: An individual activity followed by large group discussion

SPECIAL NEEDS: None.

SEQUENCE:

1. Direct students to read the case.

2. Have them respond to the questions.

3. Conduct a large group discussion.

VARIATIONS:

1. Assign as homework.

2. After completing their responses to the questions, students could engage in small group discussion.

KEY POINTS:

1. People can argue about who to send for training, and never convince one another.

2. Note that motives of racial or gender bias are not operating here, but feelings managers develop for employees. These feelings flavor their choices.

3. Contrary to what we may like to believe, passion does exist in bureaucracies and organizations.

4. You can't decide to send a person to training because you "feel good" about the decision; you have to publicly justify your choices.

Assessment: Who to Send for Training?
Process Guide

PURPOSE: The purpose of this activity is to demonstrate how personal, complex, subjective, and moral these human/ managerial choices are. By assuming different roles, students understand that many times there is no right or wrong choice to make. This activity helps students to understand that there is a need to establish a rationale for their choices without hiding from themselves the emotional and personal values they bring to the decisions. As such this activity provides a vivid demonstration of the learning section entitled *Seeing Things As We Really Are*.

STEP 1: Direct students to read the case on page 137 of the text.

STEP 2: Have them respond in writing to the questions on pp. 137-138.

STEP 3: Conduct a large group discussion, drawing on their observations regarding this experience. Additional discussion points include:

    A. While we may value objectivity, and hope to make decisions which are devoid of human emotion, such is seldom the case. Managers develop different feelings for their employees: a sense of where their employees' lives are, how training would affect employees' personal lives as well as their professional lives, managers' desires to be supportive or even punitive to employees. These feelings flavor managerial choices.

    B. Passion, biases, subjectivity, and feelings are real in organizations and bureaucracies. We may try to pretend that passion doesn't exist, but that's simply not true.

    C. You can't decide to send a person to training because you "feel good" about the decision; you have to publicly provide plausible and rational reasons for justifying your choices.

Analysis: The Shoe War
Activity Flow Sheet

PURPOSE: This activity allows students to analyze a case that illustrates impediments to sound judgment, and employees who had the right ideas but advanced them in the wrong fashion. The dilemma of how insightful employees with vision can advance their ideas in a firm where the upper management does not share their views is vividly portrayed.

KEY TOPICS: The impediments to sound judgment:

TIME ESTIMATE: 45 minutes.

FORMAT: Individual activity, work in 4-6 person groups, followed by large group discussion.

SPECIAL NEEDS: None.

SEQUENCE: 1. Instruct students to read the case .

                    2. Have them respond to the questions on page 150.

                    3. Place class members into 4-6 person groups.

                    4. Conduct a large group discussion and summarize.

VARIATIONS: 1. Steps 1 and 2 may be assigned as homework, with steps 3 and 4 taking place in class.

                    2. Particularly if step 1 is done in class, step 2 can be omitted. The questions lend themselves to interesting discussion without previously writing out responses.

                    3. If time is particularly short, one can go directly from reading the case (step 1) to the large group discussion (step 4).

KEY POINTS: 1. It is clear that George Cervantes and Ingrid Mueller were right in their proposal, but they did not advance it very well.

                    2. The proposal should not have been the first that the leadership of the company heard about the idea.

                    3. We must realize that it was very unclear to these people in the late 1970's what the future would bring.

Analysis: The Shoe War
Process Guide

PURPOSE: This activity allows students to analyze a case that illustrates impediments to sound judgment, as well as employees who had the right ideas but advanced them in the wrong fashion. The dilemma of how insightful employees with vision can advance their ideas in a firm where the upper management does not share their views is vividly portrayed.

This case also illustrates an important point in critical thinking: you have to evaluate the quality of your decisions based upon the information that was available to you at the time you made the decision.

STEP 1: Instruct students to read the directions and the case on pages 146-150.

STEP 2: Have them respond in writing to the questions on page 150.

STEP 3: Place class members into small groups of 4-6 students each to discuss the questions. See how many responses to question #3 they can generate.

STEP 4: Conduct a large group discussion, having each group report their consensus. Other discussion points may include:

A. How would you describe the qualities of Cervantes and Mueller? Note that they have good instincts, and a vision about the future. They suspect that the environment is changing, becoming more turbulent, and that it should affect the strategies of Mercury Shoe Co. Both are sensitive and insightful. They were not very astute.

B. Given that the proposal was good, what mistakes did Cervantes and Mueller make in advancing it? Basically, the proposal should not have been the first that the leadership of the company heard about the idea. It is a mistake just to write a proposal without trying to influence, persuade, and negotiate a little with the people who would be reacting to the proposal and making a decision.

C. What traps was the company beginning to fall into? Note that Mercury illustrates some of the classic traps: Not Invented Here Syndrome, this formula has worked in the past and it will work again, not doing enough environmental scanning, not open to change, not open to idea that they might be wrong, that things had changed so much that old strategies might no longer be working. The management at Mercury was not looking for new problems and solutions but was only concerned with the old problems.

D. With hindsight, it is clear with Mercury should have done. Now we can see that the environment changed, that the company should have broadened the product line, and it should have gotten into new speciality markets, such as the aerobic shoe market.

E. The critical question is, at that time, on the strength of the evidence then available, would you have made the decision to invest scarce company resources to make these changes? You can't assess the quality or effectiveness of the decisions you've made based upon how things turned out, even though that's what common sense tells you that you would do. You have to evaluate the quality of your decisions based upon the information that was available to you at the time you made the decision.

Practice: Argument Mapping
Activity Flow Sheet

PURPOSE: This activity allows students to practice analyzing arguments.

KEY TOPICS: Analyzing arguments and argument mapping.

TIME ESTIMATE: 25 minutes.

FORMAT: Small groups of 4 students each, in teams of 2 students per team; followed by large group discussion.

SPECIAL NEEDS: None.

SEQUENCE: 1. Divide the class members into groups of 4.

2. Let each team in the group choose one of the two arguments to analyze.

3. Conduct a large group discussion by summarizing the observations of the groups.

VARIATIONS: Four students could be chosen to do this as a fishbowl exercise, while the rest of the class reads the cases to decided how they would assess the arguments.

KEY POINTS: 1. There is a weak argument and a strong argument. According to tests with hundreds of students and quite a few faculty, the first one strong and the second one is weak.

2. The second argument is weak because assertions not well supported, recommendations are not founded on plausible or strong evidence, and the argument is based on limited examples and very limited data and information.

3. Using the model of looking at the claims and the data that the claims are based upon and the warrants that bridge claim and data together, then it is clear that the second argument is weak.

Practice: Argument Mapping
Process Guide

PURPOSE: This activity allows students to work in pairs, practicing analyzing
arguments.   Argument 1 is deemed as a sound argument and argument 2 is
deemed as weak.

STEP 1: Divide the class members into groups of 4. If the number of students are not
evenly divisible by 4, add one more to each subgroup.

STEP 2: Let each team in the group choose one of the two arguments to analyze. Allow
teams 15 minutes to analyze the arguments before presenting their
analysis to the other pair of classmates.

STEP 3: Conduct a large group discussion by summarizing the observations of the
groups, as well as the key points from the activity flow sheet.

Application: Implementation Plan
Activity Flow Sheet

PURPOSE: This reflective activity allows students to apply critical thinking skills to a personal situation.

TIME ESTIMATE: In class: 10 minutes to set up; over a 3 week period outside of class: approximately 3 hours; in class follow up discussion: 15-20 minutes.

FORMAT: An individual activity followed by large group discussion.

SPECIAL NEEDS: None.

SEQUENCE: 1. Direct students to the instructions on page 152.

                    2. Conduct a clarifying discussion regarding their choice of activity.

                    3. Walk through question #2 with them.

                    4. Remind them of the due date.

                    5. On the due date, conduct a large group discussion.

VARIATION: After students have individually identified their activity in question #1, divide them into small groups to discuss their critical thinking processes as teams. These small group meeting may take place outside of class during intervals during the three week period, after which individual reports can be submitted.

KEY POINTS: 1. Efforts to see things from different perspectives are information gathering devices.

                    2. All of us are disposed to considering our situations in set ways; examining our critical thinking process exposes those set ways to us. Such exposure helps us to delineate their advantages and disadvantages.

Application: Implementation Plan
Process Guide

PURPOSE: This reflective activity allows students to apply critical thinking skills to a personal situation. Their critical thinking processes are considered in terms of how they managed information.

STEP 1: Direct students to the instructions on page 152.

STEP 2: Conduct a clarifying discussion regarding what type of activity they may choose in response to question #1.

STEP 3: Walk through question #2 with them, explaining that this is a process that is an important life skill as we seek to improve our critical thinking process.

STEP 4: Remind them of the due date for their written response.

STEP 5: On the due date, conduct a large group discussion regarding their experience in completing the assignment. Summarize their responses to the last three questions of the assignment. Make the key points.

Assessment: That'll Show 'Em
Activity Flow Sheet

PURPOSE:	This activity allows students to assess their ability to identify strengths and weaknesses in a piece of writing.
KEY TOPICS:	Memo writing; making your message assessible.
TIME ESTIMATE:	20 minutes.
FORMAT:	Individual activity, then work in 4-5 person groups, followed by large group discussion.
SPECIAL NEEDS:	None, unless variation #2 is chosen, in which case blank transparencies, special markers, and an overhead projector would be helpful.
SEQUENCE:	1. Introduce the activity.
	2. Have students read and revise the memo individually, and to respond to the questions.
	3. Place students into small groups of 4-5, to discuss their revisions and the questions.
	4. Conduct a large group discussion, summarizing their revisions.
VARIATIONS:	1. Step 2 can be completed as homework, with the small groups beginning the next class session.
	2. Groups can decide on a revision, and present it to the class. This can be expedited using an overhead projector, and having each group write its revision on a transparency.
KEY POINTS:	1. The tone of the memo sends much of the message.
	2. There are no "right" answers, no one perfect memo.
	3. Organizational norms and personal style preferences may vary the revisions.
	4. Emphasize strengths and weaknesses rather than rights and wrongs.

Assessment: That'll Show 'Em
Process Guide

PURPOSE: This activity allows students to assess their ability to identify strengths and weaknesses in a piece of writing.

STEP 1: Introduce the activity by directing students to read the instructions and the memo on page 158-159.

STEP 2: Have students read and revise the memo individually, and to respond to the questions on page 153. Direct them to think about:

A. What is the tone of the memo and how is the tone developed?

B. What strengths did you find?

C. What weaknesses did you find?

STEP 3: Place students into 4-5 person groups to discuss their revisions and the questions.

STEP 4: Conduct a large group discussion, summarizing their revisions.

Observations regarding the memo: it projects a negative tone and is unnecessarily contentious, even though it is grammatically and mechanically correct. From the standpoint of what the person is trying to achieve and what reactions he/she wants or does not want to trigger in people, it is a very poor document.

Analysis: A Look at Your Own Writing
Activity Flow Sheet

PURPOSE: This activity provides students with an opportunity to improve their critical thinking as it relates to writing. They also receive feedback on their writing as well as to review the writing of a classmate and give constructive feedback.

KEY TOPICS: The entire learning section; also giving constructive feedback.

TIME ESTIMATE: 30 minutes.

FORMAT: Dyads followed by large group discussion.

SPECIAL NEEDS: Three writing samples from each student, plus the writing analysis worksheet (follows process guide).

SEQUENCE: 1. Introduce the activity; form class into dyads.

                    2. Review basic ideas for giving constructive feedback.

                    3. Have partners review each other's material.

                    4. Discuss as a large group.

                    5. Summarize.

VARIATION: Give students a few moments to critique their own writing before giving it to their partners. This can be done by asking students to detail to their partners areas where their writing skills could use improvement.

KEY POINTS: 1. Most people are self-conscious about their writing.

                    2. Everyone can improve their writing, and seeking constructive feedback provides significant help.

                    3. Writing tends to improve with practice, as well.

Analysis: A Look at Your Own Writing
Process Guide

PURPOSE: This activity provides students with an opportunity to improve their critical thinking as it relates to writing. They also receive feedback on their writing as well as to review the writing of a classmate and give constructive feedback.

STEP 1: Introduce the activity by referring to the instructions on page 160, and form class into dyads.

STEP 2: Review basic ideas for giving constructive feedback.

Basically, remind students to point out positive aspects of their partner's writing first, before explaining possible improvements.

Further, suggest that they might want to avoid being definitive and using phrases such as: You should have . . . or, You were wrong to . . . Instead, in giving constructive feedback, its best to be more tentative, using such phrases as: I might be wrong but, to me this seems . . . or, You might want to consider . . .

Explain that as partners they are not experts, but merely sharing with the writer one reader's perception.

STEP 3: Have partners review each other's material and respond to the questions on page 160.

STEP 4: Discuss as a large group. Additional discussion questions might include:

A. Did you like or dislike having your material reviewed? Explain your feelings.

B. Did the criticism you received mirror your own assessment of your writing?

C. Do you feel that you can better review and edit your own work as a result of this activity? Explain.

STEP 5: Summarize by eliciting responses from students regarding the experience.

WRITING ANALYSIS WORKSHEET

Writer's Name:_____ Date:_____

Partner's Name:_____

WRITING SAMPLE #1

List positive comments on the writer's sample:

List areas in which writer's sample may be improved:

WRITING SAMPLE #2

List positive comments on the writer's sample:

List areas in which writer's sample may be improved:

WRITING SAMPLE #3

List positive comments on the writer's sample:

List areas in which writer's sample may be improved:

Practice: Editing Exercise
Activity Flow Sheet

PURPOSE: This activity allows students to practice correcting basic kinds of writing errors.

KEY TOPICS: Finding the Right Words: The Lard Factor; The Memo: Workhorse or Deadhorse?, and Making Your Message Assessible.

TIME ESTIMATE: 25 minutes.

FORMAT: Individual activity followed by large group discussion.

SPECIAL NEEDS: Revisions to Sentences handout (follows process guide).

SEQUENCE: 1. Introduce the activity.

2. Direct students to individually complete the exercise.

3. Conduct a large group discussion.

4. Summarize.

VARIATION: This activity can be modified into a small group format after Step #2. This would permit students to share their edited versions with group members before proceeding to the large group discussion.

KEY POINTS: 1. Writing communicates more than the content; tone and clarity also communicate messages.

2. Grammatical correctness is usually not at issue. Sentences can be grammatically correct and still be unclear.

3. Small changes in wording can lead to large changes in intonation, clarity, and meaning.

4. There are no right or wrong answers to these changes. It is a matter of what the writer wishes to communicate.

5. Suggested editing changes are provided on the process guide.

Practice: Editing Exercise
Process Guide

PURPOSE: This activity allows students to practice correcting basic kinds of writing errors. It also allows them to demonstrate improvement in the use of brevity, organization of thought, and clarity.

STEP 1: Introduce the activity by referring students to the directions and sentences on page 161.

STEP 2: Direct students to individually complete the exercise on a separate sheet of paper.

STEP 3: Conduct a large group discussion, allowing students to present their edited versions of the sentences. Ask students to explain why they feel their revisions improve the original statement.

STEP 4: Summarize, using the Revisions to the Sentences handout and the students' main points.

REVISIONS TO SENTENCES ON PAGE 161

by Michael P. Thompson

1. After completing your application, please proceed to the interview section and give the interviewer your application and all other forms you were asked to complete.

   [**NOTE:** Why talk about an "application process," instead of just asking the person to complete the application? We also think its better to put everything in parallel form whenever possible. In this revision, note the imperative mood, the direct address form: "please do this, then turn in this, and fill out this" etc. The revision is also warmer and less impersonal in tone. We added a "please" and deleted the "as required."]

2. Our top priority must now be to individualize our treatment programs so we can improve our accreditation review.

3. We should put in place out new pricing guidelines immediately.

   [**NOTE:** In the original, "put in place" and "implementation" were redundant; they referred to the same recommended action.]

4. The recent assessment showed that a good deal of the auditors' time was spent rescheduling audits.

   [**NOTE:** The biggest problem with the original is the use of the passive voice ("it was ascertained" "was consumed") and the redundant words "rescheduling" and "previously arranged."]

5. You are legally entitled to information on how bidders are selected.

   [**NOTE:** This kind of sentence gives the legal department fits. We could have rewritten it even more simply by dropping the passive voice construction "how bidders are selected," and said, "how we select bidders," but this version is probably pushing the limit of clarity and directness, as it is.

   The main strategy here is to go ahead and tell people something, instead of saying that you are going to tell them, and thus indirectly telling them. Get it?]

6. The committee felt that examiners need to be more aware of the need to verify credentials, especially when dealing with new applicants.

   [**NOTE:** Watch out for any sentence that begins with the "false subject" word "it." And those prepositions: *on* the part *of* the examiners *of* the importance *of* credential verification. . . . Start chopping prepositions where possible and your writing will automatically be more focused.]

7. The manager of a large office *must* be willing to delegate authority.

   [**NOTE:** We cheated a little by italicizing must, but that's what good writers do: they use all the resources they have to get the message across.]

8. We must give our immediate support to the creation of a commission to investigate the trend of crimes against the elderly. We can do this by writing directly to the governor and by contacting other elected officials.

[**NOTE:** There's certainly no best way to do this one, but we think the original sentence is trying to carry too much lumber and has to be split in two.]

Application: You Will Report to Work
Activity Flow Sheet

PURPOSE:	This activity allows students to apply concepts from this chapter by writing a memo in response to a work situation.
KEY POINTS:	Critical thinking, memo writing.
TIME ESTIMATE:	30 minutes.
FORMAT:	Individual activity followed by large group discussion.
SPECIAL NEEDS:	Two sample memos follow the process guide. The first one is a poor example, and the second one is a good example.
SEQUENCE:	1. Introduce students to the activity.
	2. Instruct students to write a memo to all employees.
	3. Conduct a large group discussion.
	4. Summarize.
VARIATIONS:	1. Assign completely as homework, providing a due date for the assignment to be submitted.
	2. Use small group discussions, after step #2, and allowing the members, as a group, to design a memo.
KEY POINTS:	1. Effective writing skills are developed through practice; they are not an in-born trait.
	2. Often memo writing in organizations has to take into account a number of different audiences besides the persons to which the memo is addressed.
	3. There are challenges to writing a memo that is easy to understand, succinct, contains the most important information, and not too curt and not too authoritarian.
SPECIAL NOTE:	**This activity assumes knowledge of the Christine Elm practice activity on pages 133-135 of the text.**

Application: You Will Report to Work
Process Guide

PURPOSE: This activity allows students to apply concepts from this chapter by writing a memo in response to a challenging work situation. As such they apply critical thinking and principles of memo writing to a timely and difficult situation. This activity assumes knowledge of the Christine Elm practice activity in this chapter.

STEP 1: Introduce students to the activity by directing their attention to the situation on pages 161-162 of the text.

STEP 2: Instruct students to write a memo to all employees, in response to the situation. Using this as an in-class assignment with a time limit adds to the pressure of the situation.

STEP 3: Conduct a large group discussion, summarizing their major concerns. Additional discussion questions include:

A. How did it feel to have to write an assignment under such pressure? What did you do to mitigate the negative effects of that pressure?

B. What was the most difficult part of this writing assignment?

C. If you had more time and this were a work project, what additional information would you have wanted to include?

STEP 4: Summarize, using students' memos and the two sample memos provided.

MEMORANDUM

Date: March 13, 1990

To: All Employees

From: _____Vice President of Operations

Last week, the Accounting Department discovered some missing inventory. The value and amount of the missing assets could not be determined for certain. In an effort to update inventory records, it was deemed necessary by the Board of Trustees to implement an emergency inventory procedure.

In agreement with Local 365, PSE will pay all hourly employees time and a half for the hours they work at this inventory session. The work will begin on Saturday at (9:00 A.M. at Warehouse A.

Attendance at this project is mandatory for all employees, and individuals unable to attend must clear their non-attendance with their supervisors immediately. Your careful compliance with this request is appreciated.

MEMORANDUM

DATE: March 13, 1990

TO: All Employees

FROM: Vice President of Operations

SUBJECT: Emergency Inventroy Check on Saturday, March 17, 1990

All employees are to report to warehouse A this coming Saturday at 9:00 a.m. for an inventory check.

Reasons for the Check

Last week, the Accounting Department discovered some missing inventory. In an effort to update inventory records, the Board has decided to conduct this emergency accounting.

Compensation for Your Time

In agreement with Local 365, PSE will pay all hourly employees **time-and-a-half** when they exceed forty (40) hours for the week (the increase in pay begins after reaching forty hours). Lunch will be provided by PSE.

Also in agreement with the Union, employees attending will be given priority when vacation allowances are decided. If you have questions concerning this, please see your union representative.

If You Need to be Excused

If you find that you can not attend, please see your supervisor. Your supervisor needs to know if you will not be attending.

I appreciate your effotrs to make PSE run as smoothly as possible.

The Mentor Role is the first role in the Human Relations Model, and in many ways epitomizes the posture of the Human Relations School. Managers in the Mentor Role provide concern and support for subordinates, develop people and reward performance. In the words of one of the authors, "It is the concerned human role. Note that in Western society, caring and concern are seen as weak; good leaders are seen as powerful and in control. This is a mistake."

Of all the roles, the manager in the mentor role may most directly experience the tensions between the interests of the organization to control individuals, and the interests of individuals in being autonomous. Managers, as mentors, often find themselves in the middle of this tension.

Students tend to relate strongly to the mentor role competencies. The concepts involving self-understanding and communication skills are easily viewed as necessary life competencies, important to individuals regardless of chosen career. As such, these competencies are readily recognized as being immediately applicable to students' personal lives. Frequently, students find themselves enthusiastically subscribing to these competencies; they realize that many problems facing people and organizations alike are basically communication problems. Eagerly embracing these skills, they may believe that the world would be a better place if everyone practiced them. They may perceive how much happier they would be if all of their friends, loved ones, acquaintances, and professors used these skills. They may be quick to recognize where others need to improve these skills, and not so quick to realize their own need to improve.

It is not surprising, then, to find students--or anyone--believing that any problems that organizations have would be solved with the diligent use of the communication and self-understanding competencies associated with this role. And organizations often are quick to identify their problems as being based in communication. While not taking away from the importance of these skills, it may be necessary with some students to raise this issue explicitly, pointing out the need for the rest of the framework in order for organizations to function and function effectively.

While several paradoxes are apparent in the mentor role, one of the more compelling deals with communication skills: the balance between expressing ourselves clearly to others (as in feedback) and actively listening to them. The process is more interactive than it may appear to some. Providing feedback is taking the other person into account and responding to their reflections on what the speaker has said. Receiving feedback involves responsibility to ask for clarification and elaboration when needed and taking the risk of saying: "I'm not sure what you mean. . .".

On the same token, active and reflective listening involves more than being a tape player with the record button pushed, and more than just repeating back to assure surface understanding. Real listening also involves a measure of vulnerability, of feeling with the other person, of letting oneself be affected by the other. Paradoxically, there is strength in vulnerability.

The competencies in the Mentor Role: The three competencies of this role and their corresponding topics in the learning activities are:

Competency #1: Understanding Yourself and Others

Topics:
Values and assumptions
Theory X and Theory Y
Values and understanding yourself
Johari Window
Values and understanding others
Rules for practicing empathy

Competency #2: Interpersonal Communication

Topics:
A Basic model of interpersonal communication
Feedback and noise
Problems in interpersonal communication
Rules for effective communication
Reflective listening

Competency #3: Developing Subordinates

Topics:
Uses and problems of performance appraisal
Two-step process to performance evaluation
Guidelines for giving and receiving feedback

Conceptually, these are not the only competencies in this role.   Other competencies have been identified as:

Showing sensitivity and concern
Counseling and coaching
Interviewing and active listening
Career planning and development of subordinates
Giving performance feedback in effective ways
Working with problem employees
Using rewards and incentives

Which competencies to choose? We recognize that you, as the instructor, may not be able to cover all three competencies in your course. In order to assist you with your decision of which ones to choose, the following questions were posed to the authors. You may not agree with the authors; in fact, they did not always agree among themselves, as is illustrated here:

1. In teaching this course, if you could cover only ONE competency from this chapter, which one would that be and why?

One author noted: "Its tight between Understanding Self and Others, and Interpersonal Communication. Understanding the self is critical; its central to everything."

Another author said: "Interpersonal Communication. Without this, you might as well pack up the rest. Need I say more?"

2. In teaching this course, if you could cover only TWO competencies from this chapter, which two would they be and why?

One author said that in addition to Understanding the Self, the choice would be Interpersonal Communication.

Another author said, "In addition to Interpersonal Communication, the choice is Understanding Yourself and Others, because you cannot be a mentor, i.e., think about developing others, if you don't understand them. This is a personal bias with regards to management, more than it is about this role. In the 1990's and onward, the 'interpersonal stuff' is more and more important."

3. If you had an additional 5 pages of space for each COMPETENCY, what ideas and concepts would you wish to include?

Understanding Self and Others: Perception, the concept of how we select and organize information. This overlaps somewhat with "Analyzing Information" in the Monitor Role, but there is more from a human relations viewpoint on the perceptual process. Also, include a discussion on attribution.

Interpersonal Communication: Nonverbal communication - what it is and what it isn't. Nonverbal has become very overused. It might be useful to have some discussion on using and reading nonverbal communication.

Developing Subordinates: Career stages, development of subordinates through their career and life cycles. What are people looking for at different stages of their careers?

The Mentor Role and current issues: The Mentor Role bears a direct relationship to the issue of managing a culturally diverse workforce. The competencies and skills defined by the Mentor Role, including communication and feedback, prepare managers to meet the challenges of the changing composition of the workforce. It also bears an obvious relationship to ethics in the workforce. Furthermore, the skills acquired in the Mentor Role may be helpful as managers are called upon to deal with international markets and concerns.

Some questions to consider in this chapter are:

1. While the value of the competencies involved in the Mentor Role are widely acclaimed, what would be the consequences if this role were taken too far? What would it be like, for the organization and for employees, if the managers carried the Mentor Role to extreme?

2. What types of organizational designs, are more conducive to the qualities in the Mentor Role? Which are less?

3. Under what circumstances is an emphasis on the Mentor Role more appropriate, and under what circumstances is it less appropriate?

4. It has been argued that the Mentor Role is more important for managers in volunteer organizations, which lack a financial incentive and depend on people to want to be involved, than for managers in the work place. Do you think this is accurate?

A note from one of the authors: The single most valuable course he ever took was an undergraduate course in reflective listening. He spent the entire semester on this one skill. It has since proved to be his most used and most effective interpersonal skill.

**Assessment: Managerial Orientation Measure
Activity Flow Sheet**

PURPOSE: Measure students' attitudes toward managing others, and begin to increase awareness of how attitudes influence employee behavior at work. Scoring will indicate whether students have a general Theory X orientation, or an orientation towards Theory Y.

KEY TOPICS: Theory X and theory Y.

TIME ESTIMATE: 10 minutes for response and scoring; 10-15 for discussion.

FORMAT: Individual activity followed by large group discussion.

SPECIAL NEEDS: None in addition to blackboard to discuss scores.

SEQUENCE: 1. Assign students to complete the scale before reading the learning activity.

                    2. Have them score their answers and be prepared to report their score for the class discussion.

                    3. Conduct large group discussion of implications.

                    4. Summarize.

VARIATION: Steps #1 and #2 can be completed as a homework assignment.

KEY POINTS: 1. Attitudes towards employees and work affect the interaction between manager and employees.

                    2. Expectations and assumptions influence behavior and outcomes.

                    3. Awareness of one's own attitudes about values and openness to learning about the values of others are important.

Assessment: Managerial Orientation Scale
Process Guide

PURPOSE: A first step towards understanding ourselves and others is to determine what assumptions we have about people. This activity helps students to measure their attitudes toward managing others, and to increase their awareness of how attitudes influence employee behavior at work. Scoring will indicate whether students have a general Theory X orientation, or an orientation towards Theory Y.

STEP 1. Assign students to complete the scale at home before reading the learning activity. (If you wish to do this in class, allow approximately 10 minutes). Brief instructions for the completion of this activity are in the text. If you wish to elaborate, you could indicate the following:

The Managerial Orientation Scale (MOS) measures one's attitude toward management and employee performance. In this activity you will be measuring whether you think more like a "Theory X" or a "Theory Y" manager. Descriptions of Theory X and Theory Y are explained in the learning activity. Before reading that section of the assignment, fill out the MOS by noting the extent to which you agree - or disagree - with each of the items in the scale, on pp. 167-168 of the text.

STEP 2. Instruct them to score their answers and be prepared to report their score for the class discussion. Instructions for scoring at on p. 168 of the text.

STEP 3. Conduct a large group discussion of the activity and its implications. Record comments and scores on the blackboard. Suggestions of questions include:

A. How many of you scored more like a Theory X manager? Theory Y?

B. How would either of these orientations affect what a manager tends to perceive in terms of employee work behavior?

C. How would either of the orientations affect the manager's behavior? Consider this in terms of "self-fulfilling prophecy"; that is, people often behave according to our expectations of them.

D. If you were employed and had a choice to be supervised by a Theory X-oriented manager or by a Theory Y-oriented manager, which would you choose to be supervised by and why?

E. Question for students with a Theory Y orientation: can you think of situations where a Theory X approach might be more appropriate than a Theory Y? (Reverse the question and pose to Theory X students.) Can you think of situations where the reliance on either orientation to the exclusion of other considerations might be dysfunctional?

F. What organizational designs might be more conducive to the development of the Theory X orientation in its managers? Which types of structures might be less friendly to the display of a Theory X oriented attitudes? (Reverse the question for Theory Y.)

G. If you had the opportunity to develop a theory of your own, what would it be?

STEP 4. Summarize. The following is an interpretation of MOS scores:

Theory X is "shorthand" for the traditional managerial viewpoint (or set of attitudes) emphasizing control and close supervision. The assumption is that workers are lazy and must be told what to do. In fact, the assumption is that workers want to be told because they are too lazy to think for themselves, and must be coerced to work. A "soft" version of Theory X is the notion that people can be gently "prodded" to work. Low MOS scores are linked to Theory X beliefs.

Theory Y refers to a set of assumptions that different from Theory X and at times are opposite of Theory X. Theory Y assumes that workers want (or can easily learn to want) greater responsibility for and control over their own job activities. Workers are assumed to be challenged by rewards. According to Theory Y, people are generally capable to innovation and making real contributions to the organization. High MOS scores are related to Theory Y attitudes.

Notice how Theory X and Theory Y are contradictory, and yet how both are useful.

Analysis Activity: The Sherwood Holmes Case
Activity Flow Sheet

PURPOSE: Increase awareness of how prejudices, assumptions, and self-concepts influence perceptions and decisions.

KEY TOPICS: Understanding ourselves in order to understand our perceptions.

TIME ESTIMATE: About 60-70 minutes.

FORMAT: Individual, small group work, and large group discussion.

SPECIAL NEEDS: Inference sheet (follows the process guide).

SEQUENCE   1. Introduce the activity.

                      2. Give examples of observation/ knowledge/ inference.

                      3. Have students individually complete the Inference Sheet.

                      4. Divide students into 4-5 person groups.

                      5. Discuss as a large group.

                      6. Summarize.

VARIATIONS: 1. Steps #1 and #3 may be completed as homework. (Step #2 may be included in your directions). Then for the next class, after a few initial comments, the process can be completed using steps 4-6.

                      2. At step #3 students can complete the Inference Sheet in groups of two.

                      3. At step #4 the small groups can be instructed to produce a composite profile of the CEO.

KEY POINTS: 1. Inference, observation, and knowledge all have value.

                      2. The key is to be aware of which is which.

                      3. Our inferences of others usually reveal more about ourselves than about those we are observing.

                      4. Biases and preconceptions interfere with understanding and communication.

Analysis Activity: The Sherwood Holmes Case
Process Guide

PURPOSE: The purpose of this activity is to increase students' awareness of how prejudices, assumptions, and self-concepts influence perceptions and decisions. In this analysis, students have the opportunity to distinguish among observation, knowledge, and inference. Students then can proceed to explore the relationships among these three concepts. In addition, the activity is designed to help students become aware of their personal preconceptions and biases.

Step 1. Introduce the activity by referring students to the case on pages 172-175 of the text.

Step2. Give examples of observation, knowledge, and inference.

Example 1:

Observation	picture of woman and child on desk
Knowledge	people commonly place pictures of spouse and children on desk
Inference	The woman and child are probably the CEO's wife and son; the CEO is probably a man.

Example 2:

Observation	The CEO has a copy of *You Are What You Eat* in the office.
Knowledge	This publication is read by people who are interested in nutrition and health.
Inference	The CEO is probably interested in nutrition and general health.

Step 3. Have students read the case and complete the Inference Sheet.

> NOTE: Steps 1 and 3 may be assigned as homework; include step 2 in the directions to the students.

Step 4. Break them into groups and have them compare their responses. Assign a recorder to complete the group's Inference Sheet.

Step 5. Conduct a large group discussion. Suggestions to facilitate that discussion include:

A. Divide the blackboard into three parts, outlining a large Inference Sheet. Using a round-robin approach, ask for one response from each group (the recorder may respond) until the board-sheet is filled. In this way, groups can see the responses of other groups, and also see the variety of inferences.

1. Ask the class as a whole to discuss the similarities and differences among the groups' responses, and to account for them.

2. Ask the class for alternative inferences. For instance, one might infer from the picture (example 1) that the CEO has a traditional married life. In fact, he may have been widowed.

An alternative inference in example 2 is the possibility that the CEO is concerned about being overweight.

3. Other discussion questions can be used. See B below.

B. Additional discussion questions may include:

1. How do our prejudices, assumptions, and self-concepts affect our observations and decisions?

2. What are some examples from your experience where personal biases and assumptions affected your perceptions of others' perceptions of you? What did you do in these situations? What would you do differently now?

3. What sort of impressions do we gain about people we have never met by the nature of their surroundings?

4. In what ways can people contrive for others to have certain impressions by what they display in their surroundings? Can you give examples? (For instance, if a professor does most of her research and writing outside of the office, could she possibly feel compelled to make sure her office at school has a lot of books? What might students and colleagues possibly assess her performance to be if she has no books at school?)

5. How do we deal with inconsistencies in our observations of others?

6. What is the nature of the relationship among observation, knowledge, and inference?

7. What can we do to increase our accuracy in our perceptions and relationships with others?

8. What steps can managers take to more accurately view the behaviors of their employees?

9. In what ways do our inferences increase our knowledge of our own biases and perceptions? How can our inferences help us better to understand ourselves?

Step 6: Summarize by asking students to state the major points of this activity. For instance:

A. Our own biases and preconceptions can influence the inferences we make, based upon our knowledge and observations.

B. We can improve our ability to make inferences by becoming more aware of the relationship between observation and knowledge. For example, although the CEO has an issue of *Ebony* in the office, it is a surmise that the CEO is Afro-American, rather than indicating that the CEO is interested in minority concerns.

C. Inferences can be useful tools in deciphering our environment.

THE SHERWOOD HOLMES CASE INFERENCE SHEET

DIRECTIONS: Read carefully the description of the CEO's office and study the room diagram. Complete this Inference Sheet as follows:

1. In the left-hand column (observation) note data from your reading that you think are important clues about the kind of person who occupies the room.

2. In the middle column (knowledge) note any experiences that you may have had that influence your observation.

3. In the right-hand column (inference) note whatever conclusions you reach as a result of your observations.

OBSERVATION Raw data	KNOWLEDGE Experiences that Influence your observation	INFERENCE Resulting perception

Practice Activity: The Marvins are Missing, Again
Activity Flow Sheet

PURPOSE: Help students see how the same behavior observed in different employees may call for different responses.

KEY TOPICS: Values and understanding others.

TIME ESTIMATE: 50 minutes

FORMAT: Individual work, then 4-5 person groups followed by large group discussion.

SPECIAL NEEDS: None

SEQUENCE: 1. Have students, individually, read the cases of the Marvins and prepare their responses.

2. Divide students into 4-5 person groups.

3. Conduct a large group discussion.

4. Summarize.

VARIATIONS: Step #1 can be assigned as homework, with the activity resuming with step #2 the next class session. This would cut the time estimate by about 20 minutes.

KEY POINTS: 1. Different people in different circumstances require different responses.

2. Our own values, experiences, and style influence our perceptions of and responses to others.

3. Empathy can be a useful tool for understanding others and can assist the manager and employee in finding a solution to problems at work.

4. This case portrays the classic tension between organizational needs and the needs of individuals. It further illustrates the dilemma of managers who are caught in that conflictual situation.

Practice Activity: The Marvins are Missing, Again
Process Guide

PURPOSE: "The Marvins are Missing, Again" details the story of three Marvins, each of whom are absent from work. This activity is designed to help students understand how the same behavior observed in different employees may call for different responses. This activity is an opportunity tp practice empathy and understanding others.

In order to solve may problems with employees, attention to individual factors is necessary. Only by recognizing that a different approach is needed for each Marvin can the situation be optimized for the manager and the employee.

Step 1. Have students, individually, read the cases of the Marvins and prepare a response for each one. Remind students to try to use the skills discussed in the learning activity. (Allow about 20-25 minutes).

Step 2. Break students into small groups and have them discuss their responses with other group members. (Allow about 15 minutes).

Step 3. Conduct a large group discussion. Several possible discussion questions are listed below:

A. How did you respond to each of the Marvins?

B. How did your own managerial style (Theory X or Theory Y) influence your responses?

C. What were your first impressions of these three Marvins?

D. Were some people in your group more sympathetic to some Marvins than others? How did this affect your response?

E. If you were one of the Marvins, how would you need for your manager to handle your situation? What if your manager were inflexible? What effect would this have on your performance and loyalty and morale?

G. If you decided to be lenient and flexible with the Marvins, how would you handle this with your boss?

Step 4. Summarize, using students' main ideas and the key points on the activity flow sheet.

Application Activity: Understanding and Changing Relationships
Activity Flow Sheet

PURPOSE: Apply skills in appreciating individual differences, empathy, and use of perception in making inferences.

KEY POINTS: Changing perceptions and the use of empathy.

TIME ESTIMATE   30 minutes.

FORMAT: Individual activity followed by large group discussion.

SPECIAL NEEDS: None.

SEQUENCE: 1. Explain activity and direct its completion.

                    2. Explain importance of honesty in completing it.

                    3. Have volunteers share insights.

                    4. Conduct a large group discussion and summarize.

VARIATIONS: This may be assigned as homework; steps #3 and #4 could begin the next class session.

KEY POINTS: 1. Sometimes we are too busy to reflect upon our perceptions, assumptions, etc. about others.

                    2. Sometimes we fail to see the changes in them or the inaccuracies of our perceptions.

WATCH FOR: possible student resistance – not to the activity, but to completing it honestly. They may be more inclined to be candid if you give a personal example, answering the questions of the activity while giving the directions.

Application Activity: Understanding and Changing Relationships
Process Guide

PURPOSE: This activity provides a format for students to apply skills in appreciating individual differences, empathy, and the use of perception in making inferences. This activity: examines how perceptions of others have changed over time (or how they have been reinforced); details possible problems in the relationships and ways in which the respondents may have contributed to those problems; increases insight into how personal characteristics influence our relationships; encourages the use of concepts in this section to improve these relationships.

Step 1. Briefly review the questions in the activity and direct students to respond to the questions.

Step 2. Explain the importance of honesty in completing it. Emphasize that their responses are not for anyone else to read or to evaluate. Some students may especially view steps #3 and #4 as risky; however, if it becomes too uncomfortable, they can always choose another person.

The significance of this activity is highlighted by the fact that awareness of perceptions is essential to increasing our understanding of ourselves and others.

Step 3. Ask for volunteers to share insights. If you would like, give an example from your own experience to illustrate how a work relationship changed as a result of your increased awareness of your impressions and perceptions.

Step 4. Conclude by summarizing the main points brought out in the discussion.

Assessment: Communication Skills
Activity Flow Sheet

PURPOSE: Most people think they are excellent communicators. This activity helps students to understand that people tend to be self-deceptive about communication skills.

KEY TOPICS: Communication skills.

TIME ESTIMATE: 15 minutes.

FORMAT: Individual activity followed by large group discussion.

SPECIAL NEEDS: None.

SEQUENCE: 1. Introduce the activity by instructing students to identify two relationships: one that is very pleasant and one that is very painful.

                    2. Emphasize that this activity is not graded, but is for their personal use only.

                    3. Direct them to complete the questionnaire.

                    4. Have students respond in writing to the interpretation questions.

                    5. Conduct large group discussion.

                    6. Summarize.

VARIATION: Steps #3 and #4 may be completed as homework.

KEY POINTS: 1. When we are in painful relationships, we may tend to see the other person as having communication problems and feel that we do not have problems with communication.

                    2. We tend to think of ourselves as having good communication skills; it is easy to be self-deceptive in this regard.

                    3. Since we experience the consequences of a painful, dysfunctional relationship, it is in our interest to consider our role in maintaining its status.

Assessment: Communication Skills
Process Guide

PURPOSE: This activity increases student awareness of the need to examine their communication skills. While most people think they are excellent communicators, this activity helps students to realize that they bear the emotional consequences of the perpetuation of painful relationships. Students are asked to respond to a questionnaire, analyzing their communication in two relationships. One relationship is very pleasant and the other is very painful. This activity helps students to identify specific problems in the painful relationship that they need to work on.

Step 1. Instruct students to identify two relationships: one that is very pleasant and one that is very painful. Write the names of these two individuals on a piece of paper.

Step 2. Emphasize that this activity is for their use only, and their written responses will not be evaluated or read by anyone else.

Step 3. Direct them to complete the questionnaire regarding their communication with these two individuals.

Step 4. Reiterate the interpretation questions; have students respond in writing by making notes of their thoughts.

Step 5. Conduct a large group discussion. Additional questions may include:

A. How do you feel about this activity? Did you find parts of it difficult? If so, which parts, and why were they difficult?

B. Did you find that your communication behavior varied in these two relationships? How?

C. Do you consider it important to examine your communication behavior in the painful relationship? Do you think this would be a wise use of your time?

D. In reflecting on the painful relationship, how much does that person mean to you? Often we find that the hurt in the relationship would diminish considerably if we did not care about the person. The more important a person is to us, the greater the potential for pain.

E. What consequences to you experience from the maintenance of the painful relationship?

F. What specific steps could to take to improve your communication skills in the painful relationship?

Step 6: Conclude by summarizing the key points on the activity flow sheet and the main ideas in the discussion. The following may surface:

A. Both individuals identified in the activity may be very important to us - not only the one with whom we enjoy a very pleasant relationship. If the person with whom we have a painful relationship did not mean anything to us, there likely would be less pain.

B. Maintaining the painful nature of the troublesome relationship does not punish the other person, as we often would like to think. We suffer - if we didn't, we would not have identified the relationship as painful.

**Analysis Activity: One-Way, Two-Way Communication
Activity Flow Sheet**

PURPOSE:	This activity allows students to focus on the elements of communication and the barriers to effective communication.
KEY TOPICS:	Communication and feedback.
TIME ESTIMATE:	45 minutes.
FORMAT:	Dyads followed by large group discussion.
SPECIAL NEEDS:	Diagram 1, diagram 2, and the One-Way, Two-Way Communication Response Sheet for participants and for observers (all of which follow the process guide).
SEQUENCE:	1. Introduce activity and sheets.
	2. Divide students into dyads; designate one as the speaker.
	3. Have pairs sit back-to-back. Review directions. Give Diagrams 1 ONLY to speakers.
	4. Allow 5 minutes for the drawing.
	5. Have pairs sit facing each other. Review directions. Give Diagram 2 ONLY to speakers.
	6. Allow 5 minutes.
	7. Have students complete the One-Way, Two-Way Communication Response Sheet.
	8. Conduct large group discussion.
	9. Summarize.
VARIATIONS:	1. Place students into 4-5 person groups, assigning some students to be observers.
	2. One constraint with dividing the class into dyads is that it is important for the listeners to hear only their partners. An alternative is to use this as a fishbowl, perhaps using 2 or 3 dyads in different parts of the room.

KEY POINTS: Due to space limitations, they are included on the process guide.

Analysis Activity: One-Way Two-Way Communication
Process Guide

PURPOSE: The purpose of this activity is to enable students to focus on the elements of communication and the barriers to effective listening and communication. In this activity students are asked to draw a diagram based on the directions given by the partner. Through this activity they learn the importance of nonverbal signals, hand gestures, etc. that assist in the communication process. They also learn the importance of feedback provided in two-way communication.

STEP 1. Introduce the activity by referring students to the directions on page 181 of the text.

STEP 2. Divide students into dyads; designate one as the speaker. Point out that one member of the dyad will act as the speaker, giving instructions verbally, and the other will be the listener. The listener draws the figure on paper according to the information provided by the speaker. Dyad members will remain in their designated roles for both parts of the activity.

   NOTE: Dyad members should sit so that they cannot hear the interaction among the other dyads.

STEP 3. Once the students are in place, review the directions. Have pairs sit back-to-back. Give Diagram 1 ONLY to speakers. Note the following instructions on page 181 of the text:

Instruct speakers to:

Sit back to back with the listener and describe the drawing. You are to give drawing instructions without allowing the listener to see you or the figure. Do not answer any questions.

Instruct listeners to:

Sit back-to-back with the speaker and draw the figure as it is described to you. Correct your drawing as you think necessary. Do not look at the speaker; do not ask any questions.

STEP 4. Allow 5 minutes.

STEP 5. Have pairs sit facing each other. Give Diagram 2 ONLY to the speakers. Review the directions, noting the differences between instructions for this part of the exercise and instructions for the former. Note the instructions on page 182 of the text.

STEP 6: Allow 5 minutes.

STEP 7: Have students individually complete the One-Way, Two-Way Communication Response Sheet.

STEP 8: Reassemble students into a large group and discuss their responses to questions 1-5 of the One-Way, Two-Way Communication Response Sheet. The following could be highlighted in the discussion:

A. Skills needed for effective one and two way communication.

B. Difficulties encountered in each part of the exercise and their similarities to managerial communication problems.

C. The feelings that the listeners had about asking questions to the speakers. How would those feelings be different if the speakers were the listeners' bosses?

D. Advantages of two-way communication over one-way communication.

E. Examples of instructions we receive which are one-way communications.

STEP 9: Summarize by asking students what they feel are the positive and negative aspects of nonverbal communication and how these aspects can either help or hinder communication for the manager. Note the key points below:

1. Two-way communication tends to produce more accurate results than one-way communication.

2. Two-way communication permits speakers' testing of their assumptions of what how their partner is interpreting their instructions.

3. Difficulties in this activity may parallel difficulties in organizations.

4. Point out positive and negative aspects of non-verbal communication.

SPEAKER ONLY

DIAGRAM 1: One-Way Communication

DIRECTIONS: Study the series of squares below. With your back to your listener, direct him/her to draw the figures. Begin with the top square and describe each in succession, taking particular note of the relationship to each to the preceding one.

Do not allow your listener to ask any questions.

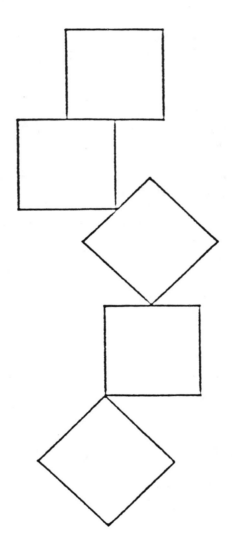

ANALYSIS ACTIVITY: ONE-WAY, TWO-WAY COMMUNICATION

SPEAKER ONLY

DIAGRAM 2: Two-Way Communication

DIRECTIONS: Study the series of squares below. Face your listener and direct him/her to draw the figures. Begin with the top square and describe each in succession, taking particular note of the relationship of each to the preceding one. Answer all questions and repeat if necessary, but do not show this paper to your listener.

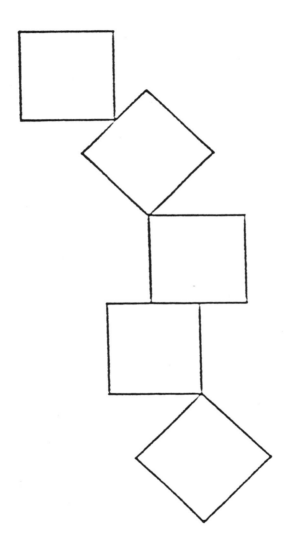

ONE-WAY, TWO-WAY COMMUNICATION RESPONSE SHEET
FOR PARTICIPANTS IN THE DYADS

Respond to the following questions and be prepared to discuss your answers in the large group discussion.

1. What were the differences between seeing and not seeing your partner?

2. What were the effects of not being able to ask questions?

3. Based on the role you played in this exercise, how would you rate your effectiveness as a listener or as a speaker?

4. What did you learn about yourself as a listener or speaker?

5. How does this experience apply to on-the-job situations?

ONE-WAY, TWO-WAY COMMUNICATION RESPONSE SHEET
FOR OBSERVERS OF THE DYADS

Compare the role players in the dyads for both parts of the activity.

1. In which part of the activity was the listener the most confident? Why?

2. In which part of the activity was the listener the most frustrated? Why?

3. In which part of the activity was the speaker the most frustrated? Why?

4. From what you observed, what were the effects of not being able to ask questions?

5. What were the effects of the two people not being able to see each other?

6. What non-verbal communication did you notice in the two-way communication? What were the benefits of it?

Practice Activity: Reflecting Feelings and Ideas
Activity Flow Sheet

PURPOSE: This activity allows students to practice reflective listening responses in order to determine the speaker's meaning.

KEY TOPICS: Reflective listening.

TIME ESTIMATE: 45 minutes.

FORMAT: Individual activity followed by large group discussion.

SPECIAL NEEDS: None.

SEQUENCE:
1. Introduce the activity.

2. Have students complete the instrument.

3. Conduct large group discussion.

4. Summarize.

VARIATIONS:
1. After step #2, divide the class into dyads and have them role-play the situations.

2. After step #2, have a demonstration fishbowl role play, give feedback, and discuss as a large group.

KEY POINTS:
1. While there is no right answer, the reflective response can be identified.

2. The reflective response (even if not accurate) can encourage the sender to further clarify the message.

3 Attending skills on the part of the responder are as important as the actual words of the response. Attending skills include: eye contact, leaning towards the speaker, and using an empathetic tone of voice.

Practice Activity: Reflecting Feelings and Ideas
Process Guide

PURPOSE: The purpose of this activity is to allow students to practice reflective listening responses in order to clarify the meaning of speaker's comments. This activity also illustrates the differences involved in making objective judgments about feelings and ideas without the help of additional information such as nonverbal cues and past history.

STEP 1. Introduce the activity by reminding students about the tenets of reflective listening.

STEP 2. Have students individually complete the instrument. Allow approximately 15 minutes.

STEP 3. Conduct large group discussion based on their responses. Additional questions include:

A. What difficulties did you have in choosing one answer instead of another? What would have helped you better determine the intended meaning?

B. Would you have responded in a way other than the choices given? If so, what responses do you consider more appropriate?

NOTE: There are no absolute right or wrong answers. Reinforce the difference between a reflective response and the "right answer." There is, in most cases, only one reflective answer given. The others may be acceptable as responses but are not truly reflective. If the students disagree with a suggested answer, ask them to justify their response and discuss it with the class members.

Suggested most reflective answers are:

1. b	6. c
2. a	7. b
3. c	8. b
4. c	9. d
5. a	10. a

STEP 4. Summarize by asking students to share their difficulties with completing this exercise. Ask if it would have helped if they could have seen and heard the speakers and why.

VARIATIONS: This activity can be expanded by adding the following steps:

STEP 5. Divide the class into dyads and have them role-play the situations. Partner A should role-play the initial remarks to the first 5 situations with Partner B responding in his/her own words using a reflective response.

Have students reverse roles for situations 6-10.

In each instance the student making the initial remarks should give the respondent feedback as to the effectiveness of the reflective response. Partners who wish to make up remarks rather than use situations 1-10 can be encouraged to do so provided they role-play and *NOT* just talk about a situation.

STEP 6. Have a demonstration fishbowl role play, give feedback, and discuss as a large group.

Application Activity: Active Listening
Activity Flow Sheet

PURPOSE: The purpose of this activity is to allow students to apply active listening skills in their interactions.

KEY TOPICS: Active and reflective listening.

TIME ESTIMATE: 45 minutes.

FORMAT: 3-person groups followed by large group discussion.

SPECIAL NEEDS: The Listening Response Sheet and the Guidelines for Active Listening sheet (both of them follow the process guide).

SEQUENCE: 1. Divide students into groups of 3.

2. Hand out the Guidelines for Active Listening sheet and review briefly.

3. Review the directions on pages 185-186.

4. Time the rounds to 10 minutes per round.

5. Have students complete the Listening Response Sheet.

6. Conduct a large group discussion, using the Listening Response Sheet and the questions supplied at the bottom of page 186.

7. Summarize.

VARIATIONS: 1. This activity can be assigned as homework, with students forming groups with other class members. Then for the next class meeting, the discussion can be initiated by referring to their responses on the Listening Response Sheet. With this variation, you may want to assign the Referee in each round to be the time keeper.

2. More than three students can be placed in a group, increasing the times a student is Referee.

KEY POINTS: 1. Listening is neither easy nor passive, but takes considerable concentrated effort.

2. Focusing on what our responses will be is a hindrance to effective listening.

Application Activity: Active Listening
Process Guide

PURPOSE: This activity allows students to apply active listening skills in their interactions. Through this activity students increase their understanding of the difficulties and energy involved in active and reflective listening.

STEP 1. Divide students into groups of 3. Give them the Guidelines for Active Listening Handout.

STEP 2. Briefly review the Guidelines for Active Listening handout. Remind students that reflective and active listening skills involve the following:

A. Paying close attention to what is said.

B. Observing nonverbal cues given.

C. Listening for both feelings and ideas.

D. Clarifying, restating and paraphrasing statements to test your understanding.

Indicate to students that in this activity they will apply these skills.

STEP 3. Review the directions on pages 185-186.

STEP 4. Inform students of the beginning and ending times for each round. The total process of speaking and summarizing should take a maximum of 10 minutes per round.

STEP 5. After the rounds, have students complete the Listening Response Sheet.

STEP 6. Conduct a large group discussion on the barriers to effective listening, using the Listening Response Sheet and the questions supplied at the bottom of page 186.

STEP 7. Summarize, focusing on the application of these skills to their personal interactions.

GUIDELINES FOR ACTIVE LISTENING

1. Try to ask only open-ended questions; avoid questions that can be answered by "yes," "no," or "I don't know."

2. Listen patiently to what the other person has to say, even though you may believe it is wrong or irrelevant. Indicate simple acceptance (not necessarily agreement) by nodding or injecting an occasional "um-hm" or "I see."

3. Try to understand the feeling the person is expressing, as well as the intellectual content. Many people have difficulty talking clearly about their feelings, so careful attention is required.

4. Restate the other person's feeling, briefly but accurately. At certain times you should simply serve as a mirror and encourage the other person to continue talking. Occasionally make summary responses such as "you think the director does not understand how this unit operates" or "you feel the manager is playing favorites;" but in doing so, keep your tone neutral and try not to lead the person to your pet conclusions.

5. Avoid direct questions and arguments about facts; refrain from saying "that's just not so," "hold on a minute, let's look at the facts," or "prove it." Allow the other person to express his or her feelings.

6. When the person touches on a point you want to learn more about, use reflective listening techniques, such as repeating or rephrasing his or her statements as a question. For example, if a person remarks " no one can ever talk to the boss around here," you can probe by replying "you say no one can ever talk to the boss around here?" or "are you saying that there is no communication between the workers and the boss?" With this encouragement, the other person will probably expand on their previous point.

7. Listen for what is not said--evasions of pertinent points or perhaps too-ready agreement with common cliches. Such omissions may be clues to a bothersome fact that the person wishes were not true.

8. Limit the expression of your own views, since these may condition or limit what the other person says.

9. Focus on the content of the message; do not try to think about your next statement until the person is finished talking.

Adapted from:
Gordon, Judith R. *A Diagnostic Approach to Organizational Behavior*, Boston, MA: Allyn and Bacon, Inc., 1987

LISTENING RESPONSE SHEET

List some of the difficulties you encountered in each of the following roles:

SPEAKER:

LISTENER:

REFEREE:

What barriers to effective listening became evident?

What did you learn about your own communication effectiveness

AS A SPEAKER?

AS A LISTENER?

AS A REFEREE?

How can you apply what you learned about yourself to your personal interactions?

Assessment: Assumptions about Performance Evaluations
Activity Flow Sheet

PURPOSE: This activity points out a contradiction between performance evaluation as an organizational requirement and the managerial posture inherent in the Mentor Role. This activity helps students understand how performance evaluations can be used to develop subordinates.

KEY TOPICS: Performance evaluation.

TIME ESTIMATE: 20 minutes.

FORMAT: Individual activity followed by large group discussion.

SPECIAL NEEDS: None.

SEQUENCE: 1. Direct students to complete the Assumptions about Performance Evaluation Questionnaire on page 187, as well as respond to the interpretation questions.

                2. Discuss interpretation question #1.

                3. Present interpretation of the questionnaire.

                4. Discuss interpretation questions #2 and #3.

                5. Summarize.

KEY POINTS: 1. Performance evaluations tend to be threatening times for subordinates.

                2. Performance evaluations perform organizational functions of justifying pay increases and promotions.

                3. Properly used, performance evaluations can be valuable tools for developing subordinates, as well as giving valuable feedback to managers.

Assessment: Assumptions about Performance Evaluations
Process Guide

PURPOSE: This activity points out a contradiction between the use of an organizational
requirement and the managerial posture inherent in the Mentor Role. Performance
evaluations typically are formal processes which advance the interests of the
organization.   However, performance evaluations may also function as useful tools in
employee development.   This activity helps students understand how performance
evaluations can be used to develop subordinates.

STEP 1.   Direct students to complete the Assumptions about Performance Evaluation
Questionnaire on page 187, as well as respond to the interpretation questions.
This should be completed before reading the learning activity.

STEP 2. Discuss interpretation question #1 as a large group. In this discussion, students may
identify the intended interpretation of the questionnaire (see Step 3).

STEP 3. Present interpretation of the questionnaire, which is as follows:

The A response in all 8 questions suggests an organization centered, formal process
orientation. A responses reflect traditional control values.

The B response suggests a participative, subordinate developmental, employee central
orientation. B responses reflect values of involvement, trust, and communication.

Discuss this assessment in terms of A vs. B answers.

Note that in many organizations, the performance evaluation process is for
organizational reasons not employee development reasons. This is why the
process is so universally detested.

STEP 4. Discuss interpretation question #2 as a large group.

STEP 5. Summarize by discussing interpretation question #3: How would you design an
effective process?

Points to note:

The importance of feedback in employee development.

The inherent threatening nature of the process, which demands additional
consideration and care for it to be a positive experience.

Analysis Activity: United Chemical Company
Activity Flow Sheet

PURPOSE: This activity allows students to analyze a situation of a conversation between a manager and a subordinate, and reframing the conversation in a way that is consistent with supportive communication skills.

KEY TOPICS: Communication and listening skills.

TIME ESTIMATE: 30 minutes.

FORMAT: An individual exercise, followed by fishbowl role-play and large group discussion.

SPECIAL NEEDS: None.

SEQUENCE: 1. Introduce the activity.

2. Direct students to read the case and write out their responses to the discussion questions.

3. Ask for two students to volunteers to role play Max and Sue.

4. Conduct fishbowl role-play.

5. Discuss the responses as a large group.

6. Summarize.

VARIATION: Students may role-play Max and Sue in small groups with observers, in addition to, or instead of, the fishbowl.

KEY POINTS: 1. Both Max and Sue benefit from using of supportive communication skills.

2. When people feel strongly about issues, it may be more difficult to use reflective listening and feedback skills.

3. Use of reflective listening and feedback enhance one's chances of identifying the real issues, and making them explicit.

Analysis Activity: United Chemical Company
Process Guide

PURPOSE: The purpose of this activity is to allow students to analyze a situation of a conversation between a manager and a subordinate. Using supportive communication skills, they reframe the conversation, allowing them to note the difficulties, as well as the benefits.

STEP 1. Introduce the activity by reminding students of the listening skills learned in Competency 2, along with the guidelines for effective feedback in Competency 3. Note the added complexities of those skills in situations where employees feel that they are being evaluated in some way.

STEP 2. Direct students to read the case and write out their responses to the discussion questions at the end of the case, on page 193.

STEP 3. Ask for two students to volunteers to role play Max and Sue.

STEP 4. Conduct fishbowl role-play. Intervene to note how points are demonstrated. Have other students step in to play Max and Sue. Note especially the emotional component of the conversation.

STEP 5. Discuss the responses as a large group. Additional discussion questions may include:

A. How did the redesigned conversation between Max and Sue help to clarify the situation?

B. Without the use of supportive communication skills, what assumptions might Sue have made regarding her value to the company?

STEP 6. Summarize, using students' main points as well as noting:

A. The emotional and conceptual differences between the original conversation and the redesigned conversation.

B. How use of supportive communication skills assists in clarifying issues.

Practice: Giving and Receiving Feedback
Activity Flow Sheet

PURPOSE: The purpose of this activity is to allow students to practice giving and receiving feedback, using a role-play situation.

KEY TOPICS: Giving and receiving feedback.

TIME ESTIMATE: 30 minutes.

FORMAT: Dyads followed by large group discussion.

SPECIAL NEEDS: None.

SEQUENCE:
1. Review with students the guidelines on page 190.

2. Divide students into dyads.

3. Review the two roles in the activity and assign roles.

4. Conduct a large group discussion.

5. Summarize.

VARIATION: After Step #3, ask for a pair to volunteer to do their role-play in front of the class, in a fishbowl activity.

KEY POINTS:
1. The effective use of feedback is essential in setting a climate of trust.

2. The effective use of feedback also hinders employees from making the wrong assumptions about "what is really being said" about the employee's value.

3. Following the guidelines for effective feedback takes concentrated effort.

Practice: Giving and Receiving Feedback
Process Guide

PURPOSE: This activity allows students to practice giving and receiving feedback, using a role-play situation. Unlike the immediately preceding analysis activity, this activity describes a situation between a manager and subordinate without detailing their conversation. Only their respective viewpoints are described.

STEP 1. Review with students the guidelines on page 190.

STEP 2. Divide students into dyads.

STEP 3. Review the two roles in the activity. Assign one student to play the role of Klaus Schultz, and the other to play the role of Martin LeFete. Allow students time to read their respective roles and to "get into them". Time the role play to 10 minutes or so.

As a variation: Conduct fishbowl role-play. Intervene to note how points are demonstrated. Have other students step in to play Klaus and Martin. Note especially the emotional component of the conversation.

STEP 4. Discuss as a large group. Discussion questions may include:

   A. How well was each guideline implemented? Were some easier to implement than others? Why?

   B. What were some of their hindrances to following the guidelines?

   C. What did you learn from the role play?

STEP 5. Summarize by asking students to list some of the barriers to and benefits from using the guidelines for giving and receiving feedback.

Application: The Coach at Work
Activity Flow Sheet

PURPOSE: This activity allows students the opportunity to apply the guidelines to their personal lives, noting when they have been the recipients of feedback the effects of such feedback.

KEY TOPICS: Giving and receiving feedback.

TIME ESTIMATE: 30 minutes.

FORMAT: Individual activity, followed by small group work and large group discussion.

SPECIAL NEEDS: None.

SEQUENCE: 1. Introduce the activity by mentioning the concept of "coach" and its relationship to feedback.

                     2. Direct students to individually write out responses.

                     3. Have students meet in groups of 4-6 to make up a composite list.

                     4. Note the mistakes that might more likely be made by managers.

                     5. Conduct a large group discussion.

                     6. Summarize.

VARIATION: Step #2 may be completed as homework, and the other steps completed in class.

KEY POINTS: 1. We have had feedback modeled to us throughout our lives.

                     2. From this modeling, we have learned how to give feedback, inheriting many of the strengths and weaknesses of our "coaches."

                     3. Skills that people learn in their personal lives often carries over to their roles as managers in organizations.

                     4. Some organizational structures are more conducive to giving effective feedback than are others.

Application: The Coach at Work
Process Guide

PURPOSE: This activity allows students the opportunity to apply the guidelines for effective feedback to their personal lives. By noting when they have been the recipients of feedback, they are able to identify the effects of feedback. They do this by identifying someone who has coached them, or given them feedback. Students individually make a list, distinguish the strengths and weaknesses of that feedback. Students then meet in groups to compile a list of common mistakes.

STEP 1. Introduce the activity by mentioning the concept of "coach" as indicating someone who helps us grow by guiding the development of our capabilities. Effective use of feedback is seen as essential to effective coaching.

STEP 2. Direct students to individually write out responses to questions 1, 2, and 3 of the activity.

STEP 3. Have students meet in groups of 4-6 to make up a composite list of the most common coaching mistakes made by people giving feedback.

STEP 4. Note the mistakes that might more likely be made by managers, and why.

STEP 5. In a large group discussion, using the round robin technique, list the common mistakes on the blackboard.

STEP 6. Summarize by asking students what can be done to avoid those mistakes.

The Facilitator Role, together with the Mentor Role, comprises the Human Relations Model of the Competing Values Framework. As such this managerial role is associated with "people skills" and attention to building cohesion and morale among employees. The manager in this role fosters collective effort and manages interpersonal conflict. Using the listening and empathetic skills of the mentor, the efforts of the facilitator are directed to groups of individuals. As such the facilitator relates well to others, builds trust, manages conflict, promotes input from others, emphasizes mutual helping, and designs and chairs meetings.

While at first glance the skills of the facilitator role may seem remote to some students, reflection will assure them that they are probably already using some facilitation skills. As they consider their social situations, for example, they likely can identify instances where they made sure that everyone present knew each other, and that everyone became a part of the conversation. In addition, conflict management is a competency to which people quickly relate, as most individuals would like to manage conflict in their lives. Furthermore, the facilitator role encompasses leadership development skills that students use as leaders of student organizations and groups.

More than any other managerial role, the facilitator role embodies important values of a democratic society. These values affirm each individual, and the importance of everyone's viewpoints and perspectives. While American society espouses these values, people work in organizations where the need for control and structure often mitigates against the advancement of these values within the organizational setting (Balk, 1990; Weisbord, 1989). It can be argued that when individuals find these fundamental values confirmed by their workplace, any degree of dissonance experienced with their work is likely to decrease. The manager as facilitator not only nurtures these values for the benefit of the individuals, but for the benefit of the organization, as well.

Unless you began the course with the Human Relations Model, you likely have demonstrated facilitation skills to your class before students get to this role. You may wish to point out to students what has transpired in the classroom as you have used facilitation techniques. You have espoused that you value the knowledge, skills, experiences, and ideas of your students. While your job as instructor is clearly to make sure that students understand concepts, you have encouraged them to participate actively in the process. This experience can be tied to organizational life. The idea of employee involvement programs in the workplace is to draw from those who are closest to the jobs. In like manner, your use of facilitation skills, as an instructor, reflects the view that, in essence, you draw from those closest to the learning tasks, involving them in the process, and valuing their input.

While the facilitator role provides managers with skills which empower employees within the organization, paradox clearly characterizes the role. Groups have tasks to do: how do you maintain group morale, while completing the task? When is participative decision making dysfunctional? When is conflict good? These questions and others demonstrate the need for individual discretion and judgment of the manager in this role.

Competency #1: Team Building

Topics:
                    Work groups and work teams
                    Roles of team members
                    Role clarity and role ambiguity
                            Task and group maintenance roles vs. self-oriented roles
                    Stages of team development
                    Informal and formal approaches to team building
                            Responsibility charting
                    Barriers to team building

Competency 2: Participative Decision Making

Topics:
                    A Range of decision making strategies
                    Who should participate - and when
                            Decision tree.
                    Increasing meeting effectiveness

Competency #3: Conflict Management

Topics:
                    Different perspectives on conflict
                    Levels and sources of conflict
                    Stages of the conflict process
                    Conflict management strategies
                    Advantages and Disadvantages of conflict management approaches
                    How to use collaborative approaches to conflict management

Conceptually the facilitator role is not limited to these competencies. Other competencies have been identified as:

                    Introducing new work procedures so as to gain employee
                            cooperation
                    Consensus building
                    Understanding group process
                    How to identify and remedy dysfunctional group behavior
                    Basic teaching and coaching skills
                    Team supervision
                    Designing group goals

Which competencies to choose? As with the other roles, you may not be able to cover all three competencies in your course. In an effort to assist in your decision of which ones to choose, the following questions were posed to the authors:

1. In teaching this course, if you could cover only ONE competency from this chapter, which one would that be and why?

The authors were split on this response. Some maintained that since the basis of the facilitator role is the ability to think in terms of relating to and working with groups, team building is the first choice because it covers group process and the roles that we play in groups.

Other authors chose conflict management because conflicts occur frequently, have potential for disruptions, and are manageable provided one learns the appropriate skills.

2. In teaching this course, if you could cover only TWO competencies from this chapter, which two would they be and why?

Some authors chose team building and participative decision making. They noted that in team building it is too easy to go into the negative zone. That is, there may be a tendency to push the group to be too cohesive, and thus to ignore the task at hand. In participative decision making there is an understanding that one needs to decide when to involve the group and when not to, and how to structure the group to allow for appropriate participation.

Other authors responded that they would choose conflict management and team building, echoing the value of team building pointed out by their co-authors.

3. If you had an additional 5 pages of space for each COMPETENCY, what ideas and concepts would you wish to include?

Team Building: Include more on group process. We would like to see more in terms of small group dynamics, process loss, structural variables, building conflict into groups, etc.

Participative Decision Making: Include more on meeting management. Stress that so much of organizational life is built around meetings. Expand this concept more. Also, add more on leading meetings as an organizational skill.

Conflict Management: Include discussion of third-party negotiation; what to do as the mediator between others' conflicts.

The Facilitator Role and current issues: The facilitator role advances for managers a posture of openness to feedback and ideas from employees. Increasingly, firms are using task forces in creating new work designs. Such task forces necessitate the use of facilitator role competencies.

Additionally, as we face an increasingly diverse workforce, the importance of such feedback from employees is even more pronounced. While the skills of managing group processes, team building, and conflict management are potentially more difficult to apply in a culturally diverse workforce, the values underlying these skills are consonant and, in fact, the competencies are appropriate for managing a diverse workforce.

Some questions to consider in this chapter are:

1. What would be the consequences if managers took the facilitator role to extreme, neglecting the other roles?

2. In what ways do the competencies of the facilitator role affirm other people as individuals of worth?

3. Why are organizations experiencing an increasing need for managers to demonstrate facilitation skills?

4. When are the competencies which define the facilitator role *not* appropriate in organizational settings?

A note from one of the authors:

"I guess my major concern about this chapter is that people not assume that every group has to be a team, that you have to include everyone in decision making, that everyone has to be good friends. Note in the integration section, the need for balance. While this role maintains a clear focus on human relations, instructors need to keep in mind the need that balance. Point out the negative aspects of too little task focus and too much participative decision making."

Assessment: Are You a Team Player?
Activity Flow Sheet

PURPOSE: This activity allows students to assess the extent to which they tend to be team players in organizational settings. In doing so, their definition of team membership is likely to become more refined.

KEY TOPICS: Leads into a discussion of the importance of work teams and work groups, and the roles of team members.

TIME ESTIMATE: 5-10 minutes.

FORMAT: Individual activity followed by large group discussion.

SPECIAL NEEDS: None.

SEQUENCE: 1. Introduce the activity.

                     2. Allow students 5-10 minutes to complete the activity.

                     3. Conduct a large group discussion.

                     4. Summarize.

KEY POINTS: 1. Teams are not just for athletic activities, but are important in organizational settings, as well.

                     2. There are many dimensions to team membership.

                     3. People can acquire the skills necessary to becoming better team members.

Assessment: Are You a Team Player?
Process Guide

PURPOSE: This activity allows students to assess the extent to which they tend to be team players in organizational settings. In doing so, their definition of team membership is likely to become more refined. Students begin to distinguish between groups and teams.

STEP #1: Introduce the activity by referring students to the questionnaire and directions on page 198. Point out that there are no right or wrong answers to these questions. Explain that they should reflect on behaviors and feelings they have experienced in the past, rather than how they feel they *should* respond. Suggest that if they finish before the other class members, to begin considering their responses to the interpretation questions on page 199.

STEP #2: Allow students a 5-10 minutes to complete the activity.

STEP #3: Conduct a large group discussion based on the interpretation questions, to lead into the learning section. Additional discussion questions may include:

A. What surprised you about this assessment?

B. Does the instrument reflect your view of what a team is? Explain.

C. How would you define the characteristics of an effective team player?

D. Do individual have to relinquish their best interests in order to become effective team players? Explain your position.

E. How do you distinguish between a group and a team?

F. How are teams important in organizations and in the workplace? When do teams tend to become very important in the workplace?

G. Why is team building necessary? Aren't groups enough?

STEP #4: Summarize, using students' main ideas and the key points from the activity flow sheet.

Analysis: Stay Alive Inc.
Activity Flow Sheet

PURPOSE: This activity allows students to work in consulting teams to analyze a dysfunctional work situation and to recommend remedies. In this situation employees seem to exhibit considerable cohesion and strong team membership. This case demonstrates the importance of task maintenance functions.

KEY TOPICS: Roles of team members, team development stages.

TIME ESTIMATE: 50 minutes.

FORMAT: Individual activity, work in 4-5 person groups, followed by large group discussion.

SPECIAL NEEDS: None.

SEQUENCE: 1. Introduce the activity.

2. Divide students into 4-5 person consulting teams.

3. Allow time for consulting team reports and discussion.

4. Conduct a large group discussion and summarize.

VARIATIONS: 1. Step #1 may be completed as a homework assignment.

2. Step #2 may be completed as an out-of-class group assignment, followed by step #3 to being the next class session.

3. The class can omit the small group work and proceed directly from individually analyzing the case to the large group discussion.

KEY POINTS: 1. Emotional closeness to group members does not necessarily constitute an effective team.

2. Teams experience various stages of team development; appropriate task and group maintenance behaviors differ accordingly.

3. Both task maintenance and group maintenance are necessary in order for the team to function effectively.

Analysis: Stay-Alive, Inc.
Process Guide

PURPOSE: This activity allows students to work in consulting teams to analyze a dysfunctional work situation and to recommend remedies. In this situation employees seem to exhibit considerable cohesion and strong team membership. This case demonstrates the importance of task maintenance functions.

STEP #1: Introduce the activity by directing students to the case and instructions on page 207-208 of the text. Explain that they will be placed into consulting teams to analyze a work situation in terms of team development and task maintenance processes. Direct them to read the case and respond in writing to the questions on page 208. This individual work is important to their group recommendations.

STEP #2: Divide students into 4-5 person consulting teams. Explain that each group is an organization consulting team that has been retained for the purpose of diagnosing the problems at Stay Alive, Inc. and suggesting remedies. Based on their responses to the questions, what suggestions would they present to the agency director and staff?

STEP #3: Allow time for consulting team reports and discussion.

STEP #4: Conduct a large group discussion. Summarize, using students' main ideas and the key points from the activity flow sheet.

Practice: Ethics Task Force
Activity Flow Sheet

PURPOSE: This activity provides students with the opportunity to practice and observe specific team building skills.

KEY TOPICS: Task maintenance behaviors and group maintenance behaviors.

TIME ESTIMATE: 50 minutes.

FORMAT: Two groups, ideally approximately 12 persons each.

SPECIAL NEEDS: Post-Discussion Questionnaire for Task Force Members and Team Building Behaviors Observation Guide, both of which follow the process guide.

SEQUENCE:
1. Introduce the activity.

2. Divide students into the two groups.

3. Give each member of Group 2 a copy of the Team Building Behaviors Observation Guide.

4. Direct members of Group 1 to take 20 minutes to generate policies and procedures to deal with the use of work time (and telephone) for personal business.

5. After the discussion is completed, give each task force member a copy of the Post-Discussion Questionnaire for Task Force Members, and give them a few minutes to complete it.

6. Conduct a large group discussion based on Group 2's observations and Group 1's reported feelings about the discussion.

7. Summarize.

VARIATIONS:
1. If time permits, have members of the two groups switch roles.

2. If there is a sufficient number of students, have several task forces running simultaneously.

KEY POINTS:
1. Team building involves a number of group dynamics principles.

2. Use of team building and group facilitating behaviors increases the effectiveness of communication and the bond among group members.

3. Both task and maintenance behaviors are necessary for effective group decision making.

Practice: Ethics Task Force
Process Guide

PURPOSE: This activity provides students with the opportunity to practice, identify, and observe specific team building skills.

STEP #1: Introduce the activity by explaining that some class members will take the role of the ethics task force members (Group 1), while the others will act as observers (Group 2). The choice of number of students on the task force is at the discretion of the instructor, but 8-12 persons is ideal. Direct students to the case and instructions on page 208-209 of the text.

STEP #2: Divide students into the two groups.

FOR GROUP 1: Care must be taken in the selection of members of the task force. It is important to remember that the goal is to achieve a positive learning experience for the students. While an overly aggressive or dominant group member is often a reality, it offers little positive discussion material for this activity. Students cannot be expected to talk about how that particular individual disrupted the entire group. Instead it is recommended that instructors select students who have strong viewpoints yet respect the viewpoints of others.

FOR GROUP 2: Announce that the remaining students will act as observers for the Ethics Task Force. Depending on the number of members in Group 2, each observer can be assigned to observe the behaviors of 1-3 task force members, and the other observers can observe the behavior of the group as a whole. Or, alternately, observers can be assigned each to watch for a different set of team building behaviors. Observers should note their observations on the Observer Guide.

STEP #3: Give each member of Group 2, a copy of the Team Building Behaviors Observation Guide. Direct them to complete the guide during the task force discussion. Students may need to be coached on what to look for as observers.

NOTE: If possible, arrange for observers to be seated so that they can both see and hear the task force members.

STEP #4: Direct members of Group 1, the Ethics Task Force, to take 20 minutes to generate policies and procedures to deal with the use of work time (and telephone) for personal business. Call time at the end of 20 minutes (or 25-30 if you prefer).

STEP #5: After the task force discussion is completed, have members announce its decision. Give each task force member a copy of the Post-Discussion Questionnaire for Task Force Members, and give them a few minutes to complete it.

STEP #6: Conduct a large group discussion based on Group 2's observations and Group 1's reported feelings about the discussion. Ask for volunteers to share their responses. Task force members may respond very differently to some of the questions, initiating meaningful discussion. In addition, observers will often be surprised at how much they perceived, and at how different their perceptions are from one another. Sometimes there may not be a lot of disagreement among observers - its just that they pick up on different things.

Additional discussion questions may include:

A. For Task Force Members: Use of work time for personal business is a volatile issue for many people. Did you have any difficulty listening to other member's viewpoints?

B. For Observers: What kinds of task maintenance and group maintenance behaviors did you notice in the task force?

C. What is your overall assessment of what happened in this group?

STEP #7: Summarize the major points brought out in the discussion.

CAUTION: Make sure that the class does not get caught up in the content or substance of this exercise but instead focuses on the process. For instance, the outcome of ethics meeting does not matter as much as how the task force reached its conclusion.

POST-DISCUSSION QUESTIONNAIRE FOR TASK FORCE MEMBERS

Indicate how you are now feeling about the group discussion that has just taken place. Draw a circle around the number that best represents your feelings.

1. **The objectives of the discussion were**

    Very clear 1   2   3   4   5   6   7 Not at all clear

2. **The abilities, knowledge, and experience of the persons in the group were used**

    Fully and effectively 1   2   3   4   5   6   7 Poorly and inadequately

3. **The level of involvement of all group members in the discussion was**

    Very low 1   2   3   4   5   6   7 Very high

4. **Control, power, and influence in the discussion were**

    Imposed on group members 1   2   3   4   5   6   7 Shared by all members

5. **Leadership functions were**

    Concentrated in 1 or 2 persons 1   2   3   4   5   6   7 Shared by all

6. **The task, norms, and standards were**

    Too vague 1   2   3   4   5   6   7 Clearly understood by all

7. **The process stimulated**

    Hardening of ideas 1   2   3   4   5   6   7 New ways of looking at issues

8. **In order to evaluate various alternatives, we developed**

    An unorganized approach 1   2   3   4   5   6   7 A logical framework

9. **Taking all things into consideration, how satisfied were you with this discussion?**

    Not at all satisfied 1   2   3   4   5   6   7 Very satisfied

10. **How committed do you feel to the conclusion or decision arrived at by the group?**

    Fully committed 1   2   3   4   5   6   7 Not at all committed

TEAM BUILDING BEHAVIORS OBSERVATION GUIDE

DIRECTIONS: Record the number and type of behaviors displayed by the persons(s) you observed. You may find it helpful to identify the person who displayed the particular behavior by writing his/her initials next to the description of the behavior.

---

1. The *Initiator*: gets the group moving; offers new ideas; suggests ways to approach a task or problem; reminds others that there is a task to perform

---

2. The *Encourager*: supports team members; encourages and raises others' ideas; builds cohesiveness and warmth; asks for contributions from quiet members

---

3. The *Information Giver*: Clarifies important facts; brings in knowledge from personal experiences; raises issues; supports opinion with fact

---

4. The *Information Seeker*: encourages others to raise facts; asks others to justify their argument; asks for further information from others

---

5. The *Harmonizer*: helps members to see past their differences; reduces tension with humor and friendliness; helps members to work together and appreciate divergent viewpoints

---

6. The *Coordinator*: brings together the activities of others; schedules activities; combines activities

7. The *Gatekeeper*: asks to hear opinions from everyone; maintains an "open gate" to others' participation; ensures that all members have opportunities to share their ideas and feelings; uses statements such as : "Let's hear him/her out."

8. The *Evaluator*: helps group assess quality of its suggestions/solutions; tests to see if the ideas will work in reality; points out consequences of implementation; points out how parties external to the group will view the solution

9. The *Standard Setter*: helps the group set goals; helps group assess the quality of the process; points out procedural matters

10. The *Summarizer*: restates ideas presented to the group; pulls together the range of ideas presented to the group; offers a decision or conclusion for the group to consider

11. The *Follower*: agrees with other members; pursues ideas and suggestions of others

Other observations:

Application: Team Building Action Plan
Activity Flow Sheet

PURPOSE: This activity permits students to apply team building principles to a situation in which they are currently engaged.

KEY TOPICS: Task and group maintenance roles

TIME ESTIMATE: In class set up time: 10 minutes; outside of class: 3 hours; in class follow up discussion: 20 minutes.

FORMAT: Individual activity followed by large group discussion.

SPECIAL NEEDS: None.

SEQUENCE: 1. Introduce the activity. Assist students in choosing a group.

2. Set a date when the 3-5 page report is due.

3. On the due date, ask for volunteers to share their experiences.

4. Conduct a large group discussion and summarize.

KEY POINTS: 1. Team building skills can be developed.

2. The skills of team building are useful in any situation where collaborative problem solving is needed.

3. Team building skills are applicable to a wide variety of situations.

Application: Team Building Action Plan
Process Guide

PURPOSE: This activity permits students to apply team building principles to a situation in which they are currently engaged. Students choose a group in which they are currently participating, and consciously alter their behavior during a group meeting in order to advance the efforts of the group.

STEP #1: Introduce students to the activity by referring them to the instruction on page 209 of the text. Explain that they are to identify a group in which they currently participate, and apply team building strategies to their participation. Assist them in choosing a group, if necessary.

STEP #2: Set a date when the 3-5 page report is due. By necessity, this date may have to be a 3-4 weeks away, due to the varying meeting schedules of the groups. Also, students may wish to use the observation forms for the previous activity as a guide.

STEP #3: On the due date, ask for volunteers to share their experiences.

STEP #4: Conduct a large group discussion and summarize.   Additional discussion questions may include:

A. What surprised you about your experience?

B. How did other group members respond to your change in behavior?

C. What were some of your challenges in implementing these changes?

**Assessment: Meeting Evaluation
Activity Flow Sheet**

PURPOSE: This activity enables students to begin to define the elements of meeting effectiveness.

KEY TOPICS: Key elements of meeting effectiveness.

TIME ESTIMATE: 20 minutes.

FORMAT: Individual activity followed by large group discussion.

SPECIAL NEEDS: None.

SEQUENCE: 1. Introduce the activity. Have students identify the specific meeting which they will assess.

2. Allow time to respond to the scale as well as to the interpretation questions.

3. Conduct a large group discussion based upon their responses.

4. Summarize students' major points.

VARIATION: After step #2, place students into 4-5 person groups to compare their responses and discuss the interpretation questions. Ask each group to identify the most effective meeting of their group members, and the least effective, and to list the characteristics of each.

KEY POINTS: 1. Meetings can be identified as more or less effective, based on discernable characteristics.

2. Meetings are important activities; considerable time is spent in meetings.

3. Many people value their time and resent time spent in poorly managed meetings.

Assessment: Meeting Evaluation
Process Guide

PURPOSE: This activity enables students to begin to define the elements of meeting effectiveness. After identifying a meeting in which they have participated, students examine their experience in the meeting, assessing the effectiveness of the meeting.

STEP #1: Introduce the activity by directing students to the instructions and questions on pages 209-210 of the text. Explain that they are to assess a meeting. It may take them a few minutes to settle on which meeting. In order to ensure that they focus on one meeting, it may be helpful to have them write down the date and time of the specific meeting.

STEP #2: Allow time to respond to the scale as well as to the interpretation questions.

STEP #3: Ask for scores results, such as:

Who assessed a meeting that was closest to a 5? Who assessed a meeting that was closest to a 1? Ask for volunteers to describe those meetings.

Who experienced wide discrepancy between the pre-scale assessment score and the scale assessment score? How do you account for the discrepancy? Are there additional factors which, to you, influence the effectiveness of a meeting?

Conduct a large group discussion based upon their responses to the scale and to the interpretation questions on page 210. Additional discussion questions may include:

A. Why are meetings important in organizations?

B. How would you define meeting effectiveness?

C. How do you feel when you are in a poorly managed meeting? Do you feel that the chairperson or convener does not hold a high regard for your time? What are some of the consequences of these feelings?

D. It has been observed that by bringing a number of people together to focus on an agenda, meetings have potential to accomplish significant outcomes. Yet often meetings are regarded as a waste of people's times. How do you account for this discrepancy between the potential of meetings and their actual outcomes?

STEP #4: Summarize, using students' main ideas as well as key points from the activity flow sheet.

Analysis: Decision by the Group
Activity Flow Sheet

PURPOSE: This activity permits students to analyze a situation in terms of
                    the advantages and disadvantages of participative decision making.

KEY TOPICS: Who should participate in decision making, and when.

TIME ESTIMATE: 30 minutes.

FORMAT: Individual activity, work in 4-5 person groups, followed by large
                    discussion.

SPECIAL NEEDS: None.

SEQUENCE: 1. Introduce the activity.

                    2. Divide the students into 4-5 person groups, asking them to take
                    on the role of Professor Mennon.

                    3. Conduct a large group discussion.

                    4. Summarize the major points made by the group.

VARIATION: The small group activity can be omitted by asking each individual
                    to take on the role of Professor Mennon. In step #3, ask for
                    volunteers to share their advice.

KEY POINTS: 1. Participative decision making is not appropriate in all instances.

                    2. When managers use participative decision making, they must be
                    committed to accept the group's decision.

                    3. Managers who use participative decision making need to be
                    clear about expectations, limits of authority, and responsibilities.

Analysis: Decision by the Group
Process Guide

PURPOSE: This activity permits students to analyze a situation in terms of the advantages and disadvantages of participative decision making. This case helps students to understand that participative decision making is appropriate in certain situations, not in all instances.

STEP #1: Introduce the activity by directing students to the instructions and the case on pages 217-218 of the text. Explain that they are to analyze this case in terms of the appropriateness of participative decision making. Ask them to read the case and respond in writing (jot down notes - nothing formal to turn in) to the discussion questions on page 218.

STEP #2: Divide the students into 4-5 person groups. Ask them to take on the role of Professor Mennon. Have them specify the advice that Professor Mennon should have given to John when he called.

STEP #3: Conduct a large group discussion, asking groups for their advice. Some important points include:

A. Intelligent participative decision making has the potential for increasing the effectiveness of performance. However, participation is not a gimmick for manipulation. John tried a superficial, quick-fix approach and it backfired. In order for group participation to work, the manager and the group need a common goal. The transition to participative decision making needs to be well considered before it is implemented.

B. John might have been able to avoid this problem by explaining why production standards were too low rather than confining his initial remarks to telling employees that the standards were too low. Further, he should have remained with the group and discussed the production standards. He failed to "communicate," air differences and provide reasons why certain actions could or could not be taken. He should have stayed with the group until he had supplied them with more information, and then asked for their opinions regarding the approaches he outlined. The ensuing discussion would have shaped a suggested course of action to follow, representing the group's opinion as well as John's.

C. It is poor practice for a manager to abdicate authority as John did in this situation. An important part of a manager's role is to provide effective leadership by offering a plan, giving reasons why, and taking into account suggestions offered by those who will be affected by the plan. Using this approach, the group's wishes and the needs of the organization can be blended into an effective program.

STEP #4: Summarize by asking students to state what they felt to be the main points of this activity.

Practice: The Sexual Harassment Case
Activity Flow Sheet

PURPOSE:	This activity allows student to practice guidelines for effective meeting management.
KEY TOPICS:	Increasing meeting effectiveness.
TIME ESTIMATE:	40 minutes.
FORMAT:	5-6 person groups.
SPECIAL NEEDS:	Effective Meetings Checklist (follows process guide) to be given to all students for future reference, but in this activity to be used by the students designated as temporary chairpersons of the review board.
SEQUENCE:	1. Divide students into small groups.
	2. Introduce the activity.
	3. Explain that each group is a Civil Rights Review Board.
	4. Charge the groups to review the evidence and make a decision.
	5. Ask the groups to meet again to consider the discussion questions on page 220.
	6. Conduct a large group discussion based on their responses and summarize.
VARIATION:	Conduct as a demonstration role play and allow the class members to observe, responding to questions 1, 3, 4, 5, and 6 of the discussion questions on page 220. The observations of the observers can be compared with those of the students who play members of the civil rights review board.
KEY POINTS:	1. Effective meetings do not occur by accident; careful planning can alter the dynamics of a meeting and increase its effectiveness.
	2. In meetings where the topics are emotionally-charged, or where difficult decisions are being made, careful adherence to effective meeting guidelines is a helpful strategy for the meeting chair.

Practice: The Sexual Harassment Case
Process Guide

PURPOSE: This activity allows student to practice guidelines for effective meeting management. A bonus to this activity is that it discusses the issue of sexual harassment in the workplace, presenting legal guidelines. For some students, this may be their first exposure to this important issue.

STEP #1: Divide students into small groups of approximately 6 persons each.

STEP #2: Introduce the activity by directing students to the case and instructions on pages 218-220 of the text. Emphasize that the purpose of the activity is not to discuss the specifics of the sexual harassment allegations and the merits of the case, but to practice effective meeting management under what would be difficult and emotionally-charged circumstances.

STEP #3: Explain that each group is a Civil Rights Review Board, convened for the purpose of considering the alleged sexual harassment of Mary Flaherty by Mike Blaggard. Instruct each group to appoint a temporary chairperson. Instruct chairpersons to read the Meeting Effectiveness Checklist, and later to respond to the appropriate points. Direct all group members to read carefully the Civil Rights Review Board Policy Guide on Sexual Harassment. They should then read the statements by Mary Flaherty and Mike Blaggard.

STEP #4: Charge the groups to review the evidence and make a decision whether action should be taken against Mike, and if so, what action. Allow 20 minutes.

STEP #5: After the discussion has been reached, ask the groups to meet again to consider the discussion questions on page 220. Ask the groups to present a list of suggestions in response to questions 6 and 7.

STEP #6: Conduct a large group discussion based on their responses and summarize. Additional discussion questions may include:

A. How satisfied were the group members with the interaction within the group and with the outcome?

B. Were techniques of effective meeting management easy or difficult to follow? Why? What is likely to get into the way?

CAUTION: You may need to make a concerted effort to focus the class discussion on the management of the meeting, rather than on the specifics of the sexual harassment case.

EFFECTIVE MEETINGS CHECKLIST

This is a checklist that you may find helpful as you conduct meetings. This ckecklist is widely applicable, although you may need to adjust or delete some of the items when appropriate.

Before the meeting:

_____ I question whether a meeting is necessary.
_____ I set objectives for the meeting.
_____ I select appropriate participants for the meeting, inviting only those who need to attend.
_____ I select an appropriate time and place to meet.
_____ I prepare and distribute an agenda in advance.
_____ I have all of the necessary material prepared in advance.
_____ I have the purposes of the meeting clearly in mind.
_____ I arrange for any necessary equipment.
_____ I set a time limit for the meeting.
_____ I allocate time for each item on the agenda.

During the meeting:

_____ I start on time.
_____ I make sure that someone is taking minutes, where necessary.
_____ I explain the purposes of the meeting.
_____ I review the agenda and check if there are necessary adjustments.
_____ I make sure that the participants know each other.
_____ I follow the agenda.
_____ I allow only emergency interruptions.
_____ I am aware of everyone's contributions.
_____ I do not let a few participants dominate.
_____ I conduct the meeting democratically.
_____ I use the participants' strong points and minimize negative roles.
_____ I pace the meeting to handle all issues on the agenda.
_____ I conclude the meeting by reviewing or restating any decisions reached and assignments made.
_____ I end on time.

After the meeting:

_____ I distribute the minutes within 48 hours, if appropriate.
_____ I periodically check with individuals as to their progress on any assignments that have been made.
_____ I have progress reports made and/or decisions executed within reasonable time limits.
_____ I place uncompleted actions under "unfinished business" for the next meeting.
_____ I analyze all feedback, formal or informal, and improve the next meeting I call.

**Application: Meeting Management
Activity Flow Sheet**

PURPOSE:	This activity allows students to apply the guidelines of effective meeting management to their personal experience.
KEY TOPICS:	Participative decision making and increasing meeting effectiveness.
TIME ESTIMATE:	In class set up time: 10 minutes: outside of class: 2 hours; in class follow up discussion: 20 minutes.
FORMAT:	Individual activity followed by large group discussion.
SPECIAL NEEDS:	Students need to attend several meetings.
SEQUENCE:	1. Introduce the activity.
	2. Explain that they are to write a report on a meeting.
	3. Assist students in the selection of a meeting.
	4. Set a date when the paper is due.
	5. Conduct a large group discussion and summarize.
VARIATIONS:	Students could complete this assignment in pairs, submitting one paper. If this option is chosen, it should be emphasized that the two students in each pair may not agree on everything, and points of disagreement should be noted in the paper.
KEY POINTS:	1. The components of effective meetings are readily observable.
	2. Running effective meetings is not a skill that comes naturally to people, but is a learned competency.
	3. Effective meetings generally result in higher quality solutions. They also improve morale by avoiding the impression that the conveners are respectful of participants' time.

Application: Meeting Management
Process Guide

PURPOSE: This activity allows students to apply the guidelines of effective meeting management to their personal experience. Students attend several meetings and write a 3-5 page report on one of them, responding to the set of questions in the text.

STEP #1: Introduce the activity by directing students to the instructions on page 221 of the text.

STEP #2: Explain that they are to observe several meetings and write a report on one of them. Emphasize that this assignment allows them to apply the principles discussed in the learning section to their experience.

STEP #3: If necessary assist students in the selection of meetings to attend. Note that by attending several meetings, they allow themselves options in the subject of their paper. Some meetings may produce richer material than others, for the purposes of the papers.

STEP #4: Set a date when the paper is due. You may need to allow 2-3 weeks.

STEP #5: On the due date of the paper, conduct a large group discussion. Ask for volunteers to share their experience. Summarize the main points of the discussion. Additional discussion questions may include:

A. Did anything surprise you about the meetings? Explain.

B. Did you feel that people's time was being respected by the meeting? Why or why not?

C. Do you think that enough attention was being made to participants' social and emotional needs? Explain.

D. Did you observe any difficult situations? If so, what were they? How were they handled? How would you have handled them differently?

E. Did one or two group members try to dominate the discussion? If so, how was this handled? Was it effective? What would you have done differently?

Assessment: How Do You Handle Conflict?
Activity Flow Sheet

PURPOSE: This activity allows students to consider various behavioral and attitudinal dimensions of handling conflict.

KEY TOPICS: This activity leads into a discussion of Robbins' three views of conflict: traditional, behavioral, and interactionist. In addition, Thomas' five conflict management approaches correspond to the three categories of conflict handling strategies: nonconfrontational (includes avoidance and accommodation), solution-oriented (collaboration and compromise), and control (synonymous with competition).

TIME ESTIMATE: 15 minutes.

FORMAT: Individual activity followed by large group discussion.

SPECIAL NEEDS: None.

SEQUENCE: 1. Introduce the activity.

2. Direct students to respond to the scale in writing.

3. Have students interpret their responses.

4. Conduct a large group discussion and summarize.

VARIATIONS: 1. After step #2, divide students into 4-5 person groups for step #3. Ask groups to report the most important points of their discussions.

2. Assigning as homework, direct students to choose three individuals with whom they have had conflict, and to respond to the scale three times, once for each individual. Write a short paper, noting any patterns of similarities, differences, and what this tells them about their approach to conflict.

KEY POINTS: 1. Conflict is not necessarily bad or something to be avoided at all costs. It can be a source of individual growth as well as organizational effectiveness.

2. Individuals often have different ways of handling conflict with different people in their lives. We might expect to handle conflict differently with our best friend than we would with the manager of a local store with whom we have a dispute.

Assessment: How Do You Handle Conflict?
Process Guide

PURPOSE: This activity allows students to consider various behavioral and attitudinal dimensions of handling conflict. Students assess their own patterns of handling conflict.

STEP #1: Introduce the activity by having students think of a person with whom they have had disagreements. Students should be encouraged to write down the person's name and recall specific instances of disagreement with this person.

STEP #2: Direct students to read the instructions on page 221 and to respond to the scale in writing. Note that there are no right or wrong answers. Remind them that it is in their interest NOT to look at the scoring and interpretation until after they have responded to the items on the scale.

STEP #3: Have students interpret their responses according to the instructions on pages 222-223 of the text, and to respond to the discussion questions.

    NOTE ON THE SCORING: A study conducted by Putnam and Wilson of 360 participants produced the following scores:

        Solution-orientation = 3.73
        Control   = 2.43
        Nonconfrontational = 2.42

STEP #4: Conduct a large group discussion based on students' reactions to the scale, and on the discussion questions. Summarize their major points.

    A. Did anything in your responses surprise you? If so, explain.

    B. How would your responses have been different with another person instead of the one you chose?

    C. How do you feel about yourself and the relationship when you consistently avoid asserting your point of view?

SPECIAL NOTE: Many people report that in conflictual situations, their objective is not to have their way, but to be understood by the other party, and to be acknowledged as holding a legitimate point of view.

Analysis: Zack's Electrical Parts
Activity Flow Sheet

PURPOSE: This activity allows students to analyze a case in terms of sources of conflict in the workplace setting.

KEY TOPICS: Levels and sources of conflict, stages of the conflict process, and conflict management strategies.

TIME ESTIMATE: 30 minutes.

FORMAT: 4-5 person groups followed by large group discussion.

SPECIAL NEEDS: None.

SEQUENCE:
1. Introduce the activity.

2. Have students read the case and respond.

3. Place students into 4-5 person groups.

4. Have the groups report to the class and discuss.

5. Summarize.

VARIATIONS:
1. Step #2 can be completed at home; begin the next class meeting with the small group discussions.

2. Omit the small group discussion and proceed directly from the individual responses to a large group discussion.

KEY POINTS:
1. Conflictual situations can be broken down into identifiable stages.

2. Once a conflict is fully developed, collaborative approaches can be used in order to manage the conflict.

Analysis: Zack's Electrical Parts
Process Guide

PURPOSE: This activity allows students to analyze a case in terms of sources of conflict in a workplace setting. This case demonstrates a highly conflictual situation involving several levels and work units in a firm.

STEP #1: Introduce the activity by directing students to the instructions and the case on page 231-232 of the text.

STEP #2: Have students read the case and respond in writing to the discussion questions on page 232.

STEP #3: Place students into 4-5 person groups each to discuss their responses and to generate a group analysis.

STEP #4: Have the groups report to the class and discuss. Additional discussion questions may include:

   A. What benefits do you think might be gained by the organization from this conflict? In other words, are there any changes within the organization that might be precipitated by this conflict? If so, what?

   B. How might individuals benefit from this conflict?

STEP #5: Summarize, the main ideas generated in the discussion as well as the key points from the activity flow sheet.

Practice: The Vacation Schedule
Activity Flow Sheet

PURPOSE: This activity allows students to practice the skills of conflict management in a role-play group decision making situation.

KEY TOPICS: Conflict management strategies.

TIME ESTIMATE: 50 minutes

FORMAT: 5-person groups, with 1-3 observers selected for each group, followed by large group discussion.

SPECIAL NEEDS: Handout describing each role (follows process guide).

SEQUENCE: 1. Divide the class into 5-person groups and assign 1-3 observers to each group.

                    2. Direct students to the instructions on page 232 of the text.

                    3. Give the groups 20-30 minutes to role play.

                    4. Conduct a large group discussion and summarize.

VARIATION: One group of carefully chosen students may role play this case in a fishbowl activity while the rest of the class members act as observers.

KEY POINTS: 1. Tendencies towards preferred conflict handling situations vary according to individuals.

                    2. Conflict management strategies are learned skills and require practice to master them.

                    3. There are frequently benefits from conflictual situations, which can be reaped if handled properly.

Practice: The Vacation Schedule
Process Guide

PURPOSE: This activity allows students to practice the skills of conflict management in a role-play group decision making situation. This activity presents students with a problem situation that requires important decisions to be made under difficult circumstances with few options available. It is the manager's job to determine what conflicts may occur and to formulate possible strategies for dealing with those conflicts. Despite its difficulty, this situation is considered commonplace for managers to encounter.

STEP #1: Divide the class into 5-person groups and assign 1-3 observers to each group. Be certain that the role players are positioned for interaction, and that the observers are able to see and hear the role players.

STEP #2: Direct students to the instructions on page 232 of the text. Explain that each group will role play the same situation, and that group members will be able to practice conflict management strategies. Distribute role descriptions to each player. Explain to the role players that, beyond the information supplied to them, they should interpret and act out the roles as they feel appropriate. They should also attempt to make the role play as realistic as possible. Answer any questions that the students might have.

STEP #3: Give the groups 20-30 minutes to role play.

STEP #4: Conduct a large group discussion based on the discussion questions on pages 232-233 of the text and summarize major points. Additional questions may include:

A. What solutions were reached by the groups?

B. Was the manager in each group satisfied with the solution?

C. How did the employees feel about the manager's approach to the problem?

D. In a situation of this type, what are the advantages and disadvantages of a manager's assumption of responsibility for a decision?

E. What kinds of conflicts arise if the manager has not thoroughly thought through the entire process?

ROLE PLAY DESCRIPTIONS

MANAGER ONLY

Background: You manage 20 people in the accounting department of a major insurance company. Vacation scheduling has always been a problem here because of the increase in activity in the summer months. This year, however, you developed a vacation schedule early, checked with your staff, and by the end of March had a schedule that showed only two people out during any one week.

Next week will be an exception to your policy. Two employees, George and Annie were already scheduled to take their vacations when another employee, Sam transferred into your unit on the condition that he could take his vacation next week as previously scheduled. George had already planned to take his family camping in Idaho and Annie was going to Hawaii for her annual family reunion. You were eager to have Sam join your staff so you decided that things would be alright, as long as nothing else came up.

1:15 P.M. Just as you were returning from lunch, Marge approached your desk with a problem. Her husband, who has been out of work for several months, has just landed a week-long job hauling goods from the next state, beginning Monday. The difficulty is that he needs her to go with him because she is the only one who knows his business operation well enough to help him on such short notice. She has not taken her vacation yet, and you know from previous conversations how important this hauling job is to their financial stability. But if Marge were gone next week, four people would be out--hardly an ideal situation for the rest of the staff.

After wrestling with the problem, you told Marge that she could take next week off. You felt that you had made a good decision; Marge always does more than her fair share of the work.

1:30 P.M. You received a call from Mike's wife. He had been out the last two days with a bad cold, but now his wife says he is scheduled for a tonsillectomy Monday and will not be in next week at all. This raises the number of people out next week to five.

1:45 P.M. As you were reconsidering the wisdom of letting Marge take next week off, Bryan strolled up to your desk. He had a job interview during his lunch hour and will be starting his new job Monday. Now you will be six people short next week; you shudder to think of the chaos that will result.

You are not sure how you are going to solve this problem. Can your unit realistically manage the next week with six people gone? If not, what are the alternatives? Should you handle this situation alone or involve others?

3:00 P.M. You have just called a meeting with George, Annie, Marge and Sam to discuss the problem. Mike and Bryan are, of course out of the schedule altogether. You have asked the workers to meet you in the conference room.

SAM ONLY

Background: It is about two o'clock on a Friday afternoon in late June. You are the newest employee in this work group, having joined the unit a month ago. Your vacation, due to begin Monday morning, was originally scheduled with your old manager in March. When you applied for this position, you were told that you could keep the same vacation week, although it would stretch the normal policy a bit. You plan to spend your vacation at a nearby lake with some friends. You are looking forward to it.

You were told that this new job would be a challenge, and nobody was kidding you! You thought that after a month in the unit you would be feeling at least somewhat knowledgeable about your new job, but sometimes trying to learn everything at once is overwhelming. You sure need a break, or maybe even a transfer back to your old unit, where you were the resident expert. Although it was boring sometimes, right now you would gladly trade some boredom for a lot of frustration. On the other hand, your new manager was really pleased to have someone with your background here and indicated that there was a lot of room for advancement.

You have decided to spend some time during the next week at the lake to think about what you want to do.

Setting: Your manager has just called a brief meeting in the conference room "to talk about a problem in next week's schedule."

ANNIE ONLY

Background: It is about two o'clock on a Friday afternoon in late June--your last day before vacation, which you scheduled with your manager in February. You are leaving for Hawaii this evening to attend your seventh annual family reunion.

There are only six hours before your plane leaves for the islands, and you can hardly wait. Years ago, when your family started this annual get--together, you looked on it as an obligation and a chore--except it was a chance to go to Hawaii again. Now, however, your perspective has changed and you really look forward to seeing everyone again (even your brother Fred, who is quite a bore until you got to know him). And this year the reunion will be special because your sister and her family will be there after spending three years in Sweden. You hope her superb wit has not changed; it has been such a long time since you two have had a good laugh together.

You just hope that things will not be as busy when you get back. The recent workload has been unreal.

Setting: Your manager has just called a brief meeting in the conference room "to talk about a problem in next week's schedule."

MARGE ONLY

Background: It is about two o'clock on a Friday afternoon in late June. Your husband Joe, who has not been able to locate any work for the past few months, called about an hour ago with the news that he has a week-long contract to haul goods from the next state beginning Monday, but he needs you to go along with him to handle the bookkeeping and other functions. You are not scheduled to take your vacation until August. You talked to your manager about the situation, and she agreed to reschedule your vacation for next week.

You were elated when Joe called with the good news about the job next week. Not only have things been pretty tight financially these past few months, but this period of unemployment has really been a drain on Joe's usually optimistic outlook. Now he has a chance to earn some money, regain his self-esteem, and maybe continue to work with this distributor. You were a bit concerned when you learned that you needed to go on this run, since you know how your absence will increase the workload in the department, and you do not want to be a burden on your friends here. But, in your mind, it is a valid, unavoidable emergency, since you are the only one who knows Joe's business well enough to help him out on such short notice.

Your manager understands the situation and has been a real friend during the crises of the last few months, providing financial counseling as well as moral support. To show appreciation, you are planning to put in a couple of hours of overtime before you leave tonight, to reduce the workload a bit.

Setting: Your manager has just called a brief meeting in the conference room "to talk about a problem in next week's schedule."

GEORGE ONLY

Background: It is about two o'clock on a Friday afternoon in late June--the last day before your vacation, which you scheduled with your manager in February. You, your wife, and two children (ages eight and nine) are leaving tomorrow morning to go camping in Idaho.

The thought of your vacation next week is just about the only thing that has kept you going all week. It has been pretty hectic here, and your morale is badly in need of that rejuvenating mountain air. It seems like years since you have spent a relaxed moment with your family, and beginning early tomorrow morning the four of you will have nine days to explore the Idaho wilderness together. You were just thinking about how excited the kids were last night as you made some last-minute plans. The thought made you smile before you turned back to the mound of paperwork left to do before five o'clock.

Setting: Your manager has just called a brief meeting in the conference room "to talk about a problem in next week's schedule."

Application: Managing Your Own Conflicts
Activity Flow Sheet

PURPOSE: This activity allows students to apply conflict management strategies to a situation which they are currently facing.

KEY TOPICS: Conflict management approaches and how to use collaborative approaches to conflict management.

TIME ESTIMATE: In class set up time: 10 minutes; outside of class: 60-90 minutes; in class follow up discussion: 20 minutes.

FORMAT: Individual activity with assigned 3-5 page paper, followed by large group discussion.

SPECIAL NEEDS: None.

SEQUENCE:
1. Introduce the activity.

2. Direct students to the instructions on page 233 of the text.

3. Assist students in selecting a conflict situation.

4. Review the assigned questions on page 233.

5. Set a due date for the report.

6. On the due date, conduct a large group discussion of their experiences and insights.

KEY POINTS:
1. Conflict management strategies are generic to all kinds of conflict, even to conflict that we experience in our personal relationships.

2. Sometimes we may resist resolving conflict. As much pain as we may receive from it, we may sometimes find ourselves prolonging the conflict in order to justify our view of the other person or of the situation.

3. The skills involved in conflict management strategies are learned, requiring attention and practice.

Application: Managing Your Own Conflicts
Process Guide

PURPOSE: This activity allows students to apply conflict management strategies to a situation which they are currently facing. After defining the conflictual situation, students examine the array of strategic options available to them, decide on which strategies to use, and plan to implement their decision.

STEP #1: Introduce the activity by explaining that students will be allowed to apply conflict management strategies to a conflict situation which they are currently experiencing. Remind them that the strategies they have studied are valid in interpersonal relationships outside of the organizational setting, as well as in the workplace.

STEP #2: Direct students to the instructions on page 233 of the text.

STEP #3: Assist students in selecting a conflict situation. If they are not currently experiencing conflict, help them recall one that did exist for them in the recent past.

STEP #4: Review the assigned questions on page 233 in detail with the students, and respond to their concerns.

STEP #5: Set a due date for the report. Because of the introspective nature of this assignment, students can reasonably be expected to complete it well within a week.

STEP #6: On the due date, conduct a large group discussion of their experiences and insights. Additional discussion questions may include:

A. Did anything about this assignment surprise you? If so, explain.

B. Which strategies did you find successful? Which strategies did you find difficult?

C. Did you find that you have a tendency to be more comfortable with one strategy than with the others? If so, why?

D. Did you find yourself resisting actions to resolve the conflict? What barriers to conflict resolution do you think people experience?

E. Do you think that some people *like* conflict? If so, why?

F. What was the most valuable thing you learned from this assignment?

The Innovator Role, along with the Broker Role, comprises the Open Systems Model of the Competing Values Framework. As such this managerial role is often associated with the organization's interaction with and response to the external environment. Managers in the innovator role find themselves engaged in creative problem solving, monitoring external trends, advocating new ideas, and responding to any environmental changes that may affect the organization.

Like other managerial competencies, the innovator role competencies reflect skills that are helpful to students in their daily lives, and which they may already be using to some extent. Living with change and managing change are important life skills, considered essential to emotional well-being. Mastery of these competencies enhances our ability to embrace life with eager anticipation and enthusiasm, and decreases any tendency to see ourselves as victims of events. Creative thinking is a skill which many people have but tend to underestimate in themselves. Hopefully this chapter may help students more fully believe in their creative abilities.

The competencies of the innovator role present a number of paradoxes to managers. It has been argued that the phrase "organizational change" is an oxymoron. While we may disagree with that view, the point of organizational resistance to change is noted. Organizations tend to be stable with many change-resistant characteristics in their design and operations. Yet change is becoming increasingly pervasive as well as salient. Managers in the innovator role need to operate within the paradoxes of adaptability and stability, or encouraging employee creativity while getting the work done.

It is important for students to understand that as organizations change to meet the demands of the future, definitive models for change do not exist. That is to say, we has yet to observe an organization which manages change perfectly. Everyone is learning to manage in the face of uncertain and opposing demands.

The competencies of the Innovator Role: The three competencies in this role and their corresponding topics in the learning activities are:

Competency #1: Living with Change

Topics:
        Planned and unplanned change
        Helping ourselves and others deal with unplanned change
        Using the organizational culture to deal with unplanned change
        Using your leadership style to deal with unplanned change
            Manager as conductor
            Manager as developer

Competency 2: Creative Thinking

Topics:
                  Developing creative thinking skills in yourself and others
                        Domain-relevant skills
                        Creative-relevant skills
                  Barriers to creative thinking
                  Task Motivation
                  Brainstorming and NGT
                  Importance of Creative Thinking in Organizations

Competency 3: Managing Change

Topics:
                  Understanding resistance to planned change
                  Designing change
                  Force Field Analysis
                  Implementing change
                  Three approaches to managing change
                        Rational-empirical approaches
                        Normative-reeducative approaches
                        Power-coercive approaches
                  Effective management of change

Conceptually the innovator role is not limited to these competencies. Other competencies have been identified as:

                  Effective risk taking in organizations
                  Fostering a creative work climate
                  How to manage organizational transitions
                  How to manage a failed innovation
                  How to see problems as opportunities
                  Understanding the present and forecasting the future
                  Recommending changes in organizational policy

Which competencies to choose? As with the other roles, you may not be able to cover all three competencies in your course. In an effort to assist in your decision of which ones to choose, the following questions were posed to the authors:

1. In teaching this course, if you could cover only ONE competency from this chapter, which one would that be and why?

      The authors agreed that their first choice would be creative thinking. One author reasoned that it is a necessary, but rare, skill. Another author added that creative thinking is more than necessary--it's imperative. Current modes of operating within organizations are inadequate in meeting the demands of the future. We need to tap all of the creative resources possible.

2. In teaching this course, if you could cover only TWO competencies from this chapter, which two would they be and why?

One author noted that, in addition to creative thinking, the next competency would be managing change, because change will be the most prevailing characteristic of organizations over then next 10 years. While most authors agreed, one author expressed the necessity of teaching all three competencies in this chapter because change will become perhaps the most salient characteristic of organizations as we approach the 21st century.

3. If you had an additional 5 pages of space for each COMPETENCY, what ideas and concepts would you wish to include?

Living with Change: Balance the discussion of resistance to change with a discussion of when change is welcomed and sought after, and how to deal with situations where the manager wants change that upper management rejects, or when a manager's employees want changes that the manager cannot agree with.

Creative Thinking: A discussion of the role of humor in precipitating a creative workplace. In fact, some classic jokes were placed in the original chapter manuscript, but due to space limitations, they were deleted from the text.

Managing Change: A discussion of some projected changes that many managers will have to deal with, such as managing a culturally diverse workforce.

The Innovator Role and current issues: Change issues involved in this role bear direct relationship to some workplace issues of the 1990's and beyond. The U.S. workforce is becoming increasingly culturally diverse. Yet most of us do not have experience in culturally diverse organizations. With no models to follow, how can we learn to manage cultural diversity?

Furthermore, as organizations find themselves operating an increasingly dynamic and fast-paced environment, they experience an intensifying need to draw on employees' creative resources in order to keep up. One of the intensifying challenges of the coming decades is ensuring human survival on this planet. It is argued that this challenge, shared by all, can be meet by people in organizations which value and advance creativity.

Some questions to consider in this chapter are:

1. How can an organization foster creative thinking among employees while maintaining a coordinated workflow and ensuring task completion?

2. Under what circumstances is it undesirable for organizations to encourage employee creativity?

3. While this chapter presents change as largely resisted by employees, is this accurate? What kinds of changes are welcomed by employees and resisted by upper management?

4. What is the relationship between fostering employee creativity and productivity?

A note from one of the authors:

Humor is not only important to fostering creativity, but it frequently is underestimated in the learning process. Unfortunately learning tends to be more associated with tedium than with fun. In the interest of advancing more humor in the classroom, here are the jokes that were left out of the text (from Koestler):

An art dealer bought a canvas signed 'Picasso' and traveled all the way to Cannes to discover whether it was genuine. Picasso was working in his studio. He cast a single look at the canvas and said: "It's a fake."
A few months later the dealer bought another canvas signed Picasso. Again he traveled to Cannes and again Picasso, after a single glance, grunted: "It's a fake."
"But cher maitre," expostulated the dealer, "it so happens that I saw you with my own eyes working on this very picture several months ago."
Picasso shrugged: "I often paint fakes."

In 1960 an anecdote in the form of an imaginary dialogue circulated in the satellite countries of the East Bloc:
"Tell me, Comrade, what is capitalism?"
"The exploitation of man by man."
"Then what is Communism?"
"The reverse."

Also, with regard to the use of analogies (Competency #2, Practice Activity), often regional speech expressions are rich with expressions that provide graphic and humorous analogies. A book which provides a number of examples from Southern speech is Diann Sutherlin Smith's *Down-Home Talk* (N.Y.: Collier Books, 1988). Some of my favorites are:

Someone's **as old as dirt.**
I'm so hungry my stomach thinks my throat's been cut.
Someone's is as **busy as a barefoot boy in an ant bed.**
I'm so depressed that I've **been down so long it looks like up to me.**
He's so poor the bank won't let him draw breath.
You've made me happier than a dead hog in the sunshine.
I'm as confused as a rubber-nosed wood-pecker in the Petrified Forest.

Assessment: Personal Acceptance of Change
Activity Flow Sheet

PURPOSE: This activity allows students to assess the extent to which they tend to accept change in their lives.

KEY TOPICS: Helping ourselves and others to deal with unplanned change. Leads into a discussion of the differences between planned and unplanned change.

TIME ESTIMATE: 25 minutes.

FORMAT: Individual activity followed by large group discussion.

SPECIAL NEEDS: None.

SEQUENCE: 1. Introduce the activity.

2. Direct students to write down their answers to the discussion questions on page 239.

3. Conduct a large group discussion.

4. Summarize.

VARIATION: After students have completed the scale items, place them into dyads to discuss the discussion questions with a partner. The discussion questions are particularly important to this activity; if students do not write out their responses, it is important that they be allowed to discuss them thoroughly.

KEY POINTS: 1. People often resist change at the time it occurs, but find themselves accepting it later. Often people are happy that the change occurred.

2. People are adaptable, and have considerable capacity for accepting change in their lives.

3. Our ability to accept change depends somewhat on prior experiences with change, but we can increase this ability with attention and conscious effort.

3. The ability to accept change is an important life skill.

Assessment: Personal Acceptance of Change
Process Guide

PURPOSE: This activity allows students to assess the extent to which they tend to accept changes in their lives. The questions permit students to indicate their level of resistance to events at the time the event occurred. Students then contrast that resistance with their ability to accept the same changes over time.

STEP #1: Introduce the activity by directing students to pages 238-239 of the text. Explain that this is a reflective activity, and suggest that they take their time in re-creating their feelings during the experiences indicated. Note that it is in their interest to be honest and emotionally thorough in their responses.

STEP #2: After students have completed the scale, direct them to write down their answers to the discussion questions on page 239.

STEP #3: Conduct a large group discussion based on their scores and their responses to the discussion questions. Additional questions may include:

A. Who had the largest difference between their two columns? Who had the smallest? How would you contrast your experiences?

B. Some people not only resist change before it happens, but *refuse to accept* the change after it has occurred. Why do you think they refuse to accept changes? NOTE: Sometimes people feel that refusal to accept change is a way to continue to object to it. In other words, if a person truly objects to the change, and then accepts it, then such acceptance may indicate that their initial objections were weak or not well-founded.

C. Why is the ability to accept change considered an important life skill?

D. What can people do to become more accepting of change in life?

STEP #4: Summarize the discussion of their major points.

Analysis: Resistance to Change
Activity Flow Sheet

PURPOSE: This activity allows students to analyze their affective response to a work situation where change is resisted.

KEY TOPICS: Using your leadership style to deal with unplanned change.

TIME ESTIMATE: 20 minutes.

FORMAT: Individual activity followed by large group discussion.

SPECIAL NEEDS: None.

SEQUENCE: 1. Introduce the activity.

       2. Instruct students to submit a short written response..

       3. Conduct a large group discussion.

       4. Summarize the major points of the discussion.

KEY POINTS: 1. Organizational changes may have emotional consequences for individuals who are affected by those changes.

       2. The emotional consequences may be unintended by those who designed the changes.

       3. The feelings of individuals are legitimate and are not open to challenge. That is to say, to assert to someone that they "should" or "should not" feel what they feel verges on nonsense and may only compound the situation. It would be appropriate, however, for someone to be told that their emotional response was not the intention of the organizational change.

SPECIAL NOTE: Students will need their responses in order to complete the following practice activity, page 247 of the text.

Analysis: Resistance to Change
Process Guide

PURPOSE: This activity allows students to analyze their affective responses to a work situation where change is resisted. By completing the questions in the first person, students can better understand some of the emotional dimensions associated with facing unplanned change.

STEP #1: Introduce the activity by directing students to pages 246-247 of the text. Explain that in this case, they play the role of a manager who is affected by an organizational change.

STEP #2: Instruct students to respond to the emotional dimensions of the experience, and to submit a short written response to question 3 on page 247.

STEP #3: Conduct a large group discussion. Note the following:

   A. Ask students what their responses were.

   B. Acknowledge that for students to share their feelings is risk-taking and requires considerable courage.

   C. It may be necessary to discuss the inappropriateness of commenting negatively on someone else's feelings.

   D. Note how none of us appreciate being told that we should not feel a certain way. Such admonishments seldom make the emotions disappear, but often merely compound the situation with additional undesirable emotions.

   E. Note the importance of dealing with others' feelings in organizational settings.

STEP #4: Summarize the major points of the discussion, noting the key points listed on the activity flow sheet.

CAUTION: Notice that the purpose of this activity is **not** to arrive at a solution, but merely to describe the emotional components of the situation. As such, *placing students in groups for discussing the questions is not advised*. In such groups there may be a tendency for students to feel that they "should" or "should not" feel certain ways, and to compare their emotional responses to those of the other group members. Such an outcome could be very dysfunctional.

Practice: Resistance to Change Revisited
Activity Flow Sheet

PURPOSE: This activity allows students to use what they learned from the analysis activity to initiate change in such a way as to mitigate any negative emotional consequences for others.

KEY TOPICS: Using your leadership style to deal with unplanned change

TIME ESTIMATE: 20 minutes.

FORMAT: Individual activity followed by large group discussion.

SPECIAL NEEDS: Student responses to the analysis activity on page 246-247 of the text.

SEQUENCE: 1. Introduce the activity by referring students to their responses to the analysis activity.

2. Direct students to the instructions on page 247 of the text.

3. Have students respond in writing to the questions.

4. Conduct a large group discussion.

5. Summarize.

VARIATION: Place students into 4-5 person groups, as upper management teams, to respond to the questions.

KEY POINTS: 1. Awareness of possible emotional consequences of our actions can be helpful as we seek to design those actions.

2. Note that the issue is often not IF the change will be made, but HOW it is presented to those who are affected by it. Often negative feelings can be avoided with appropriate implementation planning.

Practice: Resistance to Change Revisited
Process Guide

PURPOSE: This activity allows students to use what they learned from the analysis activity to initiate change in such a way as to mitigate any negative emotional consequences for others. The emphasis is not on IF the change will occur, but HOW.

STEP #1: Introduce the activity by referring students to their responses to the analysis activity.

Remind them that in the analysis activity, they played the role of a manager who was subject to unplanned change. In that role students were able to identify some possible emotional dimensions of the experience for the manager.

Explain that in this activity, they are to act as the manager's manager and change agent.

In light of the emotional dimensions which they explored in the analysis, how would they now handle the change?

STEP #2: Direct students to the instructions and questions on page 247 of the text.

STEP #3: Have students respond in writing to the questions.

STEP #4: Conduct a large group discussion. Ask the students for their answers to each question, and record them on the chalkboard. Additional questions may include:

A. Would your answers have been different if you had not completed the analysis activity? Explain.

B. How can the skills reflected in this activity apply to making changes in your personal life?

STEP #5: Summarize noting the key points from the activity flow sheet, as well as the major points made by students.

Application: Diagnosing Your Organizational Culture
Activity Flow Sheet

PURPOSE:	This activity allows students to identify the components of the culture of an organization in which they are/were involved.
KEY TOPICS:	Using organizational culture to deal with unplanned change
TIME ESTIMATE:	In class set up time: 10; outside of class: 60 minutes; in class follow up discussion: 20 minutes.
FORMAT:	Individual activity followed by large group discussion.
SPECIAL NEEDS:	None.

SEQUENCE:	1. Introduce the activity.
	2. Point out that identifying the elements of one's organizational culture is not a simple task.
	3. Help students identify an organization for this assignment.
	4. Set the date that the paper is due.
	5. Conduct a large group discussion and summarize.

VARIATION:	If the students select the same organizations, then they may be divided into teams for the purpose of diagnosing the culture.

KEY POINTS:	1. The components of organizational cultures are often difficult to identify.
	2. Organizational cultures are significant to the quality of individuals' experience within the organization.
	3. Organizational cultures are subject to change.

Application: Diagnosing Your Organizational Culture
. Process Guide

PURPOSE: This activity allows students to identify the components of the culture of an organization in which they are/were involved. This activity provides a valuable opportunity for students to " dig beneath the surface" of organizational life.

STEP #1: Introduce the activity by referring students to the questions on pages 247-248. If necessary review with students the concept of organizational culture and its components. Explain that this activity assists them in diagnosing such a culture.

STEP #2: Point out that identifying the elements of one's organizational culture is not a simple task; cultures comprise the basic assumptions of our lives, and as such, may be difficult to identify.

STEP #3: If necessary help students identify an organization for this assignment.

STEP #4: Set the date that the paper is due.

STEP #5: On the date the papers are due, conduct a large group discussion of their responses to the 4 questions on pages 247-248. Summarize the major points made by students. Additional discussion questions may include:

   A. What surprised you about this assignment?

   B. Did you find that organizational cultures are difficult to uncover and describe? What makes them difficult to describe?

SPECIAL NOTE: If you have not given special focus to organizational culture, then this activity may be considered optional. You probably should provide students with information on organizational culture in addition to what is provided in this text. If you are also using the Bowditch and Buono text, then students might find the seven dimensions on pages 242-243 of that text to be helpful in this assignment.

Assessment: Are You A Creative Thinker?
Activity Flow Sheet

PURPOSE: This activity allows students to understand that they are probably more creative than they may realize.

KEY TOPICS: Creative thinking; barriers to creative thinking. Leads into a discussion of characteristics of creative individuals.

TIME ESTIMATE: 20-30 minutes.

FORMAT: Individual activity followed by large group discussion.

SPECIAL NEEDS: None.

SEQUENCE: 1. Introduce the activity.

2. Direct them to write out responses to the three questions.

3. Conduct a large group discussion.

4. Summarize their major points.

VARIATION: After step #2 students could be placed into dyads for the purpose of discussing the interpretation questions.

KEY POINTS: 1. Creative abilities are not the sole domain of an elite group of artistically talented individuals. Virtually all individuals have some measure of creative ability.

2. Creative ability can be developed and increased.

3. The first step to increasing one's creative ability is to acknowledge one's creative potential.

4. Creativity is useful for the manager, both in dealing with people issues and in addressing nonstandard problems or issues.

5. Many people have characteristics that they have held as undesirable, but which actually are indicative of creative ability.

Assessment: Are You A Creative Thinker?
Process Guide

PURPOSE: This activity allows students to understand that they are probably more creative than they may realize. The items often refer to attitudes and behaviors which students may not have previously associated with creativity.

STEP #1: Introduce the activity by directing students to the questions on page 248. Explain that these questions will help them gauge their creative abilities.

STEP #2: Direct them to write out their responses to the three interpretation questions on page 248 after they complete the questionnaire.

> **NOTE:** Research indicates that the major difference between creative people and uncreative people is that creative people *think* they are creative.

STEP #3: Conduct a large group discussion based on their responses to the interpretation questions. Additional discussion questions may include:

A. How creative are your close friends? What have they done that leads you to regard them as creative?

B. How creative can you be at school and in your work?

C. How many of you know of children who are sometimes creative? How many uncreative children do you know?

D. Why do people stop being creative? What messages do people receive while growing up that give them the feeling that they are not creative?

E. How does creativity get forced into hiding as people move into adulthood? How can it reappear?

STEP #4: Summarize the major points made by students, as well as the key points on the Activity Flow Sheet.

Analysis: Creativity and Managerial Style
Activity Flow Sheet

PURPOSE: This activity allows students to reflect on how someone's managerial style can affect the extent to which employees will see themselves as creative.

KEY TOPICS: Developing creative thinking in others; task motivation

TIME ESTIMATE: 40 minutes.

FORMAT: Individual activity, work in 4-5 person groups, followed by large group discussion.

SPECIAL NEEDS: None.

SEQUENCE:
1. Introduce the activity.

2. Direct students to write down the name of the individual.

3. Instruct students to respond to the items.

4. Have students write their responses to the discussion questions.

5. Place students in 4-5 person groups.

6. Conduct a large group discussion.

7. Summarize.

VARIATION: Omit the small group discussions and proceed directly from step #4 to step #6.

KEY POINTS:
1. One's managerial style can have a significant influence on employees' perception of their creative abilities, as well as on their demonstrated creative activities.

2. Reflection on how others' managerial styles have affected us can assist in our understanding of how we may wish to tailor our own managerial styles.

Analysis: Creativity and Managerial Style
Process Guide

PURPOSE: This activity allows students to reflect on how someone's managerial style can affect the extent to which employees will see themselves as creative.

STEP #1: Introduce the activity by having students identify an individual for whom they have worked, either in or out of a workplace setting.

STEP #2: Direct students to write down the name of the individual, and to recall experiences with that person.

STEP #3: Instruct students to read the directions and respond to the items on page 257 of the text.

STEP #4: Have students write out their responses to the discussion questions on pages 257-258 of the text.

STEP #5: Place students in 4-5 person groups, with the charge to generate a list of strategies in response to question #5.

STEP #6: Conduct a large group discussion based on the groups' listings.

STEP #7: Summarize the key points on the Activity Flow Sheet as well as the points generated in the discussion.

**Practice: Creative-Relevant Skills
Activity Flow Sheet**

PURPOSE: This activity provides exercises that are fun to do, and which enhance students' abilities to associate previously unrelated concepts and to think differently about things.

KEY TOPICS: Creative-relevant skills.

TIME ESTIMATE: 40 minutes.

FORMAT: Individual activity and laarge group discussion.

SPECIAL NEEDS: None.

SEQUENCE: 1. Introduce the activity.

2. Give students 3 minutes to list uses of the paper clip.

3. Give students 3 minutes to list names of the restaurant.

4. Conduct a brief large group discussion.

5. Give students 5 minutes to complete the developing mental imagery exercise.

6. Conduct a brief large group discussion.

7. Give students 10 minutes to describe three problems and to apply an analogy to each one.

8. Conduct a large group discussion.

VARIATIONS: 1. Assign a short paper for the Using Analogies exercise, responding to the instructions on page 259. Be sure to specify a length and due date.

2. For steps #2 and #3, place students into 3-4 person groups or teams, charged with the generation of as many responses as possible. Give the groups 5 minutes for each exercise.

KEY POINTS: 1. With a little effort and practice, creative skills can be developed and increased.

2. Often activities which enhance our creative skills are also fun.

Practice: Creative-Relevant Skills
Process Guide

PURPOSE: This activity provides exercises that are fun to do. The exercises are designed to enhance students' abilities to associate previously unrelated concepts and to think differently about things.   With these exercises students have permission to break out of usual barriers to creative thought, and receive practice in doing so.

STEP #1: Introduce the activity by directing students to the exercises on pages 258-259 of the text.   Explain that these are activities which are fun, for which there are no right or wrong answers.

STEP #2: Give students 3 minutes to list uses of the paper clip.   Call time if necessary.

STEP #3: Give students 3 minutes to list names of the restaurant.   Call time if necessary.

STEP #4: Conduct a brief large group discussion on breaking established thinking barriers, and generate a master list of the paper clip uses and the restaurant names.

STEP #5: Give students 5 minutes to complete the developing mental imagery exercise.

STEP #6: Conduct a brief large group discussion.   Ask them what they found difficult to do and why.

STEP #7: Briefly recall to students of the uses of analogies.   Give them 10 minutes to identify and describe three problems and to apply an analogy to each one.

STEP #8: Conduct a large group discussion.   Ask for volunteers to share their problems and applied analogies.   List on the board any new analogies generated.

CAUTION: It may be necessary to guard against students who may compare themselves unfavorably with other students in the completion of these exercises. Some people may be very creative, but are just not adept at thinking of a lot of different things "on the spot." Furthermore, there are volumes of activities that accomplish the same purpose; this text had space only for a few. Don't let students become discouraged. Expanding one's creativity should be an affirming experience.

**Application: New Approaches to the Same Old Problem
Activity Flow Sheet**

PURPOSE: With this activity students identify a problem which they have, and apply their creative skills to redefining it.

KEY TOPICS: Creative-relevant skills.

TIME ESTIMATE: In class set up time: 15 minutes; outside of class: 60 minutes; in class follow up discussion: 20 minutes.

FORMAT: Individual activity followed by large group discussion.

SPECIAL NEEDS: None.

SEQUENCE:

1. Introduce the activity.

2. Read the directions with them.

3. Set a date for the submission of the papers.

4. On the submission date, conduct a large group discussion and summarize.

KEY POINTS:

1. Creative thinking skills can defuse the troublesome nature of a problem.

2. In order to apply creative skills effectively to a problem, one must sincerely want to arrive at a solution to the problem.

3. Taking a different approach to a troublesome problem can generate information which may make the problem more manageable.

Application: New Approaches to the Same Old Problem
Process Guide

PURPOSE: With this activity students identify a problem which they have, and apply their creative skills to redefining it.

STEP #1: Introduce the activity by referring students to the directions on pages 259-260 of the text. Explain that their benefit from this activity will increase in proportion to the difficulty of the problem that they choose.

NOTE: Sometimes the most troubling and urgent problems students have are personal, the details of which they may be hesitant to divulge in an assignment. Nor would they want this problem subjected to grading. Yet this activity may be most beneficial when considering such problems. If you do not plan to grade this assignment on its content (but only on its completion), you could have students complete the paper for their own use, submitting to you a short summary and response to question #8.

STEP #2: Read the directions with them, adding any explanation as necessary.

STEP #3: Set a date for the submission of the papers.

STEP #4: On the submission date, conduct a large group discussion. Ask for volunteers to share their experience. Generate from the class a master list of strategies in response to question #8.

Assessment: Changes in My Organization
Activity Flow Sheet

PURPOSE:

This activity demonstrates to students the point that the substance of a change is different from the methods through which it is implemented.

KEY TOPICS:

Designing change, implementing change, and three approaches to managing change.

TIME ESTIMATE:

In class set up time: 10 minutes; outside of class: 45 minutes; in class follow up discussion: 20 minutes.

FORMAT:

Individual activity followed by large group discussion.

SPECIAL NEEDS:

None.

SEQUENCE:

1. Introduce the activity.

2. Read the questions with the students, adding additional explanation as necessary.

3. Set a due date (preferably the next class session) for the students' papers.

4. One the due date, conduct a large group discussion.

KEY POINTS:

1. It is important to distinguish between the substance of a proposed change and its implementation procedures.

2. The procedures for implementing change affect people's perception of the substance of the change, in terms of value, feasibility, and desirability.

3. A proposed change within an organization can be needed beyond dispute, but if its implementation is haphazard and not carefully planned, the proposed change can become vigorously opposed, and ultimately fail.

SPECIAL NOTE:

Students use this activity in order to complete the first part of the practice activity on pages 269-270 entitled "Force Field Analysis."

Assessment: Changes in My Organization
Process Guide

PURPOSE: This activity demonstrates to students the point that the substance of a change is different from the methods through which it is implemented. Students compare two changes in an organization: one which is successful, and one which is unsuccessful. Students attribute the extent of success to either content of the change or to implementation procedures.

STEP #1: Introduce the activity by directing students to the instructions on page 260. If necessary assist them in identifying an organization with which they have been affiliated.

STEP #2: Read the questions with the students, adding additional explanation as necessary. Perhaps you could point to your college or university as an organization, identifying and comparing a successfully implemented change and an unsuccessfully implemented change. Examples may range from changes in admissions standards to changes in degree programs.

NOTE: It may be the case that whether or not an implemented change is successful is a judgment call. For instance, some previously all-women's colleges have become coeducational. Although apparently successful, some individuals regard such changes as unsuccessful over the long term because of concerns for declining enrollments. The important thing for this activity is for students to use their judgment as to whether an identified change is successful.

STEP #3:. Set a due date (preferably the next class session) for the students' papers.

STEP #4: On the due date, conduct a large group discussion. Additional questions may include:

A. How difficult is it to separate the substance of a change from the method of implementing it?

B. How does the method of implementing a change affect our perception of the value of the change?

Analysis: Reorganizing the Legal Division
Activity Flow Sheet

PURPOSE: This activity gives students an opportunity to analyze a case that explores issues related to frequently occurring changes in an office.

KEY TOPICS: Designing change, implementing change, and effective management of change.

TIME ESTIMATE: 45 minutes.

FORMAT: 4-5 person groups followed by large group discussion.

SPECIAL NEEDS: None.

SEQUENCE:
1. Divide students into 4-5 person groups.

2. Introduce the activity.

3. Conduct a large group discussion.

4. Summarize the major points of the groups.

VARIATIONS:
1. Depending upon the size and nature of the class, the small groups may be omitted, and the entire activity conducted as a large group discussion.

2. The case may be assigned as homework, requiring written responses to each question throughout the case.

KEY POINTS:
1. We can expect all changes to have driving forces and resisting forces.

2. It is important to understand the forces which lead to change and those which lead to resistance to change.

SPECIAL NOTE: **This activity forms the basis for the second part of the practice activity "Force Field Analysis" on pages 269-270 of the text.**

Analysis: Reorganizing the Legal Division
Process Guide

PURPOSE: This activity gives students an opportunity to analyze a case that explores issues related to frequently occurring changes in an office. This case demonstrates forces that lead to change and the forces that lead to resistance to change. Students determine what specific problems exist, what strategies they might use to solve the problem, and examine a strategy for facilitating change.

STEP #1: Divide students into 4-5 person groups.

STEP #2: Introduce the activity by directing students to the case and questions on pages 267-269 of the text. Direct them to read each section individually and, as a group, discuss the questions which follow the section. Remind them NOT to proceed to reading the next section of the case individually.

STEP #3: Conduct a large group discussion of the four discussion questions on page 269. Ask students to be as specific as possible in their responses when describing what steps Paul should take.

STEP #4: Summarize, using the main points of the groups and the key points from the activity flow sheet.

Practice: Force Field Analysis
Activity Flow Sheet

PURPOSE: This activity allows students to practice the method of force field analysis as applied to the assessment activity (page 260 of the text) entitled "Changes in My Organization" as well as to the analysis activity (page 267-269) entitled "Reorganizing the Legal Division."

KEY TOPICS: Force field analysis

TIME ESTIMATE: In class set up and small group activity: 30 minutes; outside of class writing: 30 minutes; in class follow up discussion: 20 minutes.

FORMAT: Small group activity followed by individual activity and large group discussion.

SPECIAL NEEDS: Responses to the following activities: the assessment on page 260 and the analysis on pages 267-269.

SEQUENCE: 1. Introduce the activity by directing students to the instructions on page 269-270 of the text.

2. Divide students into 4-5 person groups.

3. Conduct a large group discussion.

4. As individuals, have them conduct a force field analysis on the change they identified in question #4 of the assessment activity (page 260 of the text).

5. Assign a short paper, mapping their force field analysis and responding to the questions in the directions on page 270.

6. Conduct a large group discussion and summarize.

VARIATION: Steps #4 and #5 may be completed as homework.

KEY POINTS: 1. Force field analysis is a useful tool for considering implementing an organizational change.

2. It may not always be necessary to use every step in a force field analysis procedure. Sometimes we can short-cut our approach to match the need.

Practice: Force Field Analysis
Process Guide

PURPOSE: This activity allows students to practice the method of force field analysis as applied to the assessment activity (page 260 of the text) entitled "Changes in My Organization" as well as to the analysis activity (page 267-269) entitled "Reorganizing the Legal Division." In this activity students complete a force field twice.

STEP #1: Introduce the activity by directing students to the instructions on pages 269-270 of the text. Explain that in this activity, they are to conduct two force field analyses: one on the previous case (Reorganizing the Legal Division) and one on a change they would make in their organization, as identified in question #4 of the assessment on page 260. Have students gather any relevant materials from these activities.

STEP #2: Divide students into 4-5 person groups. Give them 30 minutes to complete the force field analysis for the Legal Division case, and to respond to the discussion questions on page 269.

STEP #3: Conduct a large group discussion. Map the force field analysis on the chalkboard, based on the responses from the groups. Discuss their responses to the discussion questions.

STEP #4: Direct students out of their groups. As individuals, have them conduct a force field analysis on the change they identified in question #4 of the assessment activity (page 260 of the text).

STEP #5: Assign a 3-5 page paper, mapping their force field analysis and responding to the questions in the directions on page 270.

STEP #6: Conduct a large group discussion and summarize. Ask students to explain the benefits of a force field analysis in implementing change.

**Application: Planning a Change
Activity Flow Sheet**

PURPOSE: This activity allows students to plan a change which is important to them.

KEY TOPICS: Designing change and implementing change.

TIME ESTIMATE: In class set up time: 10 minutes; outside of class writing: 30 minutes; in class follow up discussion: 20 minutes.

FORMAT: Individual activity followed by large group discussion.

SPECIAL NEEDS: None.

SEQUENCE: 1. Introduce the activity.

2. Assign a short paper and assign a due date for the paper.

3. Conduct a large group discussion and summarize.

KEY POINTS: 1. Sometimes we want change, we do not resist change, and still we find it difficult due to what appears to be the overwhelming nature of the change.

2. Setting target dates makes a proposed change more manageable, and assists us in bringing it to fruition.

Application: Planning a Change
Process Guide

PURPOSE: This activity allows students to plan a change which is important to them. By giving target date guidelines, the proposed change becomes more manageable for students.

STEP #1: Introduce the activity by directing students to the instructions on page 270 of the text. Encourage students to choose a change which is important to them, which they want to make, but which has been difficult for them to start. You may need to assist them in choosing a change for this activity. It may be necessary to caution students against planning something which is too grandiose or unmanageable, such as "Hitting the lottery before graduation so I can take early retirement."

STEP #2: Assign a short paper describing the experience and assign a due date for the paper. Tell them to respond in writing to the questions at the bottom of page 270.

> **NOTE:** It may be the case that for some students, the most beneficial application of this activity would be to a personal problem. However, they may not wish to submit their work on such a problem for a grade. You may wish to have them turn in an abbreviated paper which discloses that they have completed the assignment without disclosing the nature of the problem they are working on.

STEP #3: Conduct a large group discussion. Summarize, using students' main points as well as the key points from the activity flow sheet.

The Broker Role, together with the Innovator Role, comprises the Open Systems Model of the Competing Values Framework. On the organizational level the competencies of the Broker Role are closely associated with growth, expansion, and resource acquisition. As such the competencies of this role are often associated with organizational survival. On a more micro level the broker role encompasses some very interesting issues regarding authority, power, and influence in organizations. Again, the competencies of this role are often associated with individual survival within the organizational setting.

Managers in the broker role represent the organization to those outside the organization. Typical activities include: making speeches at public meetings, meeting with reporters, attending business lunches, conferences, and ceremonial events. The broker also engages in interunit and inter-organizational coordination by meeting with directors of other units and may also be involved in contract negotiations.

While this role may be perceived as primarily associated with executive functions, the fact is that the competencies of the broker role involve some very important life skills. All of us build and maintain a power base, both within the organizational setting or in our personal relationships. We also negotiate agreement and commitment; we may sometimes feel that success in our interpersonal relationships requires considerable negotiating skills! Furthermore, everyone presents ideas to others - whether informally or formally.

While several paradoxes are evident in the broker role competencies, perhaps one of the more intriguing relates to the acquisition and use of power. Power is something that most of us want and feel that we need. A measure of personal power affirms a sense that we have some control over our lives. On the other hand, we are likely to respond negatively when someone exercises power over us in a coercive, arbitrary, intimidating, or otherwise explicit manner. Since power is the *potential* to influence, it has been noted--somewhat paradoxically--that the exercise of power depletes it. To *use* one's resources reduces one's resources, i.e., lessens one's power.

Furthermore, within the organizational setting, it is argued that one gains power through empowering others. I am reminded of a story about a woman who was president of a regional coalition of local community organizations. While the woman possessed acknowledged expert, information and position power, she chose not to assert it. Instead, as she visited the local groups, she actively worked to empower the leaders of those groups to their constituents, pointing out the strengths of those leaders and the value of what they were doing. As was intended, this made the local leaders more effective in their endeavors as they sought cooperation from their constituents. Paradoxically, this also increased her power--her potential to influence. This is an illustration of how power is gained when it is given away.

The competencies of the Broker Role: The three competencies in this role and their corresponding topics in the learning activities are:

Competency #1: Building and Maintaining a Power Base

Topics:
        Power and dependency
                Misconceptions about power
        Power at the individual level
        The myth of the solitary entrepreneur
        Good power, bad power and no power
        Five sources of power
        Influence strategies
        Influence versus manipulation
        Increasing influence with superiors, peers, and subordinates

Competency 2: Negotiating Agreement and Commitment

Topics:
        Reading your organization's culture
        Four principles of Getting to Yes
            Separate the people from the problem
            Focus on interests, not positions
            Generate other possibilities
            Insist on using objective criteria
        The freedom scale: negotiating expectations up and down

Competency 3: Presenting Ideas: Effective Oral Presentations

Topics:
        Presenting ideas
        Switzler's framework for effective communication
            Set
            Sequence
            Support
            Access
            Polish
        The Importance of SSSAP

Conceptually, the broker role is not limited by these competencies. Other competencies have been identified as:

        Effective confrontation
        Building coalitions and networks
        Managing symbols and culture
        Coordinating interunit relations
        Representing your organization: effective first encounters
        Dealing with dissatisfied clients/customers/constituients
        Contract negotiations and grievance discussions

Which competencies to choose? As with the other roles, you may not be able to cover all three competencies in your course. In an effort to assist in your decision of which ones to choose, the following questions were posed to the authors:

1. In teaching this course, if you could cover only ONE competency from this chapter, which one would that be and why?

Several authors responded that they would choose "Presenting ideas" for two reasons: 1) This is an important skill in management that students get precious little opportunity to practice and explore, and 2) It seems to be the integral component of the broker role.

On the other hand, other authors argued for "Building and maintaining a power base" because this is necessary for survival.

2. In teaching this course, if you could cover only TWO competencies from this chapter, which two would they be and why?

The authors agreed: Building and maintaining a power base, and presenting ideas.

3. If you had an additional 5 pages of space for each COMPETENCY, what ideas and concepts would you wish to include?

Building and Maintaining a Power Base: More on handling responsibility without authority. When managers work in multidisciplinary teams, they often have the responsibility of getting work done though individuals over whom they have no authority. Also, more discussion on how to get, use, and maintain power through empowering others using win-win approaches. Further, a discussion of the ethics and moral issues behind exercising influence in working with people.

Negotiating Agreement and Commitment: More on third-party negotiation.

For Presenting Ideas: Effective Oral Presentations: Information on how and when to use audio-visual support in making presentations.

The Broker Role and current issues: The competencies included in the broker role are rich in implications for current issues in U. S. firms. The connections between broker and globalization are obvious: globalization requires the nurturing of strong relationships with organizations, governments, and cultures in the external environment. Furthermore, salient ethical issues surrounding the use of power and authority in organizations emerge in considering this role.

The broker role, perhaps more than any other role, represents the interacting nature of the organization with the external environment. This role represents the intensifying blurring of boundaries between organizations and their environmental components. For example, many U.S. firms are taking a more active role in educating the workforce; they are often called upon to enforce the law; and they are responding to calls for increasing social and environmental responsibility.

In addition, the broker role competencies relate to managing a culturally diverse workforce. The manager of the 21st century will certainly have to utilize brokering and mentoring skills in order to create an organizational climate which is welcoming to the voices of culturally diverse employees.

Some questions to consider in this chapter are:

1. How is the use of power within organizations related to the culture of the organization? How is the use of power related to the structure of the organization?

2. What is the distinction between power and authority? Why do people follow authority?

3. What are some ways in which one can increase one's personal power by empowering others? Under what conditions can managers empower subordinates in organizations? To what extent is it desirable to do so?

4. What are the most common patterns in the abuse of power?

5. How can a failure to develop a power base create problems for managers and the people in their work units?

A note from one of the authors:

I realize that it is difficult to take the time to allow students practice with oral presentations but it is very important. But for many students, this course may be one of their only opportunities to give some presentations and to receive supportive feedback. I encourage you to allow time and opportunity for students to improve their skills.

I feel very strongly about this because many students (MBA, MPA, and graduate accounting students) have told me that the course in Oral Communications is the most worthwhile class in our program. In seems that in degree programs, we teach students a lot of cognitive information. But in oral communication class, they have to structure and present information. Its the only place they receive real feedback.

Management is a social enterprise as much as a cognitive enterprise. Yet the degrees in management degree programs are largely cognitive. Allowing students to practice giving oral presentations gives them a rare opportunity to receive feedback on how they present themselves, and how to integrate and focus on problems and present solutions.

Assessment: A Power/Dependency Analysis of Your Position
Activity Flow Sheet

PURPOSE: This activity allows students to examine the ideas of power from
                        the perspective of the interdependence of most relationships and
                        the use of power within those relationships.

KEY POINTS: This activity leads to discussion of interdependency, of
                        stakeholders in organizations who influence the performance of
                        the organization, its access to resources, and the socio-political
                        legitimacy of the organization. From this point it's logical to
                        move to building and maintaining a power base, beginning with
                        misconceptions about power.

TIME ESTIMATE: 30 minutes.

FORMAT: Individual activity followed by large group discussion.

SPECIAL NEEDS: None.

SEQUENCE: 1. Introduce the activity.

                        2. Have students complete the diagram.

                        3. Conduct a large group discussion.

                        4. Summarize.

VARIATIONS: 1. Assign as homework.

                        2. The questions on page 274 may be used as a basis of the large
                        group discussion rather than as an individual assignment.

                        3. Following Step #2, students could be placed into small groups
                        to share their diagrams and discuss the interpretation questions on
                        page 274.

KEY POINTS: 1. What is the relationship between dependency and power?

                        2. We may have a tendency to overestimate our level of
                        dependency and the extent of our powerlessness, especially if we
                        fall victim to the Misconceptions about Power in Box 9.1 on page
                        274.

SPECIAL NOTE: **This diagram is used again in the application activity for this
                        competency on page 287 of the text.**

Assessment: A Power/Dependency Analysis of Your Position
Process Guide

PURPOSE: This activity allows students to examine the ideas of power from the perspective of the interdependence of most relationships and the use of power within those relationships.   By comparing their diagrams, they can identify factors unique to each individual situation, and explore differing perceptions of dependency.

STEP 1: Introduce the activity by directing students to the instructions on page 273 of the text. Explain that they will have the opportunity to view power from the perspective of dependence/ interdependence, and how that dependence can work both for and against them.

STEP 2: Have students complete the diagram and respond in writing to each of the questions on page 274.

STEP 3: Conduct a large group discussion. Discuss their responses to the interpretation questions and ask for volunteers to draw their diagrams on the board and explain. Some discussion questions may include:

A. How did you define dependence in order to complete the activity?

B. Do you feel that you are in a position of high or low dependence? Does this position change? If so, why and under what circumstances?

C. Do any of the people or situations reflected in your diagram tend to make you feel powerless? How? Do you think that you may tend to make others feel powerless? If so, under what circumstances?

D. Do you feel that your position of dependence can be changed? If so, how?

E. To what extend does the dependency reflected in your diagram agree with the Misconceptions about Power (Box 9.1)?   Are these truly misconceptions? Are they popular or deeply rooted in your organization? If so, why?

STEP 4: Summarize by asking students what they consider to be the main points of this activity.

Analysis:
"I Hope You Can Help Me Out": Don Lowell Case Study
Activity Flow Sheet

PURPOSE:

This activity allows students to analyze a case, exploring the uses of power and strategies for maintaining one's power base.

KEY POINTS:

Eight Influence Strategies, influence versus manipulation, and the ethics of power.

TIME ESTIMATE:

45 minutes.

FORMAT:

Individual activity, followed by work in 4-5 person groups and large group discussion.

SPECIAL NEEDS:

None.

SEQUENCE:

1. Introduce the activity.

2. Students to prepare a written response to questions.

3. Place class members into 4-5 person groups.

4. Direct the groups to discuss their responses to questions 2-8.

5. Conduct a large group discussion.

6. Summarize.

VARIATIONS:

1. Students may read the case and respond in writing as homework, followed by steps #3-#6 in class.

2. While the instructions suggest that the homogeneous groups be formed according to student responses to question #2, a point could be made to form heterogeneous groups instead. This option has the advantage of sparking lively debate in the small groups. There is some merit, however, to allowing the homogeneous groups to strengthen their position, and have the lively debate in the large group discussion.

KEY POINTS:

1. Power is the potential to influence.

2. Decisions on what to influence are often value issues, sometimes with ethical dimensions.

3. Understanding one's power/dependency relationships and one's power base helps increase one's options.

Analysis:
"I Hope You Can Help Me Out": Don Lowell Case Study
Process Guide

PURPOSE: The Don Lowell case study a typical instance of a request to use one's influence to do someone a favor. Students analyze this case, exploring the uses of power and the strategies for maintaining and/or using one's power base. Using the influence strategies discussed in the learning activity, students plan a strategy for achieving positive results. Students focus on the discussion question: What would you decide to do and why? (question 2, page 282). A very interesting discussion can be generated about values and choices, and what is appropriate in a situation like this.

STEP 1: Introduce the activity by directing students to the case and directions on pages 281-282 of the text. Indicate that in this activity they will see how sources and bases of power sometimes switch in different situations.

STEP 2: Direct students to prepare a written response to questions 1 and 2 on page 282.

STEP 3: Place class members into small groups of 4-5 students each. Have the groups composed of students who gave the same response to question 2. Hopefully you will have at least:

A. One group of those who would not get involved, and in no way try to influence the admission process.

B. One group of those who would help only by clarifying the mother's need for admission.

C. One group of those who would do everything within their power to get the mother admitted.

STEP 4: Direct the groups to discuss their responses to questions 2-8. Remind them to be as specific as possible. Have them discuss concrete methods and approaches that are being used by each character in the case study, as well as the methods and techniques they feel could be used to produce positive results given the decision they made in question 2.

STEP 5: Conduct a large group discussion, with the groups presenting their different perspectives and positions to the entire class.

Clarify that this activity involves two parts:

A. A value decision based on one's own perceptions of the situation and values relating to the uses of power.

B. Planning a strategy to reduce negative consequences and/or increase consequences of that decision.

For example, the groups which would not try to influence the mother's admission need to focus on how not to alienate Frank and how to avoid negative consequences.

The groups which would do anything to get the mother admitted need to focus on strategies to influence Sheila Hogan and to ensure that Frank "remembers" his promise.

STEP 6: Summarize, using the key points on the activity flow sheet and students' main ideas. Reiterate the positive and negative aspects of power in this situation.

Practice: The Big Move
Activity Flow Sheet

PURPOSE:
This activity is a simulation, allowing role players to demonstrate the use of particular kinds of power. Students also have the opportunity to identify and rate the effectiveness of the power exhibited by each player.

KEY POINTS:
Five sources of power.

TIME ESTIMATE:
60 minutes.

FORMAT:
Small group role play activity in 6-person groups, followed by large group discussion.

SPECIAL NEEDS:
Role play name tags or name cards, and the opening statement for each player (follows process guide).

SEQUENCE:
1. Introduce the activity.

2. Divide students into groups of 6.

3. Allow 30 minutes for the role play.

4. Direct them to complete the questionnaire.

5. Conduct a large group discussion.

6. Summarize.

VARIATION:
Conduct the role play as a fishbowl activity, allowing the other class members to observe and to fill out the Assessing Power-Oriented Behaviors Questionnaire Sheet (page 286-287).

KEY POINTS:
1. Both personal and positional power were practiced.

2. The most effective power-orientations are a product of the person, the position, the situation, and the context.

See SPECIAL NOTE at end of Process Guide.

Practice: The Big Move
Process Guide

PURPOSE: This activity is a simulation, allowing role players to demonstrate the use of particular kinds of power. Students also have the opportunity to identify and rate the effectiveness of the power exhibited by each player. As such they practice giving and receiving feedback on the role.

STEP 1:. Introduce the activity by directing students to the instructions on page 282 of the text.

STEP 2: Divide students into groups of 6. Extra participants can serve as observers. Have students in each group choose one of the six roles to play, and give out the name tags and opening statements. Remind them to read their role description, but to refrain from reading the descriptions of others.

STEP 3: Allow 30 minutes for the role play, although suggest that they stop sooner if they feel that the exchange has come to closure for the small group.

STEP 4: Direct them to complete the questionnaire and engage in small group discussion.

STEP 5: Conduct a large group discussion. Additional questions may include:

A. How did you feel during the role play? Did you feel that you were "in control" and held a strong power base? Why or why not?

B. Did the power behavior that you were given in your role match your real life power orientation, or was it one you seldom rely upon?

C. Do you feel that options were available to you? How did you develop them?

STEP 6: Summarize. Ask students what they learned from this activity that will enable them to deal more effectively with power in relationships and in organizations.

SPECIAL NOTE: This activity may take over 60 minutes. As a fishbowl, it can be particularly effective if you have astute performers who can demonstrate the use of particular kinds of power. While this activity takes a long time but certainly involves the class and can be used at a time in the course when the instructor wants heavy involvement. What may be helpful at this point is that this chapter, being late in the text, may be covered late in the course. If so, students may be experienced role players by the time they get to this activity. If there have been good discussions in class on the sources of power, this activity can be an exceptional experience for students.

THE BIG MOVE

Opening Statements for Role Play

Manager: Client Financial Services:

"As you know, I have been with the department since its founding, 10 years as manager. I have always been committed to the success of the department and the productivity and reputation of the client financial services unit is excellent."

-----------------[cut along this line]------------------

Manager: Accounting:

"I have been manager of the accounting department for several years. You know me as an objective, no-nonsense person who has the facts at hand or can get them in most situations."

-----------------[cut along this line]------------------

Manager: Purchasing:

"I have been here for 25 years. As manager of purchasing I have worked closely with all of you. You know that I have been responsible for getting many of the equipment purchases, materials, etc. that you have needed. I don't mind telling you right out that I think moving is foolish and I'm against it."

-----------------[cut along this line]------------------

Manager: Stock and Bond Transfer:

"I realize that I have not been with the department for very long. You know, however, that I come here with extensive corporate experience. Obviously I favor the move as part of our necessary and revitalizing expansion effort."

-----------------[cut along this line]------------------

Manager: Policy Department:

"The policy department has worked hard during the past few years to increase service options to clients. We are especially pleased to manage these increases while maintaining a new cost-reduction program. The two awards we received mean a lot, and we continue to work hard to achieve excellence."

-----------------[cut along this line]------------------

Manager: Personnel:

"As manager of the personnel unit, I* have been giving a great deal of thought tp this move and its implications. While I have been manager for only 8 months, I have taken the position very seriously and make every effort to know the staff and our staffing needs."

Application: Changing Your Power Base
Activity Flow Sheet

PURPOSE:	This activity helps students to think about their present level of power, using the concepts and skills learned in this competency. They also develop a plan for enlarging their power base.
KEY POINTS:	Influence strategies and sources of power.
TIME ESTIMATE:	30 minutes.
FORMAT:	Individual activity followed by large group discussion.
SPECIAL NEEDS:	Students will need their diagram from the assessment activity.
SEQUENCE:	1. Introduce the activity.
	2. Review briefly major concepts.
	3. Instruct students to complete the assignment by a specified date.
	4. Ask for volunteers to share their action plans.
	5. Conduct a large group discussion and summarize.
VARIATION:	After step 2, students may be divided into small groups for the purpose of giving one another ideas on which actions to plan.
KEY POINTS:	1. Power/powerlessness is not unchanging. Contrary to what we may sometimes feel, we can enlarge our power base.
	2. Efforts to empower ourselves are enhanced by analysis and careful planning.

Application: Changing Your Power Base
Process Guide

PURPOSE: This activity helps students to think about their present level of power, using the concepts and skills learned in this competency.   They also develop a plan for enlarging their power base. This activity is valuable in its application as a life skill, because it essentially allows students to feel empowered and in control.

STEP 1: Introduce the activity by directing students to the instructions on page 287. Remind them to use their diagram from the assessment activity for this competency.

STEP 2: Review briefly major concepts of power and dependency. Note the feelings of powerlessness that often accompanies dependency.

STEP 3: Instruct students to complete the assignment by writing a 3-5 page report and submitting it by a specified date.

STEP 4: Ask for volunteers to share their action plans with the class.

STEP 5: Conduct a large group discussion and summarize.   Additional discussion questions may include:

A. Why do some people at times resist the suggestion that they may have more power, or able to marshall more power, than they realize? What are some of the barriers to realizing our own empowerment?

B. What are some of the consequences of feeling powerless?

C. Do you believe that individuals can increase their power in organizations? Why or why not? Do some organizational structures make self-empowering efforts more difficult than other organizational designs?

D. What is it about this activity that is empowering - even before any planned action is taken?

E. How are these empowering skills valuable to one's life and relationships?

A note from one of the authors: A helpful discussion in Power, Influence and Authority is found in Cohen and Bradford's *Influence Without Authority* (N.Y.: Wiley, 1990).   See particularly chapter 6, "You're More Powerful Than You Think."

Assessment: Are You a Novice or Expert Negotiator?
Activity Flow Sheet

PURPOSE:	This activity allows students to consider the extent to which they are comfortable with negotiating in a variety of circumstances. This activity not only permits a quick self-rating, but also demonstrates the various settings to which negotiation skills apply.
KEY POINTS:	Principles of *Getting to Yes*; also relates to assertive communication skills.
TIME ESTIMATE:	30 minutes.
FORMAT:	Individual activity, work in groups of 4-6, followed by large group discussion.
SPECIAL NEEDS:	None.
SEQUENCE:	1. Direct students to the activity and instructions.
	2. Instruct them to write their responses to the questions.
	3. Place students into small groups of 4-6 individuals.
	4. Conduct a large group discussion.
	5. Summarize.
VARIATION:	In the interest of time, the activity can proceed from the individual response to the large group discussion, omitting step 3.
KEY POINTS:	1. Negotiating skills are applicable to a wide variety of circumstances.
	2. Negotiating skills have much in common with assertive communication skills.
	3. Note that combative/aggressive techniques are not considered consistent with polish negotiation skills.
	4. Using negotiating skills in various situations helps us to feel empowered good about ourselves, especially in organizational settings.

Assessment: Are You a Novice or Expert Negotiator?
Process Guide

PURPOSE: This activity allows students to consider the extent to which they are comfortable with negotiating in a variety of circumstances. This activity not only permits a quick self-rating, but also demonstrates the various settings to which negotiation skills apply. With this activity, students can understand that negotiation is an important life skill, not merely a remote concept to learn.

STEP 1: Direct students to the activity and instructions on pages 287-288 of the text.

STEP 2: Instruct them to write their responses to the questions in the margins or on separate paper. Remind them to add any items which they think may be significant.

STEP 3: Place students into small groups of 4-6 individuals. Direct them to discuss their answers, and to prepare a group response.

STEP 4: Conduct a large group discussion based on the groups' responses.

   A. How comfortable do you feel in asking for special consideration, or asking for a better deal?

   B. When is it appropriate/inappropriate to push the limits? When does asking for special consideration work? When doesn't it work?

   C. How can you apply negotiating skills to your personal relationships?

   D. How does effective use of such skills relate to our feeling good about ourselves? Usually people feel more empowered and better about themselves if they attempt a negotiation and fail, as opposed to not attempting one at all.

STEP 5: Summarize, using students' main points as well as the key points from the activity flow sheet.

Analysis:
Conflict in the Cafeteria: The Broker as Mediator
Activity Flow Sheet

PURPOSE: This activity allows students to role-play a mediation situation, using negotiating skills covered in the learning section.

KEY POINTS: Organizational culture and four principles for *Getting to Yes*.

TIME ESTIMATE: 40 minutes.

FORMAT: 4 person groups, followed by large group discussion.

SPECIAL NEEDS: None.

SEQUENCE: 1. Divide the class into 4-person groups.

                    2. Clarify assignments and directions.

                    3. Conduct the first role play (5-10 minutes).

                    4. Discuss and debrief.

                    5. Conduct second role-play (5-10 minutes).

                    6. Discuss and debrief.

                    7. Conduct large group discussion.

                    8. Summarize.

VARIATION: This activity lends itself to a fishbowl format, permitting points to be made to the class during the activity.

KEY POINTS: 1. Informal mediation is an important skill for managers to have and use. However, we believe managers should mediate sparingly and allow people the chance to work out problems on their own first.

                    2. Organizational culture affects mediation situations.

                    3. Culture and personality differences, even among people of very similar backgrounds, will influence the dynamics of the bargaining.

Analysis:
Conflict in the Cafeteria: The Broker as Mediator
Process Guide

PURPOSE: This activity allows students to role-play a mediation situation, using negotiating skills covered in the learning section. Sometimes what happens is that a manager will find herself/himself in the role of mediator involved in conflict resolution or getting a few people at cross purposes to work out their differences. This is a mediator role. The simulation gives them the opportunity to practice some of the skills of mediator, using the role of a failure mediator, and that of a success mediator.

STEP 1: Divide the class into 4 person groups. If one or two individuals remain, they may be placed as observers.

STEP 2: Clarify assignments and directions. Each group should contain the following characters:

1. Tony Lodge (or Toni, if this character is played by a female).
2. Billie Deore (or Bill, if this character is played by a male).
3. Leslie/Lester MacIntosh as a "failure" third party.
4. Leslie/Lester MacIntosh as a "success" third party.

STEP 3: Conduct the first role play (5-10 minutes). Leslie/Lester MacIntosh as a "failure" third party is involved in this first role play. Remind students to position themselves in their groups so that the key players sit in close proximity.

STEP 4: Discuss and debrief. Possible questions may include:

A. Was a solution reached? How?

B. How satisfied were the role play participants?

C. What kinds of similar experiences have the students had in the past?

D. What are the long term implications of what happened in the cafeteria?

STEP 5: Conduct second role-play (5-10 minutes). Use the same directions as the first role play. The only difference is that the student playing Leslie/ Lester MacIntosh as a "success" third party replaces MacIntosh as a "failure" third party in the role play.

STEP 6: Discuss and debrief. Possible questions include:

A. How did this role play differ from the first?

B. Were Lodge and Deore satisfied with the result?

C. What might have been done differently to obtain better results?

STEP 7: Conduct a large group discussion. Possible discussion questions include:

A. For the students who played Lodge and Deore: how did their feelings differ between the two role plays? Explore. In which role play did they feel that their feelings and dignity were the most respected? Why?

B. For the students who played MacIntosh: what were your feelings in each role play? What difficulties did you encounter? In what ways do you see yourself as skilled in mediation, and in what ways do you feel that you need to improve?

C. In what kinds of situations have you acted as a third party in an obvious misunderstanding? Why did you intervene as mediator in these situations? Why was an agreeable resolution important to you in these situations?

D. In what kinds of situations would you be prepared to act as a third party in the future?

E. Why is it difficult to make a verbal intervention in someone else's argument and not appear to be taking sides?

F. How can you use your body language to indicate both interest and impartiality as you try to give help?

G. If emotions are too high for one to talk directly to the other, can you use yourself as the channel through which one gives feedback to the other? How?

H. What would be the very first step you would take if you found that each individual really understood the other and that there were no longer any misunderstandings, but that there was really a basic value difference present?

I. What role did organizational culture play in this situation? Some examples include:

1. Lodge felt that since it was originally his/her project, he/she should determine job assignments (i.e. norms regarding who is in charge of this situation).
2. Issues surrounding equity across workers and managers.
3. Gender role issues.

J. How was power used in this activity?

K. How was persuasion used in this activity?

STEP 8: Summarize the major points of the activity, and what students have pointed out.

Practice: The Copy Machine Problem
Activity Flow Sheet

PURPOSE: Students practice the skills of bargaining and negotiation in a work-related simulation.

KEY POINTS: Four principles of *Getting to Yes*.

TIME ESTIMATE: 45 minutes.

FORMAT: Dyad activity, with several students set aside as mediators; followed by large group discussion.

SPECIAL NEEDS: None.

SEQUENCE:
1. Select 3-4 mediators. Divide rest of class into pairs.

2. Ask players to play their roles until they have an agreement.

3. Each pair should write up the policy.

4. Conduct large group discussion.

5. Summarize.

VARIATIONS: Conduct as a fishbowl activity.

KEY POINTS:
1. The copy machine is symbolic of a deeper status anxiety issue.

2. It is possible to use negotiating skills to find a solution when the positions seem mutually exclusive.

3. The bargaining strategy used to negotiate in one situation may affect future negotiations.

Practice: The Copy Machine Problem
Process Guide

PURPOSE: Students practice the skills of bargaining and negotiation in a work-related simulation. While students may not expect to work in an office setting like that occurring in this simulation, all students can expect to encounter similar occasional conflicts of interest.

STEP 1: Select 3-4 students to act as mediators. Ideally these students will have shown an aptitude for bargaining in previous activities. Divide rest of class into pairs. One person in each group should play Doyle (or Donna) Buchanan, and the other student should play Mary (or Marty) Caputo.

FURTHER EXPLANATION: Part of the conflict is that one department with customers and needs continuous copies, and the other department does a lot of production copying (large batches) on occasion. Caputo's department suffers from status anxiety: they feel like they are treated as second class citizens because they don't deal face to face with clients. Some of this needs to come out in Caputo's reaction. Caputo feels that the entire department deserves an apology. The issue of the copying machine is a *symbolic* issue. If Buchanan just tries to solve the technical problem (which in this case is easy to solve), then progress will be limited. Buchanan probably needs to get beyond the technical issues and into the personal and social issues at hand.

NOTE: This leads to a very interesting discussion of whether a manager needs to deal with the personal and social issues The authors have found that among MBA students, opinion is very divided. Half the students argue that it's not the manager's problem: if Caputo and her/his people feel hurt, that's their problem. Buchanan, a peer of Caputo's, has no concern here. The other students argue that if it is a real issue, then it is Buchanan's problem and action is warranted. Perhaps Buchanan can do more listening, go back to his/her unit and try to advance the notion that "their work is important as ours." This small case can trigger some very interesting discussions about where the responsibilities of a manager begin and end.

STEP 2: Ask students to play their roles. The pairs should reach a compromise using some of the strategies discussed in this competency. If necessary, review some basic strategies before beginning the activity. until they have an agreement or call in mediators.

STEP 3: Each pair should write up the policy and a statement that they agree to uphold it. If the managers are unable to reach an agreement, they may request the assistance of a mediator.

NOTE: If conflict levels among the pairs seems to be low, it may be necessary to increase it in order to demonstrate the major points of the activity. Managers may be told that performance evaluations are heavily dependent upon speed of service. Therefore, it is important to get copies made as quickly as possible.

STEP 4: Conduct large group discussion after all groups have reached a decision or 30 minutes have passed (whichever comes first). Possible discussion questions may include:

A. What bargaining strategies did people use?

B. What roles did the mediators play in the bargaining process?

C. How powerful were the mediators?

D. What arguments were most successful in persuading the other party to compromise?

E. How did you "read" the nonverbal communication of the manager you were negotiating with?

F. What strategies of influence did you use?

G. How was power used in solving your dispute?

H. Given what happened in your negotiation, would you approach a future bargaining session with the same individual?

I. How would you describe the negotiating climate with respect to:

1. Whether or not human nature is believed to be good, bad, or mixed.
2. Past, present, and future time orientation.
3. Individualism, teamwork, or hierarchical ordering of relationships.

STEP 5: Summarize the major points of the activity, using students' main ideas and the key points from the activity flow sheet.

Application: Negotiating Positions on the Freedom Scale
Activity Flow Sheet

PURPOSE: This activity allows students a choice of one of three ways to apply principles discussed in the learning section.

KEY POINTS: Principles of *Getting to Yes* and the Freedom Scale

TIME ESTIMATE: in class set up time: 15 minutes; outside of class: 2-3 hours over the next 2 weeks; in class follow up discussion: 15-20 minutes.

FORMAT: Individual activity.

SPECIAL NEEDS: None.

SEQUENCE:
1. Introduce the activity.

2. Review with them the three possible activities.

3. Discuss the significance of option #3.

4. Set a due date for the written work of the activity.

5. Conduct a large group discussion and summarize.

KEY POINTS:
1. Negotiating skills have wide personal and organizational applications.

2. People manage up as well as down. The freedom scale and negotiating skills enable us to perform such managing well.

3. Negotiating skills are a needed and learned activity. As with writing skills, good negotiating skills are not an inborn trait.

Application: Negotiating Positions on the Freedom Scale
Process Guide

PURPOSE: This activity allows students a choice of one of three ways to apply principles discussed in the learning section. The third option is a particularly powerful activity for understanding Onchen's freedom scale.

A note from one of the authors: A number of people have found the freedom scale to be useful in essential ways. The freedom scale is taken from William Onchen's *Managing Management Time*. Prior to the book, Onchen published the scale in what has become the most popular article ever printed in the *Harvard Business Review*, receiving the greatest number of reprint requests.

STEP 1: Introduce the activity by directing students to page 298 of the text.

STEP 2: Review with them the three possible activities, and discuss which they might like to choose.

STEP 3: Note that option #3 is particularly significant. The freedom scale is a powerful device for clarifying roles with one's boss, peers and subordinates. The authors have found it to be, in consulting and training, the most effective schema to use for role clarification in terms of accountability, reporting back, and negotiating a relationship. It takes ambiguity and potential conflict out of the relationship.

A note from one of the authors: Onchen makes the important point that when we are evaluated, it is usually based on our performance as subordinates. Ironically, we receive little training in how to be an effective subordinate because we are evaluated by "superiors".

STEP 4: Set a due date for the written work of the activity.

STEP 5: Conduct a large group discussion, allowing students to summarize what they have learned after completing the assignment.

Assessment:
The Presenter's Touch: You May Have It and Not Know It
Activity Flow Sheet

PURPOSE:	This activity allows students to assess the extent to which they may already have strong presentation skills.
KEY POINTS:	Establish that most people are better communicators than they realize.
TIME ESTIMATE:	10 – 15 minutes.
FORMAT:	Individual activity followed by large group discussion.
SPECIAL NEEDS:	None.

SEQUENCE:

1. Introduce the activity.

2. Stress the importance of honesty in this assessment.

3. Point out that most people have better oral communication skills than they realize.

4. Conduct a large group discussion and summarize.

KEY POINTS:

1. Many characteristics contribute to good presentation skills.

2. Effective presentations skills are not a matter of talent; they are learned behaviors.

3. Presentation skills are very important to managerial competencies.

4. Good oral communication skills is an even more vital skill than written communication in most American companies surveyed.

Assessment:
The Presenter's Touch: You May Have It and Not Know It
Process Guide

PURPOSE: This activity allows students to assess the extent to which they may already have strong presentation skills. This questionnaire highlights characteristics that many students may not have associated with presentation skills.

STEP 1: Introduce the activity by directing students to the questions and instructions on page 299.

STEP 2: Stress the importance of honesty in this assessment.

STEP 3: Point out that most people have better communication skills than they realize.

STEP 4: Conduct a large group discussion and summarize. Additional discussion questions may include:

   A. Did your score on the questionnaire correspond with the level of presentation skills that you tend to attribute to yourself? What surprised you about this activity?

   B. Why do you think that many people feel that they have fewer presentation skills than they actually may have?

   C. Why are good presentation skills important to the managerial role?

   D. Through what means can people most effectively improve their presentation skills?

Analysis: Applying SSSAP
Activity Flow Sheet

PURPOSE: This activity allows students to analyze presentations according to their own experience. Additionally, they learn to identify the principles of SSSAP explained in the learning section.

KEY POINTS: Switzler's SSSAP: Set, Sequence, Support, Access, Polish

TIME ESTIMATE: In class to set up: 10 minutes; outside of class: 90 minutes; in class follow up discussion: 15-20 minutes.

FORMAT: Individual activity followed by large group discussion..

SPECIAL NEEDS: None.

SEQUENCE: 1. Direct students to the activity on page 308 of the text.

2. Remind students to be as unobtrusive as possible during the presentation.

3. Students should be alerted to the possible effect of their interest in the content of the presentation, in terms of their assessment of the presentations' effectiveness.

4. Instruct students to write a 1-2 page report.

5. Conduct a large group discussion and summarize.

VARIATION: This individual activity could be assigned for completion in small groups or teams. A cautionary reminder: Care must be taken to prevent groups of students from attending lectures, classes, and other campus events, and being disruptive to the presenter by being obviously making an assessment of the presenter's style.

KEY POINTS: 1. Effective speakers vary widely in the way they adhere to SSSAP and other principles.

2. Effective speakers often present a mix of skills and their own personalities.

3. Most speakers' performance can be improved in some way; however, that realization may not prevent them from delivering an excellent presentation.

Analysis: Applying SSSAP
Process Guide

PURPOSE: This activity allows students to analyze presentations according to their own experience. Additionally, they learn to identify the principles of SSSAP explained in the learning section.

STEP 1: Direct students to the activity on page 308 of the text. Discuss with students various options of presentations they may attend. Perhaps a lecture is being scheduled in the community or on the campus that may interest them. Again, remind them of the preference **not** to use a televised presentation.

STEP 2: Remind students to be as unobtrusive as possible during the presentation.

STEP 3: Students should be alerted to the possible effect of their interest in the content of the presentation, in terms of their assessment of the presentations' effectiveness.

STEP 4: Instruct students to write a 1-2 page report commenting on the SSSAP principles and the questions on page 308. Set a deadline for this report to be handed in.

STEP 5: Conduct a large group discussion on the day that the reports are due. Discuss the questions on page 308. Summarize students' major points. Addition discussion questions may include:

A. What was the relationship between your interest in the topic and your assessment of the presentation?

B. To what extent does your feeling of liking the presenter as a person (from what you can ascertain in the presentation) affect your judgement of the effectiveness of presentation?

C. Do you think it is possible to "separate the medium from the message?" Why or why not?

Practice: You Be The Speaker
Activity Flow Sheet

PURPOSE: This activity provides students with the valued opportunity to prepare a presentation and to receive supportive feedback from peers. It also allows students to practice giving supportive feedback to others.

KEY POINTS: SSSAP

TIME ESTIMATE: 90 minutes.

FORMAT: Individual presentations to 4-6 person groups.

SPECIAL NEEDS: Sufficient copies of the Peer Feedback Form (follows process guide).

SEQUENCE: 1. Direct students to read the instructions on page 308.

2. Divide students into 4-6 person groups.

3. Remind students of the proprieties of giving constructive feedback to others.

4. Allow sufficient time in class for the presentations and feedback.

5. Conduct a large group discussion and summarize.

KEY POINTS: 1. Note that SSSAP can be used effectively in written communication as well as in oral communication.

2. SSSAP provides needed and helpful guidelines to preparing oral presentations about any subject.

3. Constructive feedback from peers is enormously helpful. This is a resource which we can tap at any time.

4. SSSAP is useful in helping people helping people learn to describe, create, and criticize.

Practice: You Be The Speaker
Process Guide

PURPOSE: This activity provides students with the valued opportunity to prepare a presentation and to receive supportive feedback from peers. It also allows students to practice giving supportive feedback to others.

STEP 1: Direct students to read the instructions on page 308. Discuss with them various options of topics they might choose on which to prepare presentations.

STEP 2: Divide students into small groups. The size of the groups is a function of how much time you wish to allow. The larger the groups, the greater the feedback, but the longer the activity will take. Note that the time allotted for the group work will be 6 minutes per group member, plus a few extra minutes.

STEP 3: Remind students of the proprieties of giving constructive feedback to others. They may wish to give the speaker a chance to be self-critical before offering their comments.

Further, suggest that they might want to avoid being definitive and using phrases such as: You should have. . . or, You were wrong to. . .   Instead, in giving constructive feedback, it is best to be more tentative, using such phrases as: I might be wrong but to me this seems. . .   or, You might want to consider. . .   or, I know I have a hard time with this, but. . .

STEP 4: Allow sufficient time in class for the presentations and feedback.

STEP 5: Conduct a large group discussion and summarize. Additional discussion questions may include:

A. Before this activity you had a level of self-assessment regarding your presentation skills. Has this activity altered that assessment? If so, how and to what extent?

B. What surprised you in doing this activity?

C. What were your feelings when you gave feedback to your peers?

D. What was the most difficult aspect of completing this activity? Why?

E. How did you find SSSAP to be helpful to you?

PEER FEEDBACK FORM

Speaker's name:_____ Date:_____
Feedback giver's name:_____

List things that worked, that were effective, about the speaker's presentation:

List some suggestions for improvement:

Speaker's name:_____ Date:_____
Feedback giver's name:_____

List things that worked, that were effective, about the speaker's presentation:

List some suggestions for improvement:

Application: You Be the Critic
Activity Flow Sheet

PURPOSE: This activity allows students to evaluate the effectiveness of their oral presentation skills. Through a written evaluation, they can identify areas in which they need to give more attention to this skill.

KEY TOPICS: SSSAP

TIME ESTIMATE: In class set up: 10 minutes; time to plan and deliver the presentation; in class follow up discussion: 15-20 minutes.

FORMAT: Individual activity followed by large group discussion.

SPECIAL NEEDS: Students must make an oral presentation in the near future.

SEQUENCE: 1. Introduce the activity.

                    2. Discuss with students when and where they may make the oral presentation.

                    3. Assign a date for the submission of the written report.

                    4. Conduct a large group discussion and summarize.

VARIATION: Divide class members into teams, having them prepare more lengthy oral presentations than the 6-minute presentations in the practice activity. With this option, delete written peer feedback.

KEY POINTS: 1. Self-evaluation is an invaluable resource to improving one's competencies.

                    2. In self-evaluation it is just as important to point out your strengths as it is to point out areas of needed improvement.

Application: You Be the Critic
Process Guide

PURPOSE: This activity allows students to evaluate the effectiveness of their oral presentation skills.   Through a written evaluation, they can identify areas in which they need to give more attention to this skill.

STEP #1: Introduce the activity by directing students to the instructions on page 308. Note that it may be necessary to provide opportunities for students to make oral presentations, or perhaps to make this an optional activity.

STEP #2: Discuss with students when and where they may make the oral presentation. Opportunities could be provided by using the small group format (as with the practice activity) with two differences: written peer feedback not required, and the increasing the length of the presentations. Students might choose from among a number of topics relating to the content of this course.

STEP #3: Assign a date for the submission of the written report.

STEP #4: On the day when students hand in their written reports, conduct a large group discussion and summarize. Discussion questions may include:

   A. What surprised you about doing this activity?

   B. What specific self-evaluation strategies did you utilize?

   C. How did the principles of SSSAP help you in your presentation?

Chapter 1 of the text presents a perspective of integrating the eight managerial roles into an overall historical and theoretical framework. Chapters 2 through 9 introduce students to competencies in each of the eight managerial roles and provide activities which enhance students' ability to integrate each role into their working and personal lives. Now chapter 10, as the conclusion, provides students with strategies, enabling them to integrate all of these roles with balance and discretion, acknowledging the intricate and dynamic inter-relationships.

This chapter challenges students to *do* something about what they have learned during this course. Chapter 10 provides students with the framework to construct and develop a plan whereby they will experience improvement in their levels of mastery of the key managerial roles. By doing this, chapter 10 advances the expectation that students are able to apply these competencies, thus affirming the value of their course work for many years to come, and perhaps for the duration of their careers.

It is important that students focus on mastery as a process and a journey. None of the authors consider themselves to be "master managers" in the sense that they "have arrived." Rather, the meaning of mastery is the ability to self-examine, to grow from experience, and to develop judgment and discernment in the application of competencies to appropriate situations.

Inherent in mastery is developing a sense of oneself. One cannot be a "copy-cat master manager." Management is simply too individual-specific. Two managers faced with identical situations, may find that dissimilar responses are appropriate because they themselves have diverse styles and different relationships with their employees. Again a central paradox is apparent: while we learn from other managers and increase our competency abilities, there is no role model of the one perfect master manager for us to copy. Each person can be said to have a master manager inside, waiting to be improved and developed, and each person's master manager is different.

Topics included in this chapter are:

        The development of Mastery
                Stage 1: novice
                Stage 2: advanced beginner
                Stage 3: competency
                Stage 4: proficiency
                Stage 5: expert
        The profile of the master
        The transformation of an aggressive achiever
        How masters see the world
        The possibility of self-improvement
                Agenda for self-improvement
                        Learn about yourself
                        Develop a change strategy
                        Implement the strategy
                        The results

Assessment: Reexamining Your Profile
Activity Flow Sheet

PURPOSE:	This activity allows students to respond again to the course preassessment discussed in chapter 1 of the text, page 23, and compare their current profile with their initial profile. It is likely that this profile will vary from their original one.
KEY TOPICS:	The profile of the master; the possibility of self-improvement.
TIME ESTIMATE:	In class set up time: 10 minutes; outside of class: 45 minutes; In class follow up discussion: 30 minutes
FORMAT:	Individual activity followed by large group discussion.
SPECIAL NEEDS:	Students will need either the software package with access to a computer, or a hard copy of the instrument (see Chapter 1 of this **Instructional Guide** for instructions and a hard copy of the questions). Students will also need their profiles from when they initially responded to the course preassessment.
SEQUENCE:	1. Introduce the activity. 2. Be certain that each student has all of the materials necessary to respond to the course preassessment. 3. Conduct a large group discussion after they have finished with the instrument and have their new profiles 4. Summarize.
VARIATION:	See Chapter 1 of the **Instructional Guide** for complete discussion of using the Managerial Practices Survey to permit students to rate each other.
KEY POINTS:	1. Everyone has areas where they may need to improve. 2. The road to mastery is a life-long journey, not a destination. 3. We can learn the managerial competencies which we lack, given time, effort, and opportunity.
SPECIAL NOTE:	**This activity is needed for completion of the practice and application activities in this chapter.**

Assessment: Reexamining Your Profile
Process Guide

PURPOSE: This activity allows students to respond again to the course preassessment discussed in chapter 1 of the text, page 23, and compare their current profile with their initial profile. It is likely that this profile will vary from their original one. This activity demonstrates for students improvement in managerial competency as a result of the experiences associated with the course, and also highlights areas of needed improvement.

STEP #1: Introduce the activity by reminding students of the course preassessment and the profile they developed at the beginning of the course. Direct students to the instructions on page 312 of the text.

STEP #2: Be certain that each student has all of the materials necessary to respond to the course preassessment.

STEP #3: Conduct a large group discussion after they have finished with the instrument and have developed their new profiles. In addition to the questions on page 312, additional discussion questions may include:

A. What did you find surprising about your new profile? Do you think it is accurate?

B. As you compare your new profile with the original from the beginning of the course, where do you find the most dramatic changes? How do you account for these changes?

C. As you look at the profiles of some of your classmates, do they match your impressions of these individuals? Why or why not?

STEP #4: Summarize the major points of the discussion, including the key points from the activity flow sheet.

Analysis: A Comparison of Two Managers
Activity Flow Sheet

PURPOSE: This activity allows students to analyze the cases of two well-known managers in terms of mastery level.

KEY POINTS: Development of mastery; the profile of the master.

TIME ESTIMATE: 30 minutes.

FORMAT: 4-5 person groups, followed by large group discussion.

SPECIAL NEEDS: None.

SEQUENCE: 1. Introduce the activity by directing students to the cases and instructions on pages 325-327 of the text.

2. Place students into 4-5 person groups.

3. Conduct a large group discussion.

4. Summarize the discussion.

VARIATIONS: 1. Step #1 can be completed as homework, with instructions to write out their responses to the three questions on page 327.

2. The small group discussion can be omitted by proceeding directly from step #1 to step #3.

KEY POINTS: 1. Performance in any one managerial role at the expense of attention to the competencies of the other roles can lead to failure and disappointment. This is the case even if one's performance in that one role is extraordinary.

2. Formalization refers to the development of a strong organizational infrastructure. This implies considerable attention to the Internal Process Model and is what enables the Open Systems Model to function well over a long period of time.

Analysis: A Comparison of Two Managers
Process Guide

PURPOSE: This activity allows students to analyze the cases of two well-known managers in terms of mastery level. These cases demonstrate the importance of balance and discretion in playing the managerial roles, especially the importance of attending to the details of the developing organizational infrastructure while undergoing creative expansion.

STEP #1: Introduce the activity by directing students to the cases and instructions on pages 325-327 of the text. Give them 10 minutes to read the cases and jot down notes in response to the questions on page 327.

STEP #2: Place students into 4-5 person groups. Have group members compare their responses to the three questions, and to develop a group response to those questions.

STEP #3: Conduct a large group discussion. On the chalkboard, list group responses to the three questions.

STEP #4: Summarize the discussion. Use the cases to illustrate the key points on the activity flow sheet. Note especially that we have likely not heard the last of Don Burr. Even if we make mistakes and fail to complete an endeavor, we can go on to better things successfully if we learn from our experiences.

Practice: The Evaluation Matrix
Activity Flow Sheet

PURPOSE:	This activity allows students to consider their level of comfort and expertise with the eight managerial roles, and to summarize their thinking on a chart.
KEY POINTS:	The profile of the master; agenda for self-improvement.
TIME ESTIMATE:	45 minutes.
FORMAT:	Individual activity followed by large group discussion.
SPECIAL NEEDS:	Their self-assessment profiles from the assessment activity on page 312.

SEQUENCE:

1. Introduce the activity.

2. While they may wish to jot notes in the matrix on page 328, suggest that they may wish to enlarge it, or even to duplicate one for each model of the Competing Values Framework in order to accommodate all of their comments.

3. Emphasize to students that this matrix is for their use after the course is completed.

4. Conduct a large group discussion after students have completed their matrix and summarize.

KEY POINTS:

1. It is important to plan for one's self-improvement development in the managerial roles.

2. The matrix takes the task of self-improvement and breaks it down into manageable steps.

3. Mastery of the managerial roles is a continuing process.

SPECIAL NOTE: This activity is needed for completion of the application activity in this chapter.

Practice: The Evaluation Matrix
Process Guide

PURPOSE: This activity allows students to consider their level of comfort and expertise with the eight managerial roles, and to summarize their thinking on a chart. The chart also specifies self-improvement steps that students can pursue after this course is completed.

STEP #1: Introduce the activity by directing students to the Evaluation Matrix on page 328 of the text. Explain that once completed, this matrix provides a summary of where they are with regard to the managerial roles. It also provides an organized plan for self-improvement, with specific steps that can be pursued after the course is over.

STEP #2: While they may wish to jot notes in the matrix on page 328, suggest that they may wish to enlarge it, or even to duplicate one for each model of the Competing Values Framework in order to accommodate all of their comments.

STEP #3: Emphasize to students that this matrix is for their use after the course is completed. They may wish to update it on an annual or a semi-annual basis. However, since it is for their use and benefit, encourage them to be thorough and honest in their responses.

STEP #4: Conduct a large group discussion after students have completed their matrix. Ask for volunteers to share their experiences and observations with this activity. Summarize the points made by the students as well as the key points on the activity flow sheet.

Application: Your Strategy for Mastery
Activity Flow Sheet

PURPOSE: This activity allows students to write a paper in which they construct a plan for managerial self-improvement and the development of mastery.

TIME ESTIMATE: In class set up time: 15 minutes; outside of class:3 hours; in class follow up activity: 30 minutes.

FORMAT: Individual activity and large group discussion.

SPECIAL NEEDS: Materials from the activities in this course, especially the assessment and practice activities from this chapter.

SEQUENCE: 1. Introduce the activity by directing students to the instructions on page 327 of the text.

2. Specify the requirements of the final paper.

3. Conduct a large group discussion.

KEY POINTS: 1. In order to begin efforts to master managerial competencies, it is first necessary to identify one's competency strengths and which competencies require improvement.

2. Long-term major self-improvement efforts require careful planning.

3. Do not be discouraged. Resist the temptation to avoid those roles which you do not happen to like. Read books which elaborate the meaning of those roles, and come to appreciate their value and significance in overall managerial mastery.

Application: Your Strategy for Mastery
Process Guide

PURPOSE: This activity allows students to write a paper in which they construct a plan for managerial self-improvement and the development of mastery. In this effort, students draw from the activities of this chapter, especially the profile (assessment activity) and the evaluation matrix (practice activity).

STEP #1: Introduce the activity by directing students to the instructions on page 327 of the text. Explain that this activity permits them to construct a comprehensive and thorough improvement plan which will be useful to them in their future endeavors.

STEP #2: Specify the requirements of the final paper: length, due date, etc., and respond to their questions.

STEP #3: Conduct a large group discussion regarding the value of such planning, and the benefit they stand to derive from this activity. Summarize and mention the key points from the activity flow sheet.